Charles John Stone

Christianity before Christ

Prototypes of our faith and culture

Charles John Stone

Christianity before Christ
Prototypes of our faith and culture

ISBN/EAN: 9783337262730

Printed in Europe, USA, Canada, Australia, Japan

Cover: Foto ©Lupo / pixelio.de

More available books at **www.hansebooks.com**

CHRISTIANITY BEFORE CHRIST.

"We should feel cheered by the words of that pious philosopher (St. Augustine) when he boldly declares that there is no religion which among its many errors, does not contain some real and divine truth."—*Professor Max Müller.*

"A man ought to honour his own faith only; but he should never abuse the faith of anybody. There are even circumstances when the religion of others ought to be honoured. And in acting thus a man fortifies his own faith and assists the faith of others."—*From King Piyadasi's Rock Inscriptions.*

CHRISTIANITY BEFORE CHRIST;

OR,

PROTOTYPES OF OUR FAITH AND CULTURE.

BY

CHARLES J. STONE, F.R.S.L., F.R. Hist. S.,
AUTHOR OF "CRADLE-LAND OF ARTS AND CREEDS."

LONDON:
TRÜBNER & CO., LUDGATE HILL.
1885.
[*All rights reserved.*]

Ballantyne Press
BALLANTYNE, HANSON AND CO.
EDINBURGH AND LONDON

SYLLABUS OF CHAPTERS.

CHAPTER I.—The monastic system of Buddhism in India, as described by the Chinese Pilgrim, Fah-Hian, in the fifth century A.D.

CHAPTER II.—Hiouen Thsang's description of Buddhist monasteries in the seventh century A.D., and of the towns, &c.

CHAPTER III.—The drama of the ancient Hindus, "Hero and Nymph."

CHAPTER IV.—The dramas of "Mâlati and Mâdhava," and of the "Necklace."

CHAPTER V.—Allegorical drama of the "Rising of the Moon of Awakened Intellect."

CHAPTER VI.—Wealth found in India by the Mohammedans in the eleventh century.

CHAPTER VII —Remains of ancient Central America, Mexico, and Peru—Romance of our mediæval days in the great Indian epic.

CHAPTER VIII.—The "Great Supporter" (Mahâbhârata epic)—Wedding presents—Ancient banquets—Fortified towns—Rules for fair fighting.

CHAPTER IX.—Philosophical aphorisms—Assembly of princes—Names of the Divine in the human—Duty of the warrior.

CHAPTER X.—Krishna as the earthly mediator—The camp, doctors. &c.—The battle array—Cookery—Yavanas (? not Greeks).

CHAPTER XI.—Magnificence of the old Indian heroes—Fêtes and amateur theatricals — Description of Krishna's city of Dwaravati—Mr. H. Chintamon on the "Divine Song."

CHAPTER XII.—The ancient deities of the Hindus—All manifestations of one Supreme Being.

CHAPTER XIII.—The incarnation of the "All-Pervading" in Krishna—Competition in feats of arms for the hand of the Princess—Krishna reveals himself to his relations.

CHAPTER XIV.—Professor Monier Williams and the "Divine Song"—Milton—The holy Fire—Krishna as the Eternal Creator—Destruction of a sceptical monarch.

CHAPTER XV.—Descent of Vishnu as Krishna for the benefit of humanity—Primeval sacrifice of Purusha (universal soul).

SYLLABUS OF CHAPTERS.

CHAPTER XVI.—Spell upon the Princess Krishnâ on account of sins in a previous existence—Krishna's wives—Association of Krishna, so also of Buddha, with the ancient philosopher Kapila.

CHAPTER XVII.—The ages of the world's history—Prominence of sacrifice—Paradise attained by charity and the other virtues.

CHAPTER XVIII.—The wreck of the universe—Survival of one holy sage, and entry into the eternal Infant's body.

CHAPTER XIX.—Krishna brings food by miracle to the Princess Krishnâ — Commencement of the "Song Celestial" (so entitled by Mr. Edwin Arnold in his translation in verse).

CHAPTER XX.—Continuation of the "Bhagavad Gita," or "Song Celestial."

CHAPTER XXI.—Infinity of Hari or Krishna—He is the sacrifice of all sacrificers—Creator of beings—The eternal man.

CHAPTER XXII.—Reconciliation of the adoration of the Divine in Shiva and Vishnu.

CHAPTER XXIII.—Account of the birth and infancy of Krishna—The tyrant Kansa endeavours to encompass his destruction, &c.

CHAPTER XXIV.—The childhood of Krishna amongst the pastoral folk—Homage done to him by Indra, the Indian Jupiter—Theatre of King Kansa prepared for a tournament.

CHAPTER XXV.—Overthrow of King Kansa's wrestlers, then of the king himself—Prototype of Washington Irving's story of the long sleep—Construction of Krishna's city.

CHAPTER XXVI.—Faith inculcated in Krishna as Vishnu upon earth—Chivalrous devotion to woman shown in the ancient Indian books.

CHAPTER XXVII.—Allegorical termination of the great Indian epic, in the style of Bunyan's "Pilgrim's Progress."

CHAPTER XXVIII.—The war between angels and devils derived from the "ancient books" of India—Professor H. H. Wilson of Oxford upon these—Hari and the Indian Venus.

CHAPTER XXIX.—Professor H. H. Wilson on the Puranas, and parallel with the Platonic Christians—The All-Pervading and the Mother of the World.

CHAPTER XXX.—Story of constancy of faith in the "Indian Preserver"—Hell from the Christian Tertullian.

CHAPTER XXXI.—Stages of existence in the "Ancient Book of the Preserver"—Constant existence of Cesava (Hari-Krishna).

CHAPTER XXXII.—End of the existing world—Vasudeva or Krishna as the Supreme and Universal Spirit—Suggestion of Archaic Buddhism.

SYLLABUS OF CHAPTERS.

CHAPTER XXXIII.—Bhagavata Purana (Ancient Book of the Blessed One)—Quotation from the Veda as to the universal embodied spirit and the primeval sacrifice—Krishna as the manifestation of the Divine.

CHAPTER XXXIV.—Doctrines of the "Ancient Book of the Blessed One" as compared with Christian Evangelicalism—Series of incarnations of the All-Pervading.

CHAPTER XXXV.—Incarnation of the All-Pervading at the end of the present world—Reconcilement of Krishnaism and Buddhism.

CHAPTER XXXVI.—M. Levêque on the Orphic theology—Quotation from Ovid's "Metamorphoses"—The Golden Verses.

CHAPTER XXXVII.—City of the "Blessed One," and his domestic relations.

CHAPTER XXXVIII.—Great period required for the systematisation of the Hindu formulas of faith, supposing the actual books to have been written within our era.

CHAPTER XXXIX.—Corroboration of the developments of both Buddhism and Krishnaism from the philosophy attributed to Kapila—Sir W. Jones as to Krishna and the Divine Spirit—Transmigration of souls in the Institutes of Manu—The individual soul united with the Supreme Soul.

CHAPTER XL.—Inscription from Buddha-Gaya with mingling of Krishnaistic ideas—Last words of the Chinese Buddhist Pilgrim Hiouen Thsang—Protestantism in India.

CHAPTER XLI.—Buddhist ritual from Nepaulese tracts—The Hindu reformer Ramanuja and others.

CHAPTER XLII.—Monasticism and adoration of the "Mother of the Universe" in India.

CHAPTER XLIII.—Succession of Buddhas—M. Emile Burnouf as to the succession of religions.

CHAPTER XLIV.—Description of the daughters of Zion in Isaiah as applicable to Hindu women in the present day—Institutes of Manu on transmigration and final beatitude.

CHAPTER XLV.—Arrian as to Ancient India—Its cities, system of "standing armies," &c.—Also the testimony of Megasthenes.

CHAPTER XLVI.—Affinities to Christianity in the ancient religions of Mexico, Peru, &c.

CHAPTER XLVII.—The cross, &c., in Mexico—Remark of Dr. Zerffi as to the striking analogies between East and West.

CHAPTER XLVIII.—"Forest" portion of the Hymns of the "Praise" Veda—Quotation from the Yajur Veda as to the Universal Spirit—Sacrifices without actual death in the Vedic ritual.

CHAPTER XLIX.—Colebrooke on the integrity of the Vedas—Agni as the first self-existent man—The Cross as exhumed by Dr. Schliemann from Troy.

CHAPTER L.—Hymns of the "Praise" Veda from the translation of M. Langlois.

CHAPTER LI.—Unity of Deity in the Vedas—The sacred Brahminical confession of faith—"Speech" as the All-Pervading.

CHAPTER LII.—Krishna, Hercules, Quetzalcoatl seeming identical; also Apollo.

CHAPTER LIII.—Upanishads from Professor Max Müller's "Sacred Books of the East."

CHAPTER LIV.—Doctrines of St. Origen as to the transmigration of souls—Theophilus of Antioch in regard to Christians holding the transmigration of souls—St. Irenæus as to the resurrection of the body, &c.

CHAPTER LV.—St. Irenæus as to the duration of the life of Christ—Paley, in his "Evidences of Christianity," as to St. Irenæus.

CHAPTER LVI.—Quotations from Christian Fathers as to Buddha, &c.—Mr. Lillie on the history of Buddha—Quotations from the rock-cut inscriptions of King Piyudasi.

CHAPTER LVII.—The Nestorian or Malabar Christians in India—Story of Mandavya—His death upon the stake and descent into Hell to punish the King of the dead.

CHAPTER LVIII.—Salem and the previous incarnation of the Divine in Melchizedek in the Bible.

APPENDICES.

I.—Mr. H. S. Ashbee in description of the Library of Tanjore.

II.—The invocation of the Mahâbhârata as compared with Froissart's introduction to his History.

III.—Buddhist temple in the Japanese village on view in London in 1885.

IV.—Adam in Ceylon.

V.—Authenticity of the inscription at Buddha-Gaya.

VI.—Hymns of the Rig Veda, from Professor H. H. Wilson's translation.

VII.—Ancient crosses found in India.

VIII.—The doctrine of the metempsychosis in Mohammedanism.

IX.—Attributes of Krishna as compared with the Odin of Ancient Germany.

CHRISTIANITY BEFORE CHRIST.

CHAPTER I.

STRANGE resemblances appear in the world's ancient faiths to the religion revealed to us in Judæa. Weird prototypes of our most sacred doctrines and ordinances are found in the ancient books of the East, and in what we know of the religions of ancient America on the one hand, and Etruria, &c. on the other. Our modern science acknowledges the doctrines of Buddhism, the religion of the "Enlightened," to have been promulgated by at least the third century B.C. Of a period in the East about coeval with that in which the Emperor Constantine professed and established Christianity in the West, we have recently had revealed to us curious and interesting pictures in the accounts of the travels of the Chinese Buddhist Pilgrims. In these the line of march of the spiritual in the material world is distinctly displayed to us at about the fifth and seventh centuries of our era. And there is much that is amazing. The travels in Affghanistan and India, in the fifth century of our era, of the first of these Buddhist Pilgrims, Fah Hian, show religious and philanthropical establishments which we have certainly held to have been of comparatively modern growth. His narrative has been translated by the Rev. S. Beal, Professor of Chinese in University College, London.

The Pilgrim describes monasteries which appear to present absolute similarities to those of the Church of Rome both in general aspect and interior regulations. He relates that all the resident priests have chambers, beds, coverlets, food, drink and clothes, provided without stint or reserve. The priests continually employ themselves in works of benevolence, or in reciting their scriptures, or remaining in profound meditation. Strangers are hospitably received and their feet washed. He also mentions convents of nuns. He describes the monks as erecting towers in the monasteries, several stories in height, in honour of their saints. He altogether indicates fashions in architecture as elaborate as our own; with political and social institutions, outside the world of the "religious," correspondingly complete. The excavated temples, monastic halls, and cells of India have lately been assigned to some centuries before and after this period. But a description of the Pilgrim's seems evidently to apply to the excavations of Elora in the province of Aurungabad. He styles them a Sangharâma of the former Buddha Kasyapa. He indicates venerable antiquity, and that they have been deserted by regular monks.

Throughout India the monastic establishments appear to have been in a most flourishing condition in the fifth century A.D. He observes that, from the time of Buddha's Nirvâna, the kings and nobles of India began to erect Vihâras for the priesthood, and to endow them with lands, gardens, houses, and also men and oxen to cultivate them. "The records of these endowments," he continues, "being engraved on sheets of copper, have been handed down from one king to another; so that no one has dared to deprive them of possession, and to this day they continue to enjoy their proper revenues."

He alludes to priests, numbered by tens of thousands, to processions, cars, images, &c.

He finds in Affghanistan 3000 monks studying the Buddhistic Scriptures styled the Small and Great Vehicles. Going south-eastwards, he passes various temples, containing 10,000 priests or more, who appear, however, to have been Brahminical. He finds Buddhism in the vicinity of the Jumna; but what he terms the worship of the deities (devas) appears to prevail in that region. He comes, however, to kingdoms in Western India, which "firmly believe in the law of Buddha." Here laymen, even kings, are not allowed to remain seated in the presence of the priesthood on any loftier seat than a carpet on the ground. He says of Madyadesa (the middle country), "The inhabitants are prosperous and happy—there are no boards of population and revenue. Those only who farm the royal demêsnes pay a portion of the produce as rent. The king, in the administration of justice, inflicts no corporal punishment; only, after repeated attempts to excite rebellion, the right hand is cut off." "The people of this country," he continues, "kill no living creature, nor do they drink intoxicating liquids; and with the exception of the chandalas, they eat neither garlic nor onions. They do not deal in living animals, nor are there shambles nor wine shops around their markets." He visits the city of Kapilavastu, and sees the ruins of the palace of Buddha's father. Here he mentions monasteries containing 600 or 700 priests, scholars, &c. He remarks that the nobles and landowners of this country have founded hospitals within the city, to which the poor of all countries, the destitute and cripples, may repair for shelter. Physicians inspect their diseases, and, according to their cases, order them food or drink, medicine or concoctions—everything, in fact, that may contribute to their ease. He states that King Ashoka constructed 84,000 pagodas; and that he presented the whole of Jambudwipa (the island of the Rose Apple, old name for India) to the priests of the four quarters, and redeemed it again in money. "He did this four times." Fah Hian alludes to what appears to have been a very elaborate system of relic worship. The "Enlightened" (Buddha) himself, assisted by his disciples, had raised a tower of 70 or 80 feet in height, as a model for all future commemorative buildings of the sort. He states that the highest tower in Jambudwipa was 470 feet in height. He mentions flags and silken canopies as articles of religious decoration.

The Pilgrim weeps in pious ecstasy at a cave where the "Enlightened" is alleged to have sat in adoration. He recounts his (Buddha's) endurance of every sort of agony for the sake of all flesh. He narrates that he left his country, wife, and child. He tore out his eyes to bestow them on another. He mangled his flesh to deliver a dove from a hawk. He sacrificed his head in alms. He gave his body to a famishing tiger. He grudged not marrow nor brains. When he became perfect Buddha, he was in the world forty-nine years, preaching the law, and converting men.

He gave rest to the wretched. He saved the lost. Having passed through countless births, amongst which he had done the above-mentioned acts of self-sacrifice, he entered Nirvana. Since that event 1497 years have passed.

The Chinese Pilgrim, then, travelling through India to learn what he could of his religion, to visit its sacred places, and to obtain copies of the Buddhist scriptures, believed that the epoch of the Enlightened was at the period at which our first great Sanscrit scholar, Sir William Jones, placed it, viz. about 1000 B.C. It appears that the Buddhist scriptures were usually learnt by rote in the monasteries, or, at all events, that copies of scriptures and their books were rare. He could not obtain one till he reached Patna, on the Ganges.

Fah Hian visits the birthplace of Buddha, and contemplates the ruins of his father's palace. The whole of his narrative seems consistent in indicating a greater antiquity for the founding of his faith than we have been disposed, in our reliance upon the Ceylonese Chronicles, to admit for it.

Altogether he displays the existence of what must have been a highly artificial civilisation, and a carefully ordered system of religious ritual, with attention to practical philanthropy. And Fah Hian's statement seems to show that the aristocratical and military classes had become as thoroughly subservient to the Buddhist clergy as ever they had or have become to the Brahminical or Romanist priesthoods. If the account which has been quoted is accurate, the lofty pretensions of the Buddhist monks may be reasonably supposed to have had a share in producing their suppression, or expulsion from India, by the regal power, or by a general revolt of the laity against these pretensions. This has usually been ascribed only to the Brahmins.

By this period of Fah Hian, Buddhism had adopted the idea of an antagonist to Buddha, extremely suggestive of the Christian Antichrist. Fah Hian relates that this person, Devadetta, poisoned his nails, in order that he might destroy Buddha; but he was sent down alive into hell. He states that Devadetta had still a body of disciples existing, who paid religious reverence to the three past Buddhas, but not to Sakia Muni (Gautauma Buddha). He mentions the existence of six heretical sects in Middle India, who "allowed the reality of worldly phenomena." "When the law of Buddha is perishing," says Fah Hian, in curious analogy to the words of St. Mark xiii. 14, "men who have acquired religious merit shall escape from destruction, and seek refuge in the mountains. Then the wicked will repent, and Maitreya Buddha will come."

Extracts from the Hindu drama of this period, in chapter iii. and following chapters, will show that besides the spiritual in religion, the spiritual in life was very assiduously cultivated. Philosophy, general education, and the fine arts seem to have been peaceably pursued, with both imagination and refinement, at the time when Rome was taken and plundered by Alaric, king of the Visigoths.

CHAPTER II.

THE Chinese pilgrim, Hiouen Thsang, visited India about two centuries later than Fah Hian. Here is an account of a monastery in Magaddha, taken from M. Stanislas Julien's translation of his travels. It appears to have been considered by the Pilgrim as the most magnificent of the monasteries of India. He describes it as surrounded by a brick-wall, and containing eight courts and several halls. Steeples were ranged in regular order, and pavilions ornamented with coral. Domes, he says, were boldly elevated to the clouds, and the summits of the temples seemed to fly beneath the vapours of the heaven. From their windows the rising of the winds and clouds could be beheld, and beneath their roofs, audacious in their height, the sun and moon might be seen in conjunction. The monastery was surrounded by water, adorned with the blue lotus, overhung by the glistening *butea frondosa* with its scarlet blossoms, and shaded by luxuriant mango groves. In the various courts the houses of the "religious" had each four stories. The pillars of the pavilions were decorated with dragons, and they had balconies brilliant with the colours of the rainbow, and with carved balustrades. Columns were ornamented with jade, painted and richly chiselled. The door-posts were elegantly decorated, and the roofs were constructed of glittering tiles, flashing every instant with variegated light. The monastery contained 10,000 "religious," who studied that collection of the Buddhist scriptures styled the Greater Vessel. Even Oxford, with its increased numbers of late years, only contains about 3000 students and resident graduates in all its colleges combined.

The travels of Hiouen Thsang testify to the existence of monasteries numbered by thousands, and Buddhist monks by tens of thousands through a great part of India at about the seventh century A.D. The religious fervour had, however, already begun to decline in favour of that particular form of devotion, for he finds many ruined and deserted monasteries. He constantly comes across relic mounds or monuments attributed to the great Buddhist monarch Ashoka, who has been assigned to about the third century B.C. In the district of Benares he finds a flourishing and dense population, the villages being close together, and many families enormously rich. Their houses are filled with rare and precious objects. He describes the people there as polite in their manners and fond of study, though few revere the law of Buddha. In the city he beholds twenty temples of the Brahminical deities, with towers of many stories, magnificent chapels constructed of artistically sculptured stone and of wood richly painted. Shady trees and streams of pure water impart their cooling charms to the scenes. He describes the statue of the god Mahesvara, or Shiva, as being made of brass and little under a hundred feet in height. "His aspect is grave and majestic, and, at his sight, respectful awe is felt as though he still lived."

To the north-east of Benares, he finds a relic monument constructed by Ashoka, and a great Buddhist monastery. By the monument is a column of blue stone, pure as a mirror, its surface being polished and clear as glass. In it the shade of the Enlightened (Buddha) might be seen. The monastery is divided into many courts, all surrounded by a wall. Here he beheld balustrades, pavilions with double stories, admirable in construction. In its midst was a *Vihara*, two hundred feet in height, with its summit surmounted by an image of the Amra tree, fabricated in gold. The bases of the building and staircases were of stone. All around this monument there were a hundred richly-adorned niches; each containing a statue of the " Enlightened " in brass, of life size. There were fifteen hundred monks in this monastery.

Mr. Fergusson seems to suggest, in his history of Indian architecture, that the epoch of its grandeur commenced at about the seventh century of our era. But the circumstantial accounts of this pilgrim, even allowing for exaggeration, appear to demonstrate that India, throughout its extent (which is about equivalent to that of Europe without Russia and Sweden), was then already filled with magnificent edifices. They were erected in stone and in wood, with decorations in the precious metals and in gems. They had towers and pinnacles, and they were constantly adorned by statues. Sacred and domestic edifices of imposing dimensions and varied architecture seem to have existed throughout the country, as in our modern Europe, by at least 600 A.D. Many were old, while there were numerous ruins in the land. At Mahâsâra on the Ganges, at its confluence with the Sona, the Pilgrim finds, for instance, a temple consecrated to Narâyanadeva, *i.e.* to the divinity, or form of divinity, also styled Vishnu, and held to have been incarnate on the earth as Vasudeva, Hari, or Krishna. He describes it as having pavilions and towers with double stories, decorated in the most brilliant manner. "The statues of the deities are sculptured in stone with marvellous art, and numerous miracles are related to have occurred there."

Of the inhabitants of several provinces he observes that they have much esteem for the cultivation of letters; sometimes he even states that they are actually ardent in study, while they are usually described as benignant in disposition and most polite in manners.

He describes the towns as generally built of brick, with walls around them, sometimes of bamboo stakes. The public edifices have their towers, belvideres, and terraces. Houses constructed of wood have tiled roofs. The form of the buildings is the same as in China. The monasteries he states to have been erected with extraordinary art, with pavilions of two or three stories in height at their angles, and the joists and beams adorned with elegant sculptures. The doors, windows, and porches are covered with paintings in different colours.

Taking his accounts into consideration, with those in the plays, and other indications which are to be found throughout the literature in the Sanskrit, the theory seems utterly untenable that the inhabitants of this continent of India learned the arts of building and sculpture in stone from the Greeks after Alexander's invasion. Considered conjointly with the old civilisation of the still vaster China, long ages of indigenous culture are suggested.

Hiouen Thsang travelled down the eastern side of India, nearly to the south of the peninsula, and ascended by the western side. In the south as well as the north he finds the intermingling of Buddhist monasteries with congregations of "heretics," frequenting the temples of the "deities." Of one district in the present Madras Presidency he observes that the people are brusque in their manners, but attached to good faith and justice, and much given to religious disputations. Of Kosala in this region, he remarks that the inhabitants are brave but violent; that there are partisans both of heresy and truth amongst them; and that they are distinguished by the elevation and brilliance of their knowledge. In Dhanakâtcheka, in the district of the river Godaveri, he remarks that their skins are black, and that they are naturally violent in their manners; still that they love to cultivate letters.[1] Here he finds many temples of the divinities and many ruined convents. In one district, bordering on the sea, he remarks that they care not for letters, but only for the pursuit of lucre. Here are the ruins of a great number of ancient convents, while many hundred temples of the "deities" (devas) are in existence.

In Dravida of the South, he states that the in-

[1] See Appendix I.

habitants shew a great respect for learned men. He observes that their language and the characters of their writings differed from those of Central India.

Altogether, in south as well as north, he finds a cultivated, literary people, usually of amiable character and honest disposition. Occasionally, as has been the case in Italy to recent times, he encounters brigands. He often finds the relic monuments, called stûpas, of one hundred or two hundred feet in height; and images of Buddha, of ninety feet in height, are mentioned, sculptured in stone as well as in brass. The numerous images of smaller size are often adorned with precious stones.

CHAPTER III.

The India of this later Buddhistic period, viz., at about the seventh century A.D., seems rather to have afforded prototypes of future European culture than copies of that of the Roman Empire. It was certainly far in advance of the Empire of Charlemagne in the west. We can trace the progress of Indian culture and spirituality backwards to the Vedas or sacred "Books of Knowledge." These have been assigned, at the latest, to the epochs of the Argonautic expedition and the siege of Troy, viz., from 1225 to 1184 B.C. From specimens of Indian poetry which will be adduced it will appear that the inhabitants of ancient India had not much to learn from the Greeks at the time of the temporary establishment of their power in the north-west, after the decease of Alexander the Great. But of course the unsurpassed perfection of Greek sculpture must be admitted, the Indian being probably over-elaborate always; but over-elaboration is suggested by their world of foliage and flowers.

It is said in the *Tatler*, No. 42, that in Wills' Coffee-house a gentleman remarked that there was no method in the world of knowing the taste of an age or period so good as by the observations of the persons represented in their comedies. At about the epochs corresponding with those of the abandonment of Britain by the Romans, the Danish invasions, the Saxon heptarchy, and Alfred the Great's victories, with his introductions of culture — extending, perhaps, to the periods of the Crusades — many elaborate dramas were produced in India. Of these, "Sakuntalâ, or the Fatal Ring,"—first translated by Sir William Jones, and lately by Professor Monier Williams—has been adapted and performed in Germany.

A play entitled "Hero and Nymph" is attributed to Kalidâsa, author of "Sakunlalâ." In this "Hero and Nymph," old artificial civilisation and spiritual love of the beauties of nature appear, such as it has been customary only to place to the credit of our own age. It has been translated by H. Hayman Wilson, late Professor of Sanskrit in the University of Oxford.

In the prelude a dialogue between "Manager" and "Actor" demonstrates that dramas were no novel institution at this epoch.

The *Manager* says—

"Many assemblies have witnessed the composition of former dramatic bards; I therefore propose to exhibit one not hitherto represented, the drama of Vikrama and Urvasî. Desire the company to be ready to do justice to their respective parts."

Actor. "I shall, sir."

Manager. "I have now only to request the audience to listen to this work of Kalidâsa with kindness and attention."

A chorus of Apsarasas, or heavenly nymphs, is introduced; and the play is altogether suggestive, in its mingling of human and supernatural beings, of our "Midsummer-Night's Dream," or "Tempest." The principal character in the piece, the king, has a Brahmin for a confidential companion. But he is by no means represented as an austere ascetic, but rather in the guise of what we should consider as a character of "eccentric comedy." Observing, for instance, that the king is sad and silent, he proposes a visit to the kitchen; because "the very sight of the savoury dishes in course of preparation will be sufficient to dissipate all melancholy ideas." On another occasion he remarks that the moon is "as beautiful as a ball of almonds and sugar."

Here is a description of the noontide heat, of another style:

> "'Tis past mid-day. Exhausted by the heat,
> The peacock plunges in the scanty pool
> That feeds the tall tree's root; the drowsy bee
> Sleeps in the hollow chamber of the lotus,
> Darkened with closing petals. On the brink
> Of the now tepid lake the wild duck lurks
> Amongst the sedgy shade; and even here
> The parrot from his wiry bower complains,
> And calls for water to allay his thirst."

The king loses the nymph by whose charms he has been fascinated, while wandering with her amidst the groves, for she has entered upon enchanted ground, and consequently been transformed into a slender vine-tree. Distracted, he searches for his beloved. He exclaims:

> "The monarch of the woods,
>   With slow desponding gait,
>   Wanders through vales and floods,
>   And rocks and forest bowers,
>   Gemmed with new-springing flowers,
>   And mourns, heart-broken, for his absent mate."

In his anxiety to obtain tidings he makes inquiries of a peacock which he sees perched upon a jutting crag:

> "Bird of the dark-blue throat and eye of jet,
>   Oh tell me, have you seen the lovely face
>   Of my fair bride, lost in this dreary wilderness?"

The peacock shows no sympathy, so the king continues to lament, now singing, while music is continually heard:

> "Yonder amid the thick and shady branches
> Of the broad *jambu*, cowers the koil, faint
> Her flame of passion in the hotter breath
> Of noon. She, of the birds, is wisest framed."

I will address her:

> "Say, nursling of a stranger nest—
> Say, hast thou chanced my love to see,
> Amidst these gardens of the blest,
> Wandering at liberty,
> Or warbling with a voice divine
> Melodious strains, more sweet than thine?"

He entreats this bird, "whom lovers deem love's messenger," to lead his steps to where she strays. He exclaims passionately:

> "Why did she leave one so devoted to her will?
> In wrath she left me. But the cause of anger lives not
> In my imagination. The fond tyranny
> That women exercise o'er those that love them
> Brooks not the slightest show of disregard.
> How now, the bird has flown. 'Tis ever thus.
> All coldly listen to another's sorrows."

After asking the swan whether he has seen her,

> "Graceful straying
> Along the flowery borders of the lake,"

and apostrophising other birds, he contemplates with envy "a royal elephant," and his mate accepting a bough snapped off from a tree. At length he perceives a gem "more roseate than the blush of the ashoka blossom." He is unwilling to take this jewel, because she is absent whose brow it should have adorned. But a voice in the air bids him take it, for it possesses wondrous virtue. Let it adorn his hand, and he will shortly cease to lament for his absent bride. He obeys, and forthwith feels a strange emotion. He gazes on a vine: "No blossoms deck the boughs, no bees regale her with their songs; silent, sad, and lonely, she shows the image of his repentant love, who now mourns for her causeless indignation. He presses the 'melancholy likeness to his heart,' and the vine changes into Urvasî." After affectionate explanations, and expressions of delight at their reunion, they return to the city, which laments its absent lord, making "a cloud their downy car." Music is heard, and the invisible voice or chorus sings:

> "The ardent swan his mate recovers,
> And all his spirit is delight;
> With her aloft in air he hovers,
> And homeward wings his joyous flight."

There is another act, however, in which the Indian Mercury, Nârada, descends to assist in the inauguration of the king's son as vice-monarch, and the chorus invokes blessings on him:

> "Son of the monarch the universe filling,
> Son of the god of the mist-shedding night,
> Son of the sage, whom the great Brahma, willing,
> Called, with creation, to life and to light."

In fact the spiritual side of life is always present in these dramas. The play ends with the following benediction from the king:—

> "May learning and prosperity oppose
> No more each other, as their wont, as foes;
> But, in a friendly bond together twined,
> Ensure the real welfare of mankind."

This drama of "Hero and Nymph" may be pronounced ultra-sentimental, but surely it cannot be denied that it indicates cultured life fitted for the reception of spiritual ideas. It not only suggests Shakespearian plays, but the masques of our ancestors, modern French *Féeries*, and the partly sentimental, partly humorous extravaganzas by Mr. Planché, which were produced on the English stage about the year 1853. "King Charming, or the Blue Bird of Paradise," is curiously recalled to mind by the king's dialogue with the peacock. In our "King Charming," however, it is not the heroine who is transformed, but the king who is changed into a "blue bird of Paradise."

CHAPTER IV.

Mrs. Manning observes, in her "Ancient and Mediæval India," that the play of Mâlatî and Mâdhava is one of the few which shares with Sakuntalâ the honour of being still occasionally read by pandits. It represents a time at which the temples of Shiva and Kâma (the Indian Cupid) were generally frequented, although Buddhists and Buddhist schools and convents were powerful.

This play is attributed to the eighth century A.D. by Professor Weber. It has a plot founded upon a dramatic device which has been frequently employed in modern times, one of the latest examples being Mr. Theyre Smith's comedietta of "My Uncle's Will." The story here is that two school companions of high rank pledged each other that so soon as their respective children should be of the right age they should be married. The father of the girl is Prime Minister to the King of Padmâvatî, supposed to be Oujein, at which place the scene of the play is laid. The father of the boy is the Prime Minister of a neighbouring kingdom to the south of Oujein. In preparation for the intended marriage the boy, or young man, is sent to study logic in a Buddhist college at Oujein, the city in which resided the future bride and her father, then its Prime Minister.

Curiously the head of this college or convent is a woman who had been nurse to the lovely Malatî. Here is a marriageable youth sent to study under a woman. We have in England our preparatory schools for boys presided over by the fair sex, but that a woman should be considered the correct head of a college in which logic is to be taught to a boy who is old enough to love, seems to have been a realisation of the "sweet-girl graduate" idea. We have our feminine colleges now in Oxford and Cambridge, and the time may be approaching when boys or young men will be sent to be under the instruction of some celebrated feminine Principal of one of them. An interchange may even take place between the seminaries at present set apart for young men and ladies respectively, and the two become commingled. "This woman," remarks Mrs. Manning, "is a Buddhist—good and conscientious, clever and scheming, and by her the whole plot of the drama is worked out." She promotes the love-making between the two, and assists them, when, owing to the command of the King, the girl is ordered to wed another instead of her lover. A former pupil of hers has, by long-continued austerities, obtained mystic powers of flying, &c.; and by her aid the dénouement is brought about, and the lovers are united." This feminine ascetic bows in adoration before the Lord of Bhavani (Shiva), showing that the Buddhists had continued the adoration of the Deity, now considered Brahminical, with that of Buddha.

The worship of the spouse of Shiva, under her terrible aspect as Kali, here called Chamunda, claimed at this epoch even human victims. One sensational incident in the drama is the kidnapping of the heroine to sacrifice her to the goddess. She is rescued from the sacrificial sword by her lover. The hero observes, on one occasion, that the damsel draws his heart like a rod of the ironstone gem. "This renders it possible," remarks Professor H. H. Wilson, "that artificial magnets, as well as the properties of the loadstone, were known to the Hindus."

The play terminates with a tag of philanthropic character, after the Buddhist Abbess has brought about the happy dénouement. The lover, blest with the object of his adoration, says:

> "My happiness henceforth is perfect ; all
> The wish I cherish, more is this, and may
> Your favour, holy dame, grant it fruition.
> Still may the virtuous be exempt from error,
> And fast to virtue cling. May monarchs, merciful
> And firm in equity, protect the earth ;
> May in due season from the labouring clouds
> The fertile showers descend ; and may the people,
> Blest in their friends, their kindred, and their children,
> Unknowing want, live cheerful and content."

When Málatí is to be wedded to the King's protégé, she escapes from her predicament by her lover's friend, who disguises himself in the bridal costume sent for her to assume in the temple of Srî (the Indian Ceres). This consisted of a corset of white silk, a red muslin mantle, with necklace, sandal, and a chaplet of flowers. Here is a description of the marriage procession conveying her to the Temple :

A hollow murmur comes upon the ear like that of rushing clouds, and as the procession draws nearer, drums that peal in joy drown every other sound. "White umbrellas float, like trembling lotuses, in the lake of the atmosphere." Banners undulate like waves as they play before the wind of the *chowris*, which hover about like swans. The elephants advance, their golden bells tinkling as they stride. They are mounted by merry bevies of damsels singing songs of rejoicing, " uttered indistinctly, as interrupted by the betel which perfumes their mouths, and blazing like rays of light with glittering jewels." And these jewels, the writer further remarks, were of variegated tints, as if they were portions of Indra's divine bow. As Mâlatî herself draws near we are told that the throng of attendants fall off to a respectful distance, and keep back the crowd with staves covered with gold and silver. Her elephant, painted with vermilion, resembles the ruddy dawn ; or with the twenty-seven pearls on her brow (an allusion to the twenty-seven lunar mansions), looks like the brilliant night. Mâlatî herself, in her deep grief, appears like some fair plant just budding into flower, but withered at the core.

Here is a speech assigned to a plotting prime minister in a play of much dramatic action, ascribed also by Professor Weber to the eighth century. It is suggestive of the words which Shakespeare puts into the mouth of the sleepless monarch. It also shows that the drama of the period was no mere spontaneous outburst of uncultured genius, but artificial, elaborated with rules, and constructed in what we have styled the " unities : "

"It will not be. Sleep flies me; nor the change
Of night or day, short intermission brings
From watchful care; whilst fate continues adverse,
And aids the crooked projects of Chânakya.
Such task is mine, as on dramatic bard
Devolves, to fix the object of the action,
Develop fitting incidents, uprear
Fruit unexpected from self-pregnant seeds,
Dilate, condense, perplex, and last reduce
The various acts to one auspicious close."

In a play called "The Necklace," attributed to King Harsha of Kashmir, who reigned between A.D. 1113 and 1125, we find a princess skilled in portrait-painting. The scene is in the garden of the palace.

The Princess Sâgarikâ has just painted a portrait of the king, with whom she has already fallen in love. In her picture he is the god of love, to whom flowers and perfumes are being presented, as in a sort of masque in which she had seen him play that part. The friend and companion with whom she has come from Ceylon discovers her, and says, "Ha! she is here, but so intent upon some painting that she does not notice my approach." The friend, Susangatâ by name, perceiving whose portrait she has taken, rallies her upon her admiration for this god of love; and saying she must give the god his bride, she adds the portrait of Sâgarikâ to the picture. This friend was in charge of the Queen's favourite talking-bird, called here a *sárika*.

The princess is rather distressed to find she has

revealed her secret. The friend says, "Be assured I will not betray you; it is more likely this prattling bird will repeat our conversation." The princess becomes much agitated; the friend cools her with lotus-leaves and fibres. Nevertheless the princess faints until aroused by confused voices behind the scenes, which announce that "the monkey has escaped from the stable;" and, rattling the ends of his broken chain of gold, he "clatters along as if a number of female feet, bound with tinkling anklets, were in sportive motion." Chased by the grooms and frightening the women, he has bounded through the inner gate.

By this device of the monkey terrifying the girls, the picture is dropt when they make their escape, and it comes into the possession of the king.

The ambassador from Ceylon is struck with admiration at the magnificence of the king's palace. He exclaims that its "avenues present a splendid scene. The eye is bewildered amongst the stately steeds and mighty elephants of war. The ear is regaled with harmonious sounds, and the heart is gratified by mixing with the throng of attending princes. The state of the King of Sinhala (Ceylon) is here effaced; and the magnificence of the entrance into every court betrays me into rustic admiration."

CHAPTER V.

Our allegories of the European literary renaissance certainly had their prototypes in India some centuries earlier, not only in the poetry of the country but in the drama. A curious play, attributed to the twelfth century A.D., which is entitled "Prabodha-Chandrodaya; or the Rising of the Moon of Awakened Intellect," is theological and philosophical in its design. Delusion is represented as king and commander of Love, Anger, Avarice, and all other sensuous powers; whilst Hypocrisy, Self-importance, Materialism, and all heresies are his allies.

On the opposite side is Reason, monarch and leader of an army of virtues. An encounter ensues between these opposing forces, but finally Tranquillity enables Reason to harmonise with Revelation. Then the Moon of Awakened Intellect can arise and illuminate mortals.

The prologue commences with an invocation to the Supreme Spirit—the primeval cause. "With reverence we approach that spotless, heavenly, self-recognising Light, which, appearing as a sea in the deceiving beams of the mid-day sun, evolved itself as ether, air, fire, water, earth." "To that highest Light the created soul returns when plunged in deepest stillness." By this is intended the conception that when the aspirations of earthly ambitions, desires, and unrest in general are extinguished in the contemplation of the Supreme Being, and in the realisation of the Spirit of All in the individual self, then the individual becomes one with the Divine.

"The light prevails when the world is filled with the ascetic followers of the Deity whose head is adorned with the crescent moon, and who is made known by the eye in the centre of his forehead" (Shiva). "But wherefore many words?" continues the manager. "The glorious Gopâla (*i.e.* the goatherd Krishna), he whose lotus feet are irradiated by the diadems of kings, . . . desires us this day to evince our joy in the accomplished victories of our prince, King Kirtivarman. For this purpose we propose to perform a drama in which personified Tranquillity shall be a leading character; and we have chosen that which is entitled 'The Rising of the Moon of Awakened Intellect.'" This piece, the manager continues, composed by the much-honoured Krishna Misra, which "the king and the multitude are eager to see," we will at once prepare. He lifts a curtain and calls. An actress appears, inquiring what it is he proposes. The manager replies as follows:—

"You are aware that Gopâla, whose fame resounds through every region, has with his sword conquered inimical kings, and has re-established our Râja Kirtivarman upon his throne. The battlefield on which the demonesses dance, proclaims his praise in far-resounding notes, whilst the little women of the Kobbolds clash together with their nimble fingers the skulls of the dead, and the wind, resounding through the frontal cavities of the slain elephants, trumpets forth his fame. This Gopala," he concludes, " having become tranquil, desires the performance of the Rising of the Moon of Awakened Intellect. Desire the performers to take their parts."

The actress asks for explanation of Gopála's tranquillity. The manager replies that it is analogous to no other proceeding in the world's history. Periods of violent activity, followed by seasons of absolute repose, are characteristic of Eternal Deity. And this Gopála, as soon as his duties had been fulfilled, conquered Karman (activity) as Reason conquers Delusion.

A voice is heard behind the scenes, which says:

"You good-for-nothing fellow! how dare you declare that Delusion will be conquered so long as I exist?"

"Ah!" says the manager, "that is Love or Káma (Desire) who, with his rolling eyes, bewitches the world. We have enraged him. Let us begone."

Love is represented as accompanied by Pleasure. He declares that Reason originates in mere books, and cannot acquire an ascendancy over his weapons, such as lovely palaces, youthful maidens, flowers amongst which the bees are humming, winds laden with the scent of jessamine, moonlit nights. Pleasure, however, thinks that Reason is a formidable opponent, but Love observes that fear is natural to the feminine heart, and he bids her remember that, although his bow is composed of sugar-cane and his arrows of flowers, that he can nevertheless, subdue the universe. Love, however, states that Saraswati (eloquence or divine wisdom) is about to appear on the earth, and that she will be a terrible enemy.

Hypocrisy is represented as a Brahman. Egotism, Deceit, Greed, and Avarice are his friends. King Delusion enters with numerous followers, and speaks superciliously of those who conceive that soul is distinct from body, and that reward can be enjoyed in a future existence. When he appears, a voice exclaims behind the scenes:

"Make ready the bejewelled crystal palace. Sprinkle the floors with sandal-scented water. Let the fountains play. Erect arches of precious stones. Plant waving flags, brilliant as the rainbow, on the palace roof."

The King declares that the Material alone is true. Nothing is known of what is beyond. Death is the end.

A Chârvâka, or materialist, appears accompanied by a pupil. These thank King Delusion for giving them and their friend Vice comfort and courage; and they warn him of a dangerous female, a strict devotee of Vishnu (the All-pervading) called Devotion. Heresy boasts that he will convince Religion, who has become the ambassador of Reason, that justice, blessedness, the Vedas, ascetic practices, knowledge of holy books, and the doctrine of rewards in future existence are all mere follies; that she will perceive the error of seeking blessedness by the abstinence from sensuous enjoyment and become indifferent to Revelation.

An ascetic of the sect of the Jains and a Buddhist mendicant appear on the scene, who are enslaved by the allurements of sense, and become intoxicated, handing one another wine-cups and dancing together in drunken frolic.

The troops of King Reason are ordered to be in readiness for action,—elephants, war-chariots, cavalry, and infantry, whose spears are said to move onwards like a forest of lotus' blossom. On arriving at the temple of Vishnu in Benares, Reason adores the deity and prays that he may grant to the world, which implores him, that Awakened Intellect may arise and that Delusion may be destroyed.

In the battle that ensues, Reason is victorious, and offers as terms of peace that Delusion should abandon the altars of Vishnu, the holy places on rivers or in woods, and also the hearts of the pious; betaking himself and his followers to such peoples as are barbarous. But Delusion is not yet conquered, and he calls Heretical Doctrine and Logic to the rescue. Then Divine Wisdom reveals herself, armed with the beneficent influence of the sacred books from the Vedas onwards; and the adorers of Vishnu, Shiva (literally the auspicious one), and of the Sun rally round her. She declares that Brahma, or primæval Light, is tranquil, changeless, and without beginning or end. From this holy Light have proceeded Brahmâ, Vishnu, Shiva, to whom man prays; and she says that the Lord of the Universe must be apprehended by means of the holy teaching of the Scriptures. Again a fierce battle is waged. Some heretics are destroyed by holy learning. Buddhists fly to the eastward, and others take refuge in distant countries. Love is slain by Right Discrimination, Anger by Patience, and Reason becomes united with Revelation. It is announced that the Moon of Awakened Intellect has arisen, that Light has entered into Mind and swallowed up Delusion and his adherents. And the drama concludes with the following "tag"—

"Now is Reason contented, now are his enemies overthrown; and I, through the favour of worshipping the All-pervading, have attained true blessedness. Now, therefore, I pray that seasonable rain may fertilise the earth, that kings may rule in peace, and that the noble-minded, who are delivered from sin by the knowledge of truth, may be safely carried across that ocean of life which is afflicted by the sorrows of egotism."

This work, observes Mrs. Manning, was little known in Europe until the year 1842, when Professor Rosenkranz of Königsberg induced a friend, who was familiar alike with Sanskrit and with Sanskrit philosophies, to make for him a new translation from Sanskrit into German. If this translator was correct in assigning it to the twelfth century of our era, it must have been written before Mahommed's capture of Benares in 1194, when he is said to have demolished the idols of a thousand temples and to have loaded four thousand camels with his spoil. During the preceding two centuries the North-Western Provinces had been overrun by the Mohammedans; and terrible destructions of life, and of temples and images, had taken place at Lahore, at Somnauth in Gujerat, and other places. Benares is described in the drama as splendid in buildings which have stolen their whiteness from the moon, adorned with many-coloured flags, and possessing gardens filled with lofty trees, and flowers of delicious perfumes. It does not seem probable that it can have suffered from the Mohammedans when this work was composed.

CHAPTER VI.

THE extracts which have been cited from this and other plays display culture, both of mind and body, of a very elaborate kind. From Mohammedan history we obtain an insight into the wealth of India at the close of this dramatic period. Mahmoud is stated to have found in the temples of Mathura, on the Jumna, five large idols of pure gold, with eyes of rubies of great value, and above a hundred images of silver. When he returned to Ghizni, he displayed, as his spoil, bullion in value £459,000, with jewels, pearls, and other precious effects, and 350 elephants. At Somnauth he found a spacious hall, with its lofty roof, supported by fifty-six pillars, covered with plates of gold, and inlaid with precious stones. One pendent lamp spread a refulgent light over thousands of small images in gold or silver, ranged around the temple. In the midst stood a great idol of marble, which he caused to be broken in pieces, and in which an immense quantity of jewels were discovered. The treasure which he took from this celebrated sanctuary is stated to have amounted to 20,000,000 *dinaurs*, computed to be equal, at the lowest computation, to £9,166,666, 13s. 4d. In this establishment, besides 2000 Brahmins, there were 500 dancing girls, 300 musicians, and 300 barbers. In the south of India, as well as in the north, an almost incredible amount was obtained of wealth—in gold, precious stones, pearls, elephants and horses, &c. &c. The Mohammedan soldiers are said to have thrown away their spoil in silver as too cumbersome to carry on the march, such was the abundance of gold. They reported that no persons wore bracelets, chains, or rings of any other metal than gold; and all the plate in the houses of the great, as well as in the temples, was of beaten gold.

At about this period the enthusiasm of Europe was

engaged in the crusades for the recovery of the Holy Sepulchre. Notwithstanding the amenities of chivalry, and the rising beauty of Gothic architecture, it can scarcely be contended that our civilisation was then so advanced as that indicated in these Indian plays of the epoch ranging from the first to the twelfth century of our era. In the year 455, Rome had been taken and sacked by the Vandals under Genseric. In 476 the Western Empire came to its end, and Odoacer the Goth assumed the title of King of Italy. In the sixth century Justinian, in the Eastern Roman Empire, had reformed the law, and published the code which became the foundation of jurisprudence in Europe upon the revival of learning in the West. But Gibbon observes that at every step, as we sink deeper into the decline and fall of the Eastern Empire, the annals of each succeeding reign impose upon the historian an ungrateful and melancholy task. "The subjects of the Byzantine Empire, who assume and dishonour the names both of Greeks and Romans, present a dead uniformity of abject vices. A succession of priests or courtiers tread in each other's footsteps in the same path of servitude or superstition." In the fourteenth century Constantinople was besieged, in the fifteenth captured by the Turks, Mohammedanism thus conquering the two great Aryan civilisations of the Hindus in Northern India and of the Greeks in Eastern Europe at about the same period. The zeal of Christianity had been manifested in religious war so early as the sixth century. "Vitalian," says Gibbon, in chapter xlvii. of his History, "with an army of Huns and Barbarians, for the most part idolaters, declared himself the champion of the Catholic Faith. He depopulated Thrace, besieged Constantinople, exterminated sixty-five thousand of his fellow-Christians, till he obtained the recall of the bishops, the satisfaction of the Pope, and the establishment of the Council of Chalcedon, an orthodox treaty reluctantly signed by the dying Emperor Anastasius;" who was considered to have offended against the true Trinitarian doctrine of the Church. The seventh and eighth centuries are described as a "period of discord and darkness, when much science and literary accomplishment had disappeared, to reappear in the dawn of restoration in the ninth century." India possessed certainly at this epoch science as well as art in high development. In the Code of Manu, by at least a thousand years before the Code of Justinian, laws had been promulgated for the regulation of commerce, the conveyance of property, and the duties of rulers, as well as regulations for moral and religious observances. Curiously at about the time when monasticism in India was declining, it was obtaining its full influence in Europe in the establishment of the Dominicans and Franciscans in about the year 1210 A.D. But imposing as may have been the extent and flourishing condition of the monastic bodies in Europe, the revelations of the Chinese Pilgrims certainly exhibit a more amazing spread in India of their system in Buddhism, which seems precisely analogous to that of our begging Friars. Considering it in conjunction with the culture displayed in the plays, it seems impossible to conceive the Eastern civilisation to have been imitated from the West. Indeed this is demonstrated by allusions in the Vedas, admitted by all scholars to have been compiled in their present form ·by at least the time of David, in the eleventh century B.C. Certainly the spiritual was marching with progressing civilisation. And the accounts of the Chinese Pilgrims of the fifth and seventh centuries testify to an extraordinary amount of religious fervour side by side with the worldliness depicted in the drama.

CHAPTER VII.

AT this period, corresponding to the "Flight" of the Prophet Mahomet from Mecca to Medina, and to the firm establishment of the use of images in the Catholic Church, as Gibbon informs us, China boasted to have had a code of laws for nearly 2000 years; while the art of block-printing had been known there for four centuries. The religions of Brahminism and Buddhism in India each possessed a voluminous body of sacred writings, the latter of which had been adopted in China. In India also existed numerous essays of a scientific, and poems of elaborate and fanciful but always spiritual character. The general life of these great countries, embracing populations at least twice as extensive as those of modern Europe and America combined, was widely cultured. In the rules of civilised warfare, in the social ceremonies and in the love of the beautiful, our modern states were certainly forestalled. There was not that extent of barbarism or ferocity which mingled with the grandeur and literary culture of Rome. Greece, if not equalled in taste or surpassed in temporary power, had been excelled in the permanence and stability which has even to this day marked the institutions of the populous realms of Asia to the east of the Indus.

In Central America, Mexico and Peru, magnificent temples and palaces were in existence, with colleges of priests, educational establishments of a religious character for both sexes, and a most elaborate devotional ritual, combined with exceedingly careful and apparently long-matured systems of political economy.

Prescott, in his "Conquest of Peru," observes that "no man could be rich, no man could become poor in Peru." "The law was constantly directed to enforce a steady industry and a sober management of a man's affairs." In regard to religion, temples were in every city, and altars smoking with burnt-offerings.

Of its ruins Prescott observes that "some find in them a warrant for an antiquity of thousands of years. Trees, which measure nine feet in diameter, have shot up in the midst of buildings." Accumulations of vegetable mould are found nine feet above pavements. Between Vera Cruz and the capital of Mexico "stands the venerable relic called the Temple of Cholula. It is a pyramidal mound, built, or rather cased, with unburnt brick, rising to the height of nearly 180 feet. The popular tradition of the natives is that it was erected by a family of giants, who had escaped the great inundation, and designed to raise the building to the clouds; but the gods, offended with their presumption, sent fires from heaven on the pyramid, and compelled them to abandon the attempt."

Mr. George Squier, in "Incidents of Travel and Exploration in the Land of the Incas," observes that "the temple of the sun was the principal and probably the most imposing edifice, not only in Cuzco, but in all Peru, if not in all America. The accounts of its splendour and riches left by the conquerors, and in which they have exhausted the superlatives of their grandiose language, have been so often reproduced as to be familiar to every intelligent reader. They represent the structure as being 400 paces in circuit, with high walls of finely cut stones. The chronicle, erroneously attributed to Sarmiento, states that the writer never saw but two edifices in Spain comparable with it in workmanship. The cornice of the walls, outside and in, was of gold, or plated with gold, as were the inner walls. At the eastern end was a great plate of gold representing the sun; and, ranged beneath it, in royal robes, and seated in golden chairs, were the desiccated—some say embalmed—bodies of the Inca rulers. This plate, all of one piece, spread from one wall to the other, and was the only object of worship in the building. Surrounding the court were other separate structures, dedicated respectively to the Moon, Venus, the Pleiades, Thunder, Lightning, and the Rainbow. There were also a large saloon for the Supreme Pontiff, and apartments for attendants. All these are described as having been richly decorated with gold and silver."

In Mr. Norman's "Rambles in Yucatan, or Notes of Travel through the Peninsula; including a Visit to the remarkable Ruins of Chi-Chièn, Kabah, Zayi, and Uxmal," he remarks of the first:—

"For five days did I wander up and down among these crumbling monuments of a city which, I hazard little in saying, must have been one of the largest the world has ever seen. I beheld before me, for a circuit of many miles in diameter, the walls of palaces and temples and pyramids, more or less dilapidated. The earth was strewed, as far as the eye could distinguish, with columns, some broken and some nearly perfect, which seemed to have been planted there by the genius of desolation which presided over this awful solitude. After the most careful search I could discover (amongst the Indians) no traditions, no superstitions, no legends of any kind."

He remarks that "the buildings which are now in

the most perfect state of preservation, are the temple, castle, pyramid, and other erections, upon a succession of terraces composed of rubble, embedded in mortar, held together by finished walls of fine concrete limestone; the sides of which are invariably located with reference to the four cardinal points, and the principal fronts facing the East."

All this must signify an educated and cultivated people with a spiritual life. Their traditions seem to have pointed to the West for their origin; while the Etrurians, Pelasgi, &c. appear to have evidently descended from the East. The account of the origin of the Babylonian Empire in Genesis xi. 2, and the mystery in which the commencement of art and science in Egypt is involved, seem to suggest the regions of tropical and sub-tropical Asia [1] for the starting-points of the march of the spiritual. The Hindus, on the evidence of language, &c., are acknowledged to be our cousins. Certainly their devotional and didactic scriptures — their moral, philosophical, scientific essays, and their epic, idyllic, and dramatic poems and fables, &c. &c. seem to demonstrate the most complete ancient advance in the spiritual to have taken place amongst them. While suggestive of our own culture, and that of the Greeks and Romans, there is so much that is purely characteristic of India that all seems to be indigenous. Their culture appears

---

[1] See "Cradleland of Arts and Creeds," by C. J. Stone, chaps. x., xii., &c.

to be much more in harmony with our European life than that suggested by the monuments of Egypt and Babylon, or even by the records of Greece and Rome. If we consider Europe as a whole during the last three centuries, with its warlike aristocracies, its religions and priestcraft, its absolutisms, and, on the other hand, its free commercial cities, its art, architecture, and literature, the institution of chivalry and its general code of manners, we find strikingly analogous constitutions of all kinds in the descriptions of the Sanskrit literature. Mohammedan influence and the depression of conquest had not then affected India. Venison, mutton, and strong potations nourished the old warrior race there. The rules for fair fighting in the field are more elaborate than those which have been promulgated in European warfare. In regard to the softer side of life, in the constant admiration of the charms of nature, in the luxury and artistic taste displayed in the adornments of dwellings, and in the devotion of the brave to the fair, the romance of our mediæval days seems suggested, combined with the luxuries of the present time. Whether the great Indian epic poem, the "Mahâbhârata," which gives us so much information upon these points, be relegated to the tenth or thirteenth centuries before our era, or ascribed to some centuries after its commencement, seems to signify little in considering the life depicted in it. An indigenous civilisation appears to be displayed, demanding many thousands of years for its development when we compare with it our own civilisation and the three thousand years of historical culture which we know to have preceded it. Certainly neither the classical civilisations of the Mediterranean, Babylon nor Egypt, nor the Roman Empire, seem to be able to claim parentage for the life and ideas displayed in its pages. It appears to show the life of the Aryan race—the race akin to the Greeks and ourselves—on the plains of the Upper Ganges at the period before the Buddhistic influence was widely extended.

CHAPTER VIII.

The Mahábhárata[1] (Great Bharata, that is, "supporter," from the old name of India) poem consists of about 215,000 long lines, as Professor Monier Williams of Oxford has observed. Whether it has been composed by one or several poets, it is remarkable not only for the grandeur of its size, but the completeness of its conception. Milton's "Paradise Lost" seems great in dimensions as in merit, but it only extends to about 10,600 lines, and the "Paradise Regained" contains about 2100. Even the voluminous Spenser's "Fairy Queen" has only some 30,000 lines. It is difficult to conceive that this "Great Bharata" poem can have been composed at or after the epoch of the Chinese

[1] See Appendix II.

Pilgrims. It was formerly assigned by European scholars to some period before the fifth century B.C., but of late years portions have been attributed to centuries within our era. By the Hindus it is ascribed to Divine revelation at about 3000 B.C. The culture revealed in its pages is elaborate; but it seems to appertain to an earlier age than the era of Buddhist monasticism.

It contains accounts of passages in the life of Hari, Krishna, or Vasudeva, as he is variously styled, amongst many other appellations, who is held to have been the divine Nárâyana (or he who moves upon the waters) incarnate upon the earth. But it does not afford a succinct history of his whole life, seeming to infer that the readers or auditors of the poem are acquainted with it. The narrative of his parentage and youth is given in the last book as an appendage. The main subject of the poem is a great civil or dynastic war, from which many efforts have been made to deduce historical facts; but the whole epic bears the aspect of being poetical or allegorical rather than historical. A mass of ancient legends have been gathered together in it. Didactic discourses on points of religious doctrine, moral and ceremonial conduct, the rules of fighting, &c. &c. are continually introduced, as delivered by Krishna, or the venerable or virtuous kings, chieftains, and prelates, who form the characters in the work. From the significations of their names these have an allegorical aspect; especially as many of them are related to have been incarnations of various Brahminical divinities, and some to have been miraculously born. A remote tradition seems apparent in the marriage of the five princes, the heroes of the story, to one princess. But the poet has smoothed over this legend—certainly repugnant to the ordinary minds either of the inhabitants of ancient Bharata or of modern Hindustan—by asserting that the five were, in reality, only incarnations of the same divinity under different forms.

When the marriage takes place, an Arch-Brahmin presides in the sacramental ceremony at the sacred fire, and offers prayers. The wedding procession is gorgeous with robes, bouquets, ornamented cars, golden garlands, &c. The antiquity of the custom of bestowing presents upon the bride and bridegroom is shown by the enumeration of the gifts sent on the occasion by the divine Prince Krishna, who is a relation of the husband. These consisted of golden ornaments embellished with precious stones, costly vestments, tissues of various countries, coverlets of furs, and glittering gems. He also sent couches and chairs of various kinds, hundreds of vases incrusted with diamonds and *lapis lazuli*—accompanied by servants born in many countries, endowed with youth, beauty, and good manners, and splendidly attired. He also presented them with well-trained elephants of great size, with horses excellent and well trained and richly adorned, and with cars handsomely embellished and resplendent with golden studs. Finally, he sent a quantity of unstamped gold, and millions of golden pieces of money. On another occasion, amongst the presents sent by Krishna are enumerated cars drawn by four horses, with garlands of bells, and with coachmen who had been instructed by able masters; also one thousand radiant damsels, with one hundred thousand horses from the district of Balkh.

Dr. Hunter observes that "glass was already known to the Hindus in the time of the Mahâbhârata, in which we read that at the *raja-surya* of Yudishthira, one of the royal pavilions was paved with 'black crystal,' which Duryodhana on entering mistook for water, and drew up his garments lest he should be wetted."

Yudishthira (firm in battle), the elder of the virtuous princes who are associated with the divine Krishna, being themselves indeed incarnations of inferior divinities, is described as banqueting on venison and wild boar, with fruits, sweetmeats, and various potations. The company is entertained with instrumental music, singing, and dancing. The palace is described as immense and beautiful, adorned with statues and precious stones, and surrounded by lakes, lovely with the red and blue lotus, &c. The sage Narada, a semi-divine personage, comes to them, and is declared to be versed in all the ancient histories, expert in logic, and greatest of doctors in his knowledge of the six philosophical treatises, acquainted with the true nature of peace and war, and capable of absorption by contemplation in that One, who is at the same time Two and Many. He tenders the king advice concerning the regal duties—

"Let thy ministers," he says, "who should be well acquainted with the treatises on politics, carefully keep secret thy counsels. Let thy kingdom be securely defended, that it may not be even insulted by enemies."

He inquires whether the king's fortresses are well stored with water, corn, arms, engines of war, soldiers, workmen, and money. Does his Arch-Brahmin duly announce the times of sacrifice? and, after proper ablutions, does he explain to him the position of the stars?

Is the general of his army truly a hero? Are his officers skilled in the use of arms? and does he give his army a proper allowance of pay and rations? For, remarks the sage, if the day passes without their receiving either pay or rations, the soldiers may behave in a manner suggested by the indigence of their master, which has been recognised as a cause of very great evils. When he marches to meet the enemy, the king is to be careful to throw out advance guards, and also to protect the rear of his army. "But," the sage wisely demands, "do you conquer yourself before attempting to vanquish others? March valiantly to battle," he says, "but when you have gained the victory, become yourself the protector of your enemy."

The king must have secretaries to regulate his expenses. He is asked whether his societies of handicraftsmen are composed of honest folk? for, says the sage, it is only by the practice of the arts and handicrafts that the world can exist in easy prosperity. Are his villages formed for defence after the fashion of the towns? Are his decrees proclaimed in the midst of the assembly of the people? Is he surrounded by a bodyguard, in red and splendid attire, with sabre in hand? Then inquiries are made concerning his medical men; and he is warned against materialism, falsehood, rage, negligence, sloth, and idleness; together with such persons as avoid those who possess knowledge.

The sage further inquires as to whether the tax-collectors have recourse to impositions, such as extorting false dues from foreign merchants who visit the country; whether the king looks into the state of the agriculture, whether regular relief is extended to labourers, and protection given to the blind, to idiots, &c.

On another occasion Krishna depicts a fortified town, and sets forth the manner in which it is beleaguered. Its arched gateways, arsenals, wide streets, and engines of war are mentioned. Additional defence to the moats surrounding it is afforded by pallisades. The attacking army encamps everywhere around the city, except in the cemeteries and temples of the deities. The true warrior is said never to abandon the field of battle. He will not strike one who has already been smitten to the ground, nor one who renders himself a prisoner, nor a woman, nor a child, nor an old man, nor a warrior who flies, or with his weapons broken.

Flights of arrows are described as concealing everything in their density like clouds. Cuirasses and many weapons are enumerated. Amongst various species of lances, swords, &c., appears a word (*bhoucoundis*) which M. E. Burnouf and others have held to mean firearms.

CHAPTER IX.

Such aphorisms as the following, from the Mahâbhârata, must surely have been the product of a highly cultivated age.

Politeness is especially displayed by the happy. Holy Scripture is the grandest of riches. Health is the greatest of gains. Contentment the greatest of pleasure. Humanity the highest duty. That man is happy who can abandon avarice. A son is a man's soul. A wife is the friend given by destiny. A mother is of great weight upon earth. That man does not live, although he breathes, who gives nothing to these five—to the deities, guests, servants, the Manes, and to his soul.

Renown is the aim of the dancer and comedian,

good living that of the servant; fear is the lot of the king.

Cupidity keeps us from heaven. Patience supports disputes. Science is the explanation of the true nature of things. Pity is the desire of good towards all beings. Anger is an enemy difficult to conquer. Avarice is a malady without end. A man without pity is wicked. Constancy is immobility in duty, while folly is ignorance thereof.

Neither birth, prayer, nor the knowledge of Holy Scripture, but only good conduct, can bestow the real quality of a Brahmin.

"Truth is the ladder for mounting to heaven; as necessary as is a vessel for traversing the sea. Patience is the virtue of the feeble and the ornament of the strong. These two men are over Paradise—a master endowed with patience, a poor man who can find the means to give. These two have a part in the disc of the sun—a religious mendicant absorbed in meditation and a warrior wounded to death, with his face towards his enemy. These three doors open to hell —desire, anger, and avarice. Let not a king take advice from the idle, the unscientific, or from dancers. Let these remain in thy house with the surroundings of prosperity—an old father, an unfortunate Brahmin, a poor friend, and a sister with her children. This indicates a period before the prevalence of Sati, or the immolation of the widow on her husband's pyre."

Here is a suggestion of sea voyaging being within

the general cognizance of the readers or audience of the poem: a vessel is said to be hated by those who have traversed the worst part of the sea.

The iron-tipped arrows and barbed shafts may be extracted from a man's body, but it is impossible to pull out the dart of a word which has buried itself in the depths of the heart. Do not estimate a Brahmin by his recitations of low-voiced prayer, but by his never abandoning truth. By truth immortality may be attained. Covetousness, desire, and anger achieve man's ruin. Death does not devour that man who, duly awakened by his reflections, smites those vices which have taken possession of him. Poets utter praises of death; but death is negligence, while vigilance is immortality. The warrior who has read the Vedas, if he is slain in battle, he is exalted to Paradise; and so also the merchant who has read, and distributed his wealth, and so the man of inferior class.

In the *Oudyaga* division of the Mahâbhârata a description is given of an assemblage of princes. This is held in a court, vast, white with marble, decorated with gold, glistening, and suggesting the splendour of the moon. It was sprinkled with the most precious sandal. It was furnished with chairs, dazzling in decorations, constructed of wood, iron, ivory, or gold, on which were thrown coverlets elegantly designed. The princes are costumed in the richest robes, with celestial ornaments. They are powdered with sandal; and they have great bouquets of flowers. They drink even to inebriety, of spirituous liquors. The forms of ceremonial address are minutely described, corresponding to the modern *salaam* of the Hindu, *i.e.* in the lowly bending of the body and the joining together of the hands in attitude of supplication, &c. It was no crude conception of deity which, having adopted what we hold to be the Christian truth of the Divine manifested in the Human, uttered these words of Krishna—That he is called *Vasou*, because he abides in all creatures; then, from his divine birth, comes the name of *Vasoudéva*. He is called Vishnu (the All-pervading) from his grandeur. From his unification in God, know that his name of *Mádhava* is derived; and his name *Madhouka* because he is formed of all true nature. He is called *Krishna* on account of his union with this dark-blue colour; also he is styled the White Lotus, the supreme habitation, the immortal and imperishable God with the blue-lotus eyes. He is styled Hrishikésa for ruling over the organs of sense, and Naràyana for his march upon the waters. He is everlasting. He assists at the birth of every being, good or evil. He names each creature, for he possesses the science of everything. He reposes in truth, and truth in him; for he is the truth. He is styled Govinda (the herdsman), and the eternal duty. It must be remembered that herdsman precisely corresponds to our shepherd. Flocks of sheep are not kept by Indians. They do not breed mutton for eating. The pastor there can only be a herdsman.

Krishna advocates peace, still he propounds the sacred duty of the warrior in terms which would be received with the highest applause amongst the chivalry of Europe. He says that defeat is no better than death. The duty of the warrior is to seek victory or death in battle. Death has many advantages over the incurring of reproach. Cynical wisdom is apparent in the remark that Brahmins, friends, and relations themselves turn away from a poor man. The Brahminical author or authors of this work frequently assert that the true Brahminhood depends upon the spirit of the Brahmin's deeds and life, not upon his mere hereditary association with the order; but care is taken to inculcate the constant propriety of supporting the Brahmins. At all great ceremonies accounts are given of vast numbers of presents bestowed upon them—golden pieces, cattle, fruits, golden adorned cars, &c. &c. It must be allowed that our modern priesthoods and ministers of various denominations have also secured for themselves as corporations their fully due proportion of the wealth of the communities with which they are connected.

In reading this great poem it is not that a few gems of high religious feeling, or of pithy wisdom, or rare poetical descriptions, suggesting high culture, are to be extracted from masses of matter worthless except from an archæological point of view. On the contrary, earnest devotional addresses which would be perfectly suitable to a modern pulpit, worldly-wise apophthegms, accounts of the magnificence, taste, and luxuries of life, and of carefully educated political and social order, abound throughout its pages. Continually the apparent polytheism is shown to express the attributes or aspects of one eternal, omnipresent, and omniscient Supreme Spirit; incarnated upon earth in many forms, but especially and entirely in the Prince of many appellations, who is, in modern times, more particularly known as Krishna. The enthusiastic love of the beauties of nature is ever apparent; whether exulting in the grandeur of mountains, the loveliness of sylvan scenes—rich in the flowers which, in India, bloom in gorgeous tints on forest trees, in the beauty of tropical gardens, or perhaps most fervently in dilating on the tranquil charms of waters, exquisitely adorned with the blue and crimson lotus, &c. Flowers are showered upon triumphant heroes, cities on ceremonial occasions are odorous with the sandal and other perfumes. Meats of many styles of cookery, sauces and sweet-meats, intoxicating liquors of various kinds, are also recounted at banquets with admiration; but the more refined delights certainly seem to inspire, in the higher degree, the poetic ecstasies of the author. And constantly truth, courage, purity of soul and gentleness are extolled. Ceremonial acts of religion are enjoined; but the highest aspiration of holiness is declared to be the seeking after union with the Divine through meditation and faith.

There are many eccentric legends in the poem, but

like those in our own Scriptures, they appertain to a past age. In Christianity the stories of the temptation of Eve by the Serpent, of the Ark, of the speaking of Balaam's ass, and of the strength of Samson residing in his hair, &c. &c., have been credited as truthful facts of ages of miracles, which have ceased in the present day. These ancient stories are held to be divine, and are reverently read throughout Christendom. And so the curious legends in the Mahábhárata of the wonderful doings of old patriarchs and saints, and of the first manifestations of the Divine to the human, are still esteemed sacred amongst the Hindus. It would certainly seem that there has been no advancement of indigenous thought in India since the epoch of this poem. An immense number of old stories and allegories are collected in it, with stores of didactic sayings on all topics, religious and secular; and with frequent and varying illustrations of the real unity of the Divine. The numerous conceptions of the Hindu Pantheon are shown repeatedly to be in reality only forms of one Supreme Spirit, who is in all and everything. Altogether, like the discoveries of geology in respect to the history of the earth, these revelations of the great Indian epic seem to open to our conceptions a remote past of civilisation.

CHAPTER X.

KRISHNA endeavours to mediate between the inimical parties in the poem, and goes as ambassador. (*Vide* trans. by Hippolyte Fauche, vol. vi., p. 126, *et seq.*) Before setting out, he bathes and solemnly performs the due matutinal ceremonial; adoring the sun and fire, and inclining before the Brahmins. His car is armed for the journey. It is adorned with moons and crescent moons, and with brilliant standards, and it is styled a charming object of art. Birds and beasts of good augury are said to follow his march. His friends, the five "virtuous" princes, accompany him to some distance from their capital; and when they bid him adieu, "Firm in Battle," the eldest, addresses him as "Lord of all beings, eternal god of gods; whom the man exempt from passion ought to obey." Saints assemble from all parts to greet Krishna, whom they style, "this god, become a warrior prince." "Courtesans and kings," they say, "contemplate thee who art the verity." As Krishna advances thunder is heard and rain falls in a cloudless sky. The seven great rivers of Scinde turn their courses from East to West. Darkness prevails over all the world, except upon his own route. The women assembled upon his line of march overwhelm with flowers of the sweetest fragrance "this grand being, whose happiness is found in the welfare of all creatures." In traversing the various towns and kingdoms the inhabitants all come forth to behold him. When he alights he gives orders to groom the horses in due accordance with the treatises on their treatment. Brahmins invite him to repose in their houses, described as adorned with precious stones. Everywhere he constitutes the topic of conversation; and it is agreed that pleasure will result to those who treat him with due honour, and pain to those who do not receive him. The roads are watered; the gates of the towns are decorated to receive him; while the inhabitants throng in cars or on foot. Crowds of charming women are upon every palace. The hymns of poets, bards, and minstrels, the sweet chants of women and concerts of tambourines and drums, flutes and conch shells, accompany him.

When Krishna's mission has failed to preserve peace, and war has been declared, the tumult of a vast encampment is powerfully described, the noise of men, horses, elephants, horns, cars, and engines of war. Then there is the putting on of cuirasses, &c., and the whole is described as in commotion like the waves in a tempest. Market-places are established in the camps. Doctors and surgeons are mentioned, duly provided with instruments and learned in the treatises on medicine. Cars, armoured elephants, cavalry and infantry are described as numbered by tens of thousands. And a district having been selected for the camp, well watered, shaded by woods, with abundance of turf, the king surrounds it with cemeteries, temples, altars, &c., and then constructs a palace for himself. Mountains of weapons are provided—bows and arrows, coats of mail, maces, battle-axes, iron arrows, sabres, standards, &c. The warriors have vestments ornamented with gold, and even golden cuirasses and coats of mail.

If they had not, in those days, quite arrived at the civilised neatness of the breechloading rifle as an engine of destruction; if they had not altogether reached to the extent of Christian culture in designing weapons of war in general, they had, at all events, manifested considerable imagination in conceiving and skill in completing these. Besides all the varieties of spears, axes, and swords, they had arrows which were shot through tubes as well as from the ordinary bows; and they had some species of shells filled with boiling water, and they threw from their chariots burning balls. They had also the mysterious firearms to which allusion has been made, the nature of which does not seem to be known. The proportion of the troops is stated to have been—one car to ten elephants, to each elephant ten horsemen, to each horseman seven foot-soldiers. It seems to have been customary for the troops of each description to engage with one another, cavalry with cavalry, infantry with infantry, &c. That the general equipment of the whole was brilliant, may be inferred from the foot-soldiers being described as wearing golden garlands.

Several of the heroes who are on the side of the

princes opposed to those whose cause is espoused by Krishna, appear to feel that it is hopeless to expect to conquer as he is against them; but they conceive themselves to be bound in honour, and in the true spirit of our mediæval chivalry, to fight on.

The allegorical nature of the poem seems to be shown in Krishna's friends, the virtuous Princes, having preferred his alliance without armies, and himself engaging not to bear arms in the contest, to that of hosts of warriors without him.

The army is described as drawn up in different array on each of the days of battle—in a half moon, a cross in the form of an eagle with its wings outstretched, a lotus, and in other fanciful forms. The air is darkened with the flights of arrows. Heroes, in their chariots, even send showers of arrows from their single bows, such is the rapidity of their fire. Their aim is so exquisite that they are described as cutting in sunder lances hurled at them, or other arrows in their flight; employing arrows with a crescent head for slicing purposes. Allowing for the exuberant imagination and exaggerations of the poet, it must still appear, from the descriptions of the shooting, that archery had been brought to a pitch of perfection not surpassed by our magnificent English long-bowmen of the Cressy and Poictiers period. The uproar of the battle is heightened by the sound of the drums and conch-horns. Flaming darts are thrown. The cavalry have barbed javelins and swords with glittering points.

After the mêlée, in confusion upon the field of battle are banners, the embroidered caparisons of horses, and rich coverlets of variegated colours, javelins, maces, tridents, hooks to seize the golden ornaments of the enemy, glistening scimitars, arrows feathered with gold, golden cuirasses, tiaras, and helmets, swords inlaid with gold, with ivory hilts; amidst bodies, decapitated heads with their earrings, aigrettes, &c., batons of command made of *lapis lazuli* or precious stones, severed arms of cavaliers with their bracelets on them, turbans of divers hues, with golden half-moon crests, &c. Surgeons are mentioned as coming with their instruments to extract the arrows from the wounded. The chieftains are described as eagerly ascending their war chariots, burning as ardently with the desire of victory as merchants with that of gain when they embark upon the great ships. When victory has been obtained, the hero is celebrated in songs chanted by the bards, minstrels, and poets. But attention is continually turned towards Krishna, in whom are said to be victory and eternal glory. He, in reply to laudations of himself, says, I cease not to work for the preservation of the entire world. And he declares that death is merely the destruction of the body; the soul will live again.

Amongst a list of evil-doers those who commit suicide are reprobated, with those who maintain atheistic or infidel opinions.

Though the Hindus have been blamed for possessing

no histories of their country, it is not impossible that many valuable historical MSS. may have perished, for bards are said to be especially learned in the ancient histories.

Comfitures, patès, various kinds of cakes, rice boiled with sweetmeats, &c., condiments flavoured with rum, in addition to meats "artistically prepared," with carefully seasoned gravies, &c., and various kinds of intoxicating liquors, seem not only to have been enjoyed by the warriors, but by the Brahmins to great extent. There are even said to have been rivers of ingeniously made potations. And their revels were accompanied by songs as in Northern Europe.

Throughout the poem, on the other hand, honour, courage, patience, truth, and tenderness are lauded in precept and example. But to become inebriated after a gay banquet seems to have been regarded with no more abhorrence than in England during the Georgian era, when the clergy as well as the gentry indulged freely in all the pleasures of the table. The descriptions of the life of the heroes of the poem, associated as they are with allusions to the excellence of agriculture, and the admirable work of artisans, and with the civilised form of the warfare, suggest a set of men corresponding to those of that period rather than to those of such an age as the Homeric in Greece. Culture and grandeur of archaic civilisation appear in the noble pages of the *Iliad* and *Odyssey*; but the frequent allusions in this Indian epic to treatises on the various branches of the political and social arts, and the allegorical rather than descriptive nature of the poem itself, indicate an epoch which may be styled literary.

Perhaps our sixteenth century, which produced Shakespeare and Spenser, and which was witnessing the revival of classical learning—and of Protestantism—corresponds more accurately with the age of this Mahâbhârata epic than the Georgian period. As has been observed, it is difficult to conceive that it can have been written after Buddhistic monasteries and relic monuments had overspread the land. It is also difficult to conceive that the invasion of Alexander, and the subsequent establishment of the Greeks upon the north-west of India, can have attracted no more attention than appears in allusions to people styled Yavanas—in a manner certainly not at all suggestive of the Greeks. As this term Yavana, which was bestowed upon the Greeks, was subsequently applied to the Mohammedans, it is evident that it may have been employed to designate the people of the Bactrian region before the advent of the Greeks. In fact, the word seems clearly to have been applied to the inhabitants of that district, or to some neighbouring territory, before it fell under the power of Alexander's successor. The epoch of the poem would therefore appear to have been earlier than the latter half of the fourth century B.C. at the latest. Portions or episodes may, of course, have been introduced afterwards, but the descriptions of the civilisation, and the doctrine of faith in the manifestation of the Supreme Spirit in Krishna, appear throughout the work. They are not merely episodical. They have an aspect of distinct antiquity. In the episode called the Bhagavad Gîtâ, or Divine Song, Krishna especially reveals to his favourite Prince Arjouna that release from transmigrations upon earth and union with the Divine may be attained through faith in himself. But if the association of this doctrine with Krishna could be shown to be within our era, its deduction is evident from the doctrine of union with the Divine taught in the older Platonic-like philosophies. The six great systems of the ancient Hindus or Bharataus, with their elaborately-framed logical modes, &c., seem to take the antiquity of cultured life further backwards even than this poem.

CHAPTER XI.

BENEATH the gorgeous azure of the Indian sky, and in the dazzling sunshine, the ancient Indian armies must have presented a most brilliant aspect at this period, when a poet, or poets, became inspired to compose the Mahâbhârata. As has been observed, it is difficult to conceive that this was after the monastic system of Buddhism had become established in the land, and from the thirteenth to the fifth century B.C.

seems to have been the more likely epoch. Allowing for the heightened colouring of the descriptions, as we can scarcely suppose the pictures to have been drawn from no model, we may conceive the "pomp and panoply of glorious war" to have been marvellously glittering. The chieftains wore tiaras of gold, and bouquets of flowers also of gold. Their banners were heavily emblazoned with the same, and had many devices which have descended to us in mediæval heraldry. Their four-horsed chariots clanged and sparkled with bells, and their arrows were winged with peacocks' or herons' plumes. Lances and great maces were decorated with ribands of golden tissue; their weapons in general, their bracelets, and the dangling jewels of their head-dresses glittered with precious stones. The horses and elephants were caparisoned with colour and magnificence. The warriors also had umbrellas and fans like the old Japanese swordsmen. One great and pious hero is represented as having been only vanquished after being so transfixed with arrows that he is enabled to repose upon them. They support him from the ground. Upon this couch of seeming torture he has the courage and constancy to remain for some time, uttering many moral reflections. A tremendous combat with clubs is described; and it is stated that it is unfair to strike below the waist in a club-fight, as in a modern English boxing-match.

To return from war to the stage, the Harivansa

(or history of the family of Hari), the last book of the Mahábhárata, has been ascribed to about the period of our Plantagenet monarchs; but again the descriptions of India in the travels of the Chinese Pilgrim render it difficult to conceive its having been written at that epoch. It also suggests the fifth century B.C. rather than a later period.

Fêtes are described as given on the occasion of a great sacrifice of Vasudeva (the name of Krishna's father, but often applied to Krishna, or Hari, himself). The narration suggests that amateur theatricals were in vogue at the period. Firstly, an account is given of an apparently professional actor who charms them by his admirable light-comedy style, and his power of universal mimicry, which had been especially bestowed upon him by the Brahmins at his request. Then the principal members of Krishna's tribal family disguise themselves in the garb of comedians. One is described as becoming what we should call the "leading man" of the company, another is the "low comedian," and the rest take various parts. With them are conjoined ladies distinguished by their graces and talents, and an orchestra is added. Concealed under the guise of the characters which they were to enact, they arrive in a popular quarter of the city; and five houses are assigned to them for residences, and hospitalities and presents conferred upon them.

At the representation they firstly perform a drama upon the subject of the Ramáyana epic, the actors being in suitable costumes. After the customary prologue it is related that many interesting scenes ensue, which evoke enthusiastic applause; and precious stuffs and gems are bestowed upon the performers. After the principal piece, recitations, &c., are given. The King causes a handsome theatre to be constructed, and therein concerts are held of wind and stringed instruments, also vocal, with choirs of women. A play is performed entitled the "History of Couvéra (the god of riches) and the Loves of Rambhâ (a nymph of Indra's heaven)." And now a passage suggests that not only were they careful to attire their characters in fitting costumes, and not only were women allowed to perform as upon our modern stage, but that they actually had our scenic effects. It is related that the decorations, by a magical effort of the art of the Yadavas, represented, in its natural aspect, Mount Kêlâsa—the Olympus of the Hindus.

The description of Krishna's city of Dwaravati, or Dwârvaka, suggests a capital not unworthy to be placed by the side of our modern Paris. Its turrets overlook parks, flower gardens, plantations, canals, and basins of water, walls resplendent with gold, woods, and the distant mountains. Its arcades are enriched with gold and precious stones, and it is surrounded by deep moats and lofty ramparts glistening with yellow stucco, on which are placed engines of war capable of killing a hundred men at a shot. The town contains eight principal streets and six grand squares, with a wide road running around it. In these streets the ladies and great men could display their cortéges without crowding, for seven chariots could go abreast. The houses had staircases enriched with gold and precious stones, and the windows had golden lattices. In Krishna's palace were a thousand crystal columns, and it was chiefly constructed of precious stones. When Krishna enters the city in triumph vases of agreeable liquors are placed here and there, the heads of the corporations come to meet him, and the women shower flowers upon him from the housetops, &c. The allegories contained in this work are not only religious and moral, but astronomical and meteorological.

Mr. Hurrychund Chintamon, in his commentary on the "Divine Song" (Bhâgavad Gîtâ) of the Mahâbhârata, observes that its object is the removal of those mists of error which hide from man the beauty of his own spiritual nature. The Prince Arjouna addresses Krishna as "Thou All," and Krishna is declared to be "Him in whom we live, and move, and have our being, and without whom nothing is—the origin of all birth, death, might, wisdom, and goodness." Mr. H. Chintamon remarks that all this beautiful poem is but an allegory, in which the opposing forces represent Passion and Intelligence. Reason, in the form of Krishna, advises Arjouna (Mind) to wage war against Passion, Pride, &c. Intelligence, Devotion, Patience, Contentment, Friendship, Compassion, Tranquillity, Retirement, Intellect, Revelation, and Science are respectively opposed to Passion, Irreligion, Anger, Avarice, Falsehood, Pride, Envy, Haughtiness, Injury, Enjoyment, and Hypocrisy.

Constantly in the "Great Bharata" faith is urged in the divine upon earth, suffering in sympathy with man. Hopes of union with the Supreme Being, through and in that manifestation, are held forth. These appear to afford distinct analogies to Christian doctrines. Gentleness combined with courage, charity, patience, and universal love are in it continually exalted for admiration. Altogether not merely suggestions, but the actual teaching of Christianity, seems to be contained in it, as will be shown in quotations —not accidentally, or in episodes, but in the design and completion of the whole.

Krishna, under his various appellations, is invoked and adored as divine, with unvarying constancy of assertion; and self-sacrifice is inculcated as the supreme example of religion.

CHAPTER XII.

LET us suppose that additions or interpolations have been made in this "Great Bharata" since the time of Christ. Our Gospel narratives, nevertheless, cannot be reasonably conceived to have suggested all the Christian analogies of the poem. Actual Christianity might have been considered to have formed the basis of some of them if we had found them isolated. But the work contains such immense profusion of allegories, variety of legends, and multiplicity of the forms of doctrines, in which the unity of Deity, and faith in His manifestation in Krishna, is set forth. These seem to render the supposition humanly untenable that they have been all imagined from the suggestions of the Christian faith introduced into India in the first ages of the Church. Their connection is too evident with the religious ideas and philosophical expositions of those Indian scriptures which are acknowledged by all the science of our day to be pre-Christian. The "Great Bharata" poem seems to be a stupendous and profusely variegated and ornamented commentary upon the following texts in the Institutes of Manu :—" Of all duties the principal is to acquire a true knowledge of one supreme God; that is the most exalted of all sciences, because it ensures immortality." . . . " Him some adore as present in elemental fire, others in Manu, lord of creatures, or more distinctly present in Indra, regent of the clouds and the atmosphere, others as the Most High Eternal Spirit."

This ancient Indian code of laws is attributed usually to about the ninth century B.C., but some modern commentators have argued it to be later. Whether earlier or later, its originality is undoubted. The association of divinity with an earthly prince had also been suggested in the following text of Manu :—" A king, even though a child, must not be treated lightly from the idea that he is a mere mortal; no, he is a powerful divinity, who appears in human shape." From this suggestion, to conceive the Almighty incarnate in an actual or mythical monarch, of extreme valour and sagacity, seems a sequence absolutely prototypical of Christianity. Even the celestial King of birds is in his turn shown to be only One with the Supreme Spirit of the Universe. But especially this Supreme Spirit is to be worshipped as Nârâyana, moving on the waters, incarnate upon earth as Krishna for man's benefit. The divisions of the poem commence with the following adjuration: "Honour Nârâyana and Nara, greatest of men, the goddess Sarasvati (divine wisdom), and Vyâsa (meaning compiler or collector, a holy sage, alleged author of the work), and then recite this poem, which gives the victory."

Nara, always coupled with Narayana, is incarnate upon earth as Arjouna, a brilliant young prince, and constant friend of Krishna. As Krishna is invoked as the incarnation of the Supreme Spirit, so Arjouna is said to be the incarnation of, or son of, Indra, chief regent of the elements. Krishna means the dark one, Arjouna the white or shining one.

The darkness of Krishna in one place is explained by the idea that the colour of the Deity metaphorically changes with the ages of the world. As we are now in the fourth, the black, equivalent to the classical Iron Age, it has become dark in correspondence with it. Now Krishna, or Hari, as has been observed, does not seem to be introduced into the "Great Bharata" epic as any novelty. It seems to assume that those to whom the poem is addressed will be acquainted with his name, and that they will already be believers in his divine office. The poem is said to have been inspired by the Creative Power, and to be in harmony with the four Books of Knowledge (Vedas).

Having been first recited in royal presence, it is then recorded in the introduction to have been narrated before holy sages, and the supposed bard thus commences—

"When I shall have done homage to the Primitive Man, to Isana, the adorable, the honoured, the absolute Being, the Right, the Eternal One, to him who is revealed and unrevealed, the essence of the ineffable monosyllable, the non-existent, or rather to that which at the same time exists and does not exist, who is All, who is above that which exists and which does not exist, to the Creator, the ancient, supreme, imperishable; to the All-pervading, called also Hrishikésa and Hari, the chief of beings—pure, without sin, happy and bestowing happiness; I will declare the holy purpose of the admirable work of the magnanimous Vyâsa, which many bards are recounting, which lives in the abridgments and developments of Brahmins," &c.

Further on the old blind monarch, who is one of the principal characters in the story, says: "When I have heard how, in the interest of the world,

Maghava-Vasudeva came to incarnate his universal soul on this earth, of which he is the sole energy"—He seems to assume here that it is merely a new narration of an acknowledged story. Again, before Krishna himself appears upon the scene, he is called "the imperishable and blessed Vasudeva, who is, assuredly, the truth, immortality, purification, and sanctity itself—the eternal Brahman, the Supreme Certainty, the Light without end, whose divine works the sages have related, who at the same time exists and exists not, from whom the universe derives its origin, who is the commencement and development, the birth, death, and resurrection of beings."

CHAPTER XIII.

THE author of the work adopts a very self-opinionated view of its comprehensiveness, and declares that there exists no legend upon the earth which rests not its basis upon this recital; and its perusal is declared to be capable of effacing all sin except the sin against Mahâdeva (Great God, or Great Shining Being literally). Mahadeva is one with Shiva, the third person in the Hindu trinity.

After Krishna under some one of his names has been frequently mentioned, the following account of his incarnation is given :—" To favour the worlds, the illustrious divinity, who receives the adoration of the world, Vishnu, incarnated himself in the womb of Devaki (the Divine One), and became the Son of Vasudeva. He who is without beginning or end, the God, Creator of the world, the Imperishable, the Chief of beings, the Universal Soul, Nature, the All-power, the Principle of life, the Creator of all; he whose essence is goodness, the Immortal, the Infinite One, the Swan, the adorable Narâyana, he who nourishes all, who is not born—the ineffable Purusha (universal soul),—He willed, for the increase of virtue, to be born in the race of men."

Krishna is first introduced in the epic under the following circumstances:—The hand of a princess is offered to any prince or noble who can win her in competition of feats of arms at a species of tournament. On such an occasion great distributions of riches of various sorts are made to Brahmins. Hither, it is said, come kings, and sons of kings, and sacrificers—students in the Veda, firm in their vows, and admirable young men of many countries, also actors, poets, athletes, &c. The "virtuous" princes come whose side in the war Krishna espouses, and who have been ejected from their rightful heritage in a manner which recalls to mind the banished duke and his followers in Shakespeare's "As you like it." And as they make their journey it is related that they read the "Books of Knowledge." Outside the city grand preparations are made for the competition. Pavilions are raised with porticoes, arcades, and commodious staircases.

They are adorned with elegant carpets, couches, and seats. They are perfumed with aloes and sandal, and decorated with wreaths of flowers.

Here we have the first meeting of Krishna with these virtuous princes, his friends and relations; and he certainly appears upon the scene as one supposed to be familiar to the reader of the poem, also represented as known to the public present at this sort of tournament described in it. After diversions of comedians and dancers, &c. &c., on the sixteenth day of the fête the princess, who is in competition, elaborately costumed, descends into the amphitheatre to display herself. Then religious ceremonies are performed, the musical instruments are silenced, and it is solemnly proclaimed that whoever draws a bow of tremendous strength, and shoots five arrows in succession through a ring, shall have the princess to wife, provided his qualifications in respect to manly vigour, beauty, and birth are satisfactory. Krishna, who has not yet made himself known to them, falls into reverie as he recognises the exiled princes under their disguise as Brahminical students. The disguised princes are victorious, much to the delight of the Brahmins present, and to the disgust of the aristocratic warriors, who exclaim that they are not qualified to win the prize. Then Krishna informs the assembled kings that the princess has been legally won, and he comes to the disguised princes, embraces the feet of the eldest, and says, "I am Krishna." In this incident Krishna appears, as is frequently the case, more as a wise prince than as a divine person; for on being asked how he knew them in their disguise, he simply replies that no others could have accomplished the deed. But the Prince Arjouna, before accomplishing the feat of bending the bow and shooting the arrow, has thought of Krishna as divine. He has bent in reverence to Indra, Isana (Shiva), and Vishnu; and he also has rendered homage in thought to Krishna. At the conclusion of this part of the narrative it is said that the "God-made man departed quickly, accompanied by Baladeva, his brother."

Krishna is certainly a charming conception, a beautiful ideal of man. It can easily be comprehended how such a hero can have become too beloved by the Hindus to be easily deserted for the object of adoration set before them by Christian missionaries. There is but one association connected with him calculated to render him odious in the eyes of Europeans, viz., the plurality of wives. But in the manner in which this attribute of his personality is narrated, and in other particulars, such as his colour, the antiquity of the conception seems certainly demonstrated, especially as it is associated with the strange marriage of the princes, his associates.

Honour, the sanctity of the plighted word, and general benevolence, are always connected with the sanctity of faith in Krishna as the divine manifested upon earth. But the brilliant, joyous, and even voluptuous sides of life are not considered to be incompatible with religion. Great ascetics and hermits are constantly held up to admiration and accredited with superhuman powers; but even these ascetics seem, upon occasions, to indulge in gaiety. So in mediæval Europe,[1] while the Christianity of nobles and knights, burghers and peasants, appears to have corresponded with this aspect of the Krishna religion, monks and hermits co-existed who are held not to have been invariably superior to carnal gratification. There is much in the "Great Bharata" epic which suggests our mediæval conceptions of mingled chivalry and religion.

CHAPTER XIV.

TILL the puritanical and "evangelical" elements were introduced into or revived in Christianity, some three or four centuries ago, there does not seem to have existed so distinct an idea of the separateness of the divine and profane in the Catholic Church. In Buddhism the misery and worthlessness of worldly existence was preached, and true happiness inculcated to be found in the entire abnegation of self and its desires. In the religion of Krishna, although tremendous austerities and fearful penances were extolled, the

---

[1] See Appendix IX.

general conception of religion was more worldly. It certainly seems to correspond, as has been suggested, with what may be conceived to have been the religion of one of our mediæval knights-errant. The spirit of devotion seems akin to that which induced Count Robert of Paris to take his stand before the Chapel of our Lady where four cross-roads met, as Sir Walter Scott narrates. Here, in mingled adoration of the Madonna and his lady-love, he dared any knight to combat who might pass. Even in the sacred Bhagavad-gita, the "divine song" of the "Great Bharata" epic, Krishna exhorts the Prince Arjouna to do his duty as a warrior, before declaring his universal divinity and propounding a system of pious philosophy. The feasting, with strong meats and potent potations, described in the poem, again brings the life generally depicted into juxtaposition with our mediæval days rather than with modern Hinduism.

Professor Monier Williams of Oxford is amongst some scholars who seem to conceive that the didactic discourses in the "divine song" present an aspect so analogous to Christian doctrine that they must be derived from it. But similar teaching, equally Christian in conception, seems to pervade the poem so continually, that this especially Christian-like portion may be more reasonably argued to be a spiritual development in old India, logically to be expected from the context of the work. The Hindus have seemed so slow in taking advantage of the efforts of Christian missionaries in our age, and translations of the Bible, that it is difficult to comprehend how they can so eagerly have adopted Christian ideas eighteen hundred years ago. But of course the difficulty may be explained by supposing the divine aid to have miraculously accompanied early apostles in India. In that case the Hindus must be regarded as Christians who have exaggerated and altered the life of Christ, while retaining a resemblance in many incidents, and assigned Him to their own part of the world.

As Milton, 1600 years after the promulgation of our faith, became inspired to glorify the work of redemption in his great epic, so the more ancient Aryan poet, or poets, would seem to have become inspired to recount the glories of Krishna, and the grandeur and goodness of actual or imaginary heroes devoted to him. It would appear that, as in the case of our own poet, the belief of the multitude must have been necessary to yield the requisite inspiration for such a stupendous and often sublime work. It has been asserted by European critics to have been a compilation by "crafty Brahmins" to promote their own ends. But their system is complete without the aid of Krishna. It would seem probable, if the work was dictated by Brahminical design, that this happened after Krishna had become the veneration of the people, in order to associate him with Brahminism.

The stories of Krishna in this poem connect him with the sun and the holy fire (Agni). And his constant association with Arjouna, the incarnate Indra, seems to signify the Supreme Spirit, associating with and directing the Regent of the Elements, the Monarch of Heaven and of the divine beings. Agni, the sacred fire of the earlier scriptures, as will be shown in quotations from the Vedas, is invoked in those "Books of Knowledge" as the mediator between the divinities and men. He is thus addressed in the "Great Bharata"—"Thou art the mouth of the gods, the purifier and the sacrifice; thou conveyest the offering to the deities; the Vedas are born of thee. Thou art the admirable light, the breath of life. Thou art the Holy One. O supreme Energy! purify me by the truth."

So is Krishna addressed as the soul of the Vedas, Hari, greatest Being in the world, the eternal Origin, the Sustainer of that which has been, of that which is, of that which will be, the asylum assured to the unfortunate, &c.

It is said in the *Sabha* division of this "Great Bharata" that Narayana, the adorable lord of the world, was born in the race of Yadu. He shone upon earth like the queen of the stars in the midst of the constellations. "This Hari, exterminator of enemies, whose might all the gods adore, behold him, dwelling upon earth, like a child of Manu." The expression, "child of Manu," is frequently used in this poem. It would seem to signify child of the first self-existent man-type.

"Oh, is it not marvellous!" is exclaimed in this

Sabha portion of the epic, "that the Being existing by himself, should take unto himself the form of this warrior, endowed with such vigour?" Subsequently the king, whose cause Krishna espouses, answers to a holy sage that he has heard of the actions of Krishna since his birth, who has brought happiness on earth for all creatures. He then recounts his praises, his knowledge, his universal good qualities, his liberality, science, humility, firmness. He calls him the Father, the perfect Founder of worlds, the Sovereign, the Soul; "in effect," he continues, "the generation and fortune of worlds is in Krishna; this universe, and all which exists, moveable and immoveable, has its cause in Krishna. He is invisible Nature, the eternal Creator, the Superior of all beings, the Intelligence, the grand Soul, the Wind, the Light, the Water, the Heaven and the Earth; he is all. All which exists, composed of four elements, has its root in Krishna—the sun and the moon, the constellations, the planets, the cardinal points—all subsist in Krishna, the Vedas, kings, and Mount Meru—the way of the universe, however far it may extend on high, below, on all sides, everything has for its head, in the worlds and amongst the divine beings, the adorable Cesava."

This is uttered in an assembly of kings and chieftains at which Krishna is present. A prince impetuously exclaims that he will place his foot on the head of any one who doubts it. At this a shower of flowers falls on his head from heaven, and invisible voices applaud him. But one of the monarchs present says that although Krishna may have worked miracles, sustained a mountain for seven days, &c., it is nothing wonderful. In fact, he admits Krishna's power, but contends that it does not reach to the marvellous; and he then proceeds to inveigh against Krishna. The latter replies that he has promised to endure offences worthy of death from this monarch to the hundredth time, but that this has arrived. He then thinks of his discus. The glittering weapon, evidently typical of the sun, comes to his hand at the thought. He casts it, and cuts off the head of the unbelieving king. Forthwith prodigies occur. Rain falls in a cloudless sky, with lightning, &c.

Though inculcating gentleness and mercy, Krishna slays the unrighteous, both demons and men.

CHAPTER XV.

THE happiness of the earth, according to the "Great Bharata" poem, had been ruined by demons entering into the forms of men and animals. The Earth (personified), heavily oppressed by the weight of her burden, and tormented by fear, implores succour of that God who is the parent of all creatures. She sees Brahma, surrounded by divine beings, sages, heavenly nymphs, &c., and prays for deliverance. Brahma orders the gods (devas=divine beings) to get sons to contend against the demons (Asuras), and they all proceed to become incarnate in the world. But first they go to the heaven of Nârâyana, or Vishnu—" to him of the yellow robe, the brilliant one, with the charming eyes;" and Indra, chief of the heavenly host, says to him, " Be incarnate thyself in a portion of thy substance." And Vishnu assents.

In concert with the deities, Indra makes with Nârâyana arrangements for the descent upon earth. Vasudeva, the father of Krishna, is alleged to be himself a portion of the immortal God of gods; and Baladeva, the brother of Krishna, is also an incarnation of Vishnu, considered as Sesha, the serpent, type of eternity.

Krishna's infancy, his escape from the reigning tyrant who has been informed that a child will be born of Krishna's mother for his destruction, his youthful days amongst the cowherds, &c.—these stories are not related till the end of the "Great Bharata." A book, the Harivansa, containing them has been added. But that the story of his pastoral life is not a later invention is shown by the epithet, " Lover of the shepherdesses," being applied to him, &c. &c.

Under the name of Cesava, he is thus addressed by the sage Vyâsa, the alleged author of the poem, who is supposed to have been his contemporary, and who appears among the personages of the work attributed to him: "Thou art the beginning and the end of all beings, thou art the treasure of penitences, the eternal sacrifice; thou art Hari, Brahma, the sun and moon, time, the earth, the cardinal points, the creator, and the grandest of men. Thou art slayer of Madhu (the demon), the supreme way. Thou destroyest the demons by hundreds. There exists in thee neither anger, nor envy, nor falsehood, nor cruelty. At the end of an age of the world thou withdrawest all beings into thyself, and thou then becomest this world. At the beginning of the world's age, it is from the lotus of thy navel that Brahmâ is born, father of all things, moveable and immoveable." Krishna replies to him, "That which belongs to me, belongs to thee. Every one who hates thee, hates me."

Again, Krishna is addressed thus: "In the first creation of beings thou wast the only patriarch—thou wast the creator of all worlds. Thou art Vishnu, thou art the sacrifice, the sacrificer and the victim. Patience and truth art thou. Thou art the sacrifice which is truth. Thou art the Eternal, the way on which the holy march, soul of beings, without cessation in action. The constellations, the worlds, and the guardians of worlds all subsist in thee; thou art the lord of all beings, of those who are divine, and of those who are born of Manu."

The meaning of the expressions, sacrifice and victim, as applied to Krishna, would seem to have been suggested by his being regarded as the universal soul. Evidently sacrifice had grown into an institution before the religion of the Vedas became systematised. Sacrifice produced benefits apparently to the priests, who received presents, or obtained the victims. It was as requisite for them to procure the offerings of the people as for the priests of modern days to receive their stipends. From such reasons, or from superstitious feelings of veneration, sacrifice became regarded as something so essential to life that the deities were said to have produced the world by offering up universal, primeval soul in sacrifice. Victims, even in the Vedas, had begun to give place to the bloodless rice-cake, or offering of the juice of the moon-plant. And when Krishna came to be regarded as the soul of the world, he was styled the sacrifice, the victim. As Purusha, universal soul, he seems to have been the sacrifice. Purusha is said, in the Veda, to be the whole universe, which has been, and whatever shall be, and the lord of immortality.

"The gods performed a sacrifice with Purusha as the oblation. This victim, Purusha, born in the beginning, they immolated on the sacrificial grass. Purusha is recognised as having a personality as the universe, or rather as the soul of the universe; and he is also Vishnu, Bhagavat, Nârâyana, *i.e.* the all-pervader, blessed, he who moves upon the waters, &c., incarnate on earth as Krishna, and in numerous other forms in all times and all worlds."

Sacrifice, reading of the scriptures, alms, penitence, truth, patience, the suppression of the sensual desires, the contempt of riches—these are said to be the eight branches into which is divided the way of duty.

As the sacrifice rather corresponds to the sacrament of our Christian altars than to the old blood sacrifices, these eight would seem to precisely constitute what are considered the proper qualities of Christianity. And that form of Christianity which contemns ceremonies, and derides the efficacy of works, except as the fruit of faith, is also inculcated in the "Great Bharata," though not so constantly and strenuously perhaps as in the Bhagavata Purana and other writings sacred to Krishna.

CHAPTER XVI.

In consoling the Princess, who becomes the bride of the princes his friends, Krishna exhibits his absolute reliance in himself. "The Himalaya," he says, "shall be broken, the earth be split in fragments, and the grand basin of waters dried up before his words shall have been uttered in vain."

It is related of this Princess that, in a former birth, owing to sins committed in a still previous existence, she was unable to find a husband, notwithstanding her beauty and accomplishments. The single condition being considered disgraceful in the ancient civilisation, before Buddhism had spread with its recommendations of celibacy, she prayed earnestly for a husband in five emphatic repetitions.

She was informed from heaven that the spell which ruled her life in this respect, in chastisement of her former actions, could not be removed in this existence, but that she should have five husbands in her next life. She replied that she only desired one, not five spouses; but she was informed that her five emphatic prayers had each been separately answered, and that she must have the five husbands. And so it happened that the five semi-divine princes, brothers, won her in the competition of feats of arms, and together married her.

Krishna, on the other hand, has numerous wives. It appears to have been conceived that the Deity, incarnate upon earth, would dwell amongst humanity in all that was considered most highly becoming to a man. Marriage was held to be a sacred institution. Even the Brahminical student, who might continue in his studies till middle life, and who might retire to the hermit existence at the end of his days, was bound to become the married man and householder for a time. Krishna, however, even exhibits an apparent licentiousness which recalls to mind the vagaries of the classical divinities. But this is alleged to have been mere illusion. Ascetic celibacy has occasionally been adopted amongst his adorers. The stories of his amours certainly seem to have been suggested by astronomical observations. The sun and moon and constellations appear to have been the foundations upon which many fanciful tales have been based, which, as time went on, became more and more materialised.

One of the morals which the "Great Bharata" appears to be intended to teach is the sinfulness or folly of gambling. The chief of the virtuous Pandu princes cannot resist an invitation to play. He protests that he does not desire to gamble, but he succumbs to temptation, and finally loses kingdom and everything with the dice. At length he stakes the Princess, who, however, indignantly repudiates his right to do so. The affair ends by these princes going forth into the forests, stript of all their possessions, and burning to avenge an insult which has been put upon their wife. In consoling her, Krishna utters the words which have been quoted at the beginning of this chapter. He remarks that women, dice, the chase, and ardent liquors precipitate men from the summit of their prosperity; that great blame in the eyes of wise men is seen in gambling; and he says that he would have stopped the play if he had been present. He then relates various deeds of war which had occasioned his absence, for not only is Krishna the incarnate Nârâyana, a husband, but an ardent warrior. He has become incarnate, in fact, to deliver the world from demons and tyrants, but also to instruct it in virtue and goodness, and lead it into the way of happiness by faith in himself. Doubtless the former view of his office was the more ancient. But the characters of the moral teacher and the warrior are so indissolubly intertwined, and both are so evidently in sequence with ideas of the Vedas, that it is impossible to aver that the moral side only has been attributed to him after acquaintance with our Gospel dispensation.

Krishna, in this warlike character, seems to have been naturally adored by the warriors of North-Western India, and under corresponding forms by the old warlike tribes of Northern Europe, while the peaceful Buddhistic doctrines were obtaining a hold amongst the milder races of the East. In the gentle precepts of Pythagoreanism these last seem to have obtained a footing upon the Mediterranean, developing into Platonism, and eventually displaced by Christianity.

Although Krishna is concerned in these wars for the destruction of depraved humanity, he deprecates unnecessary wars, and endeavours to act as mediator between the opponents in the great war narrated in this poem.

Nara and Nârâyana are said to have descended upon earth to accomplish what neither divine beings nor holy men could perform—to relieve the earth of the burden which oppressed it. "The fortunate, All-pervading Spirit has come upon the earth (Vishnu); he is the adorable God, Hari, the Invincible, named also Kapila" (*Mahábhárata Vanaparva*).

Now Kapila, with whom Hari, or Krishna, is thus connected, is the reputed founder of one of the six great Indian systems of philosophy. Professor Weber of Berlin remarks, in his "History of Sanscrit Literature," that "Kapila, the originator of the Samkhya system of philosophy, appears in it raised to divine dignity itself" (*i.e.* in a book which the Professor classes amongst Vedic literature). Kapila, in fact, became regarded as an incarnation of Vishnu or Naràyana. Kapila is also associated closely with Buddhism. Professor Weber observes that the close connection of Kapila's tenets with Buddhism—the legends of which uniformly speak of him as long anterior to Buddha— proves conclusively that the system bearing his name is to be regarded as the oldest system of philosophy. Krishna and Buddha are therefore both connected with the same philosophical system, which is undeniably to be assigned to a period previous to Buddha's epoch, in about the fifth century B.C. And this again corroborates views concerning the antiquity of Krishna. In fact, Krishna and Buddha were really different aspects or the same realisation of the need of a Divine Being to lead mankind to happiness by an actual revelation on earth in Person.

It is exclaimed in this *rana* division of the "Great Bharata," that Krishna is the ancient god descended upon the earth. "He is the eternal deity. Brahmins who know the Books of Knowledge (Vedas), men who possess science of universal soul, are assured that the magnanimous Krishna is the eternal deity. Govinda (the Herdsman) is the greatest of purifiers. He is the saint of saints, the most fortunate of the fortunate, the everlasting god of gods—he is imperishable, the supreme lord, Hari, whose soul is inconceivable in thought—the pure and primitive essence of life."

Succour is implored of the God who bestows succour —the august Nârâyana, who has had no birth. The deities (devas) say to him, Thou art our creator, author, and destroyer of the world—king of the king of the deities.

Again it is said that Kapila is the Vasoudevide, *i.e.*, Krishna, the son of Vasudeva.

Then Krishna is invoked by the mystic syllable Om (or Aum), signifying the divine union of three in one. Om, adoration to the Preserver of the Universe, adoration to thee, distinct from the universe, Sovereign of the deities; thou art Agni (fire), Varuna (sovereign of the waters); thou art the Divine Seed of Right; the earth is thy body.

CHAPTER XVII.

WE commonly use the word "gods" in translation of the Sanscrit *devas*, which means, literally, *shining beings*. The ancient Bharatans imagined a heaven of powerful and brilliant personages who ruled the elements, directed the course of the planets, and interfered with the life of humanity upon the earth. They also conceived regions of darkness inhabited by beings corresponding to our demons. But the word god, which we apply to the Supreme Ruler of the universe, is scarcely an accurate appellation for these sublime but still created and not everlasting heavenly beings. The stars must have naturally suggested habitations for superhuman, glittering persons. After it had been perceived that the whole universe of stars and planets was in motion, while the polar star remained seemingly fixed, a beautiful legend originated connected with this adoration of Bhagavat, or Vishnu, Krishna, &c. A young prince, Dhruva (Firm), who, in despite of temptations and trials, remained constant in faith to him, was conceived to have been translated to this fixed point in the highest heaven, where he was established, nearest to Bhagavat, and ever devoted to him. The seven stars of the Great Bear were supposed to be seven great sages. Then the dark, tumultuous army of clouds coming up in the rainy season in gloomy mass, awe-inspiring in their weird forms, seemed an array of evil spirits invading the realms of light. Hence came stories of wars between the heavenly and dark-angel hosts. When Bhagavat or Nârâyana had come to be adored as the Supreme Spirit, it was he who delivered the heavenly beings from the demons. All, indeed, had proceeded from him. All beings and all things must eventually return to him. Meanwhile the idea gradually grew, apparently from about 1500 B.C. at least, that he was frequently present on earth, in some form or other, to relieve suffering, and lead to bliss here and hereafter.

In the first of the four ages of the world, corresponding to the Golden, Silver, Bronze, and Iron Ages of the classics, eternal virtue is related to have reigned. There were no divine beings nor demons. Creatures did not die; there were no human sacrifices, wars, or hatred. The Cause, incorporeal, reigned alone. The Soul of all beings, Narâyana, was then white. The Brahmin, regal, merchant, and labouring classes preserved their distinctions, and all creatures loved their occupations. They had but one God. They followed the same ceremonial. Man was given solely to duty; he obtained the supreme way in association with the Universal Soul.

In the next ages sacrifice had become requisite, and passions had become prominent. Vishnu, or Narâyana, assumed the yellow and red colours, and the Books of Knowledge became divided into four. Alms and penitence were necessary, maladies and sufferings increased upon the children of Manu, who is the son of the Self-Existent. At length, in the dark or Iron Age, Vishnu became black (*i.e.* manifested as Krishna, the dark one). Calamities followed; then the Deity descended to save the world and created beings from destruction.

"Above the heavenly palace of Brahmâ even is the abode of Narâyana, the Master, Supreme, who has had no beginning, who will have no end, who is called the Nature of the nature of all beings; whom the deities themselves cannot behold in his beauty, composed of all splendours. This place of Vishnu is more ardent than the sun or fire; its brilliance can scarcely be sustained by deities or demons. There the Master of creatures, the Nature of all things, the Being existent of himself, illumines in his grandeur all beings. In his presence the stars give no light. To him, Hari-Narâyana, devotion conducts all those who are wedded to supreme penitence."

All this was not mere abstract religion. By charity and truth, it is said, heaven may be attained. Truth is more estimable than any mere purposeless contemplation of charity; but charity in any reality is more estimable than even truth. "How can heaven be reached? how can a man assure himself of the fruit of his works?"

Man pressing on, without sloth, can arrive at Paradise by his works, associated with the merit of doing harm to no living being, by charity, and by the other virtues. Truth, the suppression of desires, penitence, charity, persistence in virtue,—these must ever be profitable to man.

Religious ceremonies are especially enjoined to Brahmins, and the other classes are to present offerings to them. In fact, a religion of rites, repentance, and good works is apparent. But the "Great Bharata" continually connects these works with faith in Krishna, while the Puranas ("ancient books") still more strenuously urge this doctrine.

"First," says a holy sage in the "Great Bharata,"

"homage must be offered to the Self-Existent, to the Ancient, Immortal, Eternal, Indistinct—to him of the Yellow Robe, Creator and Destroyer, the Pure, to him who is the Source and Energy of all. Even the Vedas know not what this Man knows. All marvels here below have their completion in him."

CHAPTER XVIII.

HEAVEN and earth have passed away, and will be destroyed again.

In the wreck of the universe it is narrated that one most holy sage alone survived. Nothing remained but a waste of waters, without even atmosphere; but holy ascetics are continually gifted with powers even transcending those of the deities, when they are absorbed in Nârâyana. This sage, Markandeya, swam with the waters, but found no asylum. Presently he perceived a sacred Indian fig-tree. Beneath it was an infant, who told him to rest there. "Enter," he says, "into my body."

The sage enters, and sees the entire world, with kingdoms and cities, the ocean with its sea-monsters, and the River Ganges, the four castes, the deities, and their enemies the demons, &c. And travelling for one hundred years, he still cannot find the limit of the infant's body. But at length he emerges, and again sees the child lying under the branch of the tree, in yellow robe and luminous with splendour.

The saint adores him, saying, "O God, I desire to know thee, thou who art sublime in this illusion of thy grandeur. All powerful deity was in thee. Infinite Power, how was all the world in thy body?"

The God of gods replies, "Even the deities know me not in truth, but for love of thee I will recount how I precede creation. Thou hast placed thyself under my protection, and I have shown myself to thee. It is a great lesson from the Books of Knowledge which is given thee. The intellectual waters existed before the material. This work of intelligence was done by me. Hence am I called Nârâyana; my birth is in eternity, and I shall have no end. I am the creator and destroyer of all beings. I am Vishnu, Brahmâ, and Sakra, and the monarch of the dead. I am Shiva, and Soma, and the Patriarchs. I am the Sacrifice, O thou greatest of Brahmins. The fire is my mouth, the earth my feet, the sun and the moon my eyes, the heaven my head, and the wind my breath. The Brahmins are my mouthpiece, the warriors my arms, the merchants and farmers my thighs, the labourers my feet. The Books of Knowledge have issued from me. I am the sun, and Agni (the material fire). My law disposes beings towards truth, penitence, and the absence of malignity towards all creatures. When virtue diminishes and vice increases, then I create myself and enter into a human body. I am the Soul of all. I bring joy to all the universe. The faithful honour me in all ways throughout the world. The universe sleeps while I am under the form of an infant—I, who am no infant, while Brahmâ awakes not. Under the form of Brahmâ he will arise and create the world and its beings."

This god, says the sage who recounts these marvels, is Krishna, Hari, Govinda. "Go," he continues, "and seek succour of him who gives succour."

He is asked what limit this age of the world will have, and he replies in terms eminently suggestive of the accounts of the end of the world in our Scriptures. Truth, he says, will be lost, the classes intermingled, atheists will abound, and Brahmins will become merely disputatious. Husbands and wives, fathers and sons, will be at enmity. Darkness, sin, misery, and shortened lives will ensue. Then trees and gardens will be destroyed. The lower classes will preach, and the Brahmins become their disciples. The temples will be in ruins, wars will prevail, rains will become overwhelming, and the constellations will lose their brilliance. The stars will only show sinister auguries. At length fire will consume everything, no asylum will remain, and only groans of anguish be heard.

At length on the ruins of the world will come the new age. Brahmins will again be recognised as the first of classes. Then will arise the Brahman Kalkî, surnamed the Glory of Vishnu, surpassing in beauty, energy, and intelligence. From his thought will be born chariots of war, warriors, and weapons. He will be king, victorious in virtue, monarch of the entire world; and he shall bring the celestial favours upon earth. He will immolate the barbarians, and prepare the great sacrifice of the horse (in significance of universal dominion). Then the children of Manu, by his example, will obtain happiness, and the destruction of robbers will ensure tranquillity. Vice will be exterminated. Virtue will return. Temples to the deities and holy hermitages will be revived. And the faithful will replace heretics.

This would certainly seem to suggest a period for, at all events, this portion of the poem, when Buddhistic ideas, antagonistic to Brahminical supremacy, were gaining ground. But it seems scarcely probable that it was written after Buddhism had apparently become a state religion under Ashoka. Though Brahminism continued to exist when that form of faith had become so prominent, in its councils, canons of scripture, monastic establishments, and in the favour of a powerful monarch, it is difficult to conceive that the poet could have alluded to it, except in more elaborate manner, considering his usual prolixity. If this view be correct, these passages must have been written at least three hundred years B.C.

The "Great Bharata" contains an account of a king of Yavanas, who comes from beyond the north-western borders of India, to combat with Krishna, and who is eventually slain in a mystic manner. It seems, however, almost impossible that the King of the Yavanas in the poem can have symbolised Alexander and his invasion, or other Greek influence. The idea of blackness is associated with him, and in fact no suggestiveness of the Greek appears except the name. Altogether this poem, and its accounts of the manifestation of the divine in Krishna and his doctrine, seem to appertain to a grand civilisation which was in existence in the present British India by the fifth century B.C. That civilisation was then ancient, elaborate, and artificial in laws, commerce, arts, and arms. India has retained to this day a valiant class of warriors; but in those days, as in mediæval Europe, war seems to have been more generally the pastime of an aristocratical class. The Brahmins, however, were preaching docility, gentleness, temperance; and they subdued the haughty warriors by assertions of their own transcendent powers. They taught that the curse of a Brahmin possessed terrific and certain force, and they also taught that no house of king or chieftain was complete without its Brahmin chaplain. Indeed the connection of warriors and Brahmins is very similar to that of the combined barons and priests of mediæval Europe. But the priest of the Papist Church in his celibacy has rather resembled the Buddhist than the Brahmin.

CHAPTER XIX.

The Princess Krishnâ, who, in this transmigration, had received the five husbands, after having to remain single in her previous life, reposes implicit faith in the power of Krishna. Wanting food during the time when she and her husbands are outcasts and wanderers on the face of the earth, she thinks of him. She calls him, in her heart, the Imperishable Son of Devaki—the protector of the world, the soul of the world, and its author. "Oh Lord," she says, "Way of those who want a way, protect me in thy compassion, O God, thou beginning and end of beings—thou Supreme Root!"

Cesava comes to her and says, "Krishnâ, I am hungry; give me to eat, and I will do all that you desire." She replies that she has no food. He rejoins that she must bring him a seething-pot; and for the moment she thinks that he is making fun of her. But speedily dishes of all sorts are produced from it, and beverages as well as eatables to entertain a number of Brahmins who have arrived and craved hospitality.

Krishna, in this aspect of the beneficent friend, continually affords prototypes of Christ. But the warrior-king is always his accompanying character. He is said to have descended upon earth to chastise the wicked and save the virtuous. "This adorable Vishnu now is named, here below, Krishna. The exploits of this august god, without birth, without beginning or end, adored in all the worlds, are celebrated by the sages. He is called Krishna, the Invincible, who bears the club, discus, and conch shell."

"This deity (Krishna) is adorned with a diadem, and clad in a robe of yellow silk. He is versed in all the sacred treatises. He is the supreme Divinity, and Arjouna is ever protected by him."

It is in the so-called episode of Bhagavad-gîtâ or Divine Song that the system of Krishna is especially displayed.

This portion of the Mahâbhârata was translated by Mr. J. Cockburn Thompson a generation ago. It has been styled an episode, and its nature is certainly episodical, but it arises naturally out of the context, and is in no way a separate portion of the whole.

When the princes entered upon the great war, Krishna, although he had engaged himself not to become a combatant in the contest, consents to act as Arjouna's charioteer.

As they are advancing amid the martial din of drums, trumpets, and conch shells, Arjouna has just raised his grandly-powerful bow, when he says to Krishna, "Stay! Imperishable One! Let the car remain between the armies." At the sight of his relations on the other side, whom he is to destroy, he is seized with profound compassion. Can good, he inquires, come from this slaughter of those his connections? "Krishna!" he says, "I desire neither kingdom, nor pleasure, not even the empire of the three worlds (heaven, earth, and hell) at this cost." And he sits down upon the seat of the chariot.

The slayer of (the demon) Madhou addresses him, with his eyes full of tears. "Whence comes, Arjouna," he inquires, "this failure of spirit?" He tells him that it is his duty to fight, and consoles him for the slaughter by saying that in reality it is of no consequence. Notwithstanding death, there will be no real cessation of existence. Just as in this life we behold in their turn infancy, maturity, and old age, so, after this life, another body will be obtained, and the wise need not be troubled with what happens here. The contact with *matter* causes both pleasure and pain. These things must be endured, for they are not everlasting; in their turn they are born and die. The man who can regard pleasure and pain as equal is wise, and he participates in immortality. These bodies come to an end, but the soul is eternal, imperishable. He who thinks the soul can be killed is unable to distinguish between soul and body. The soul will pass into a new body, just as the body takes new clothes. Soul is invulnerable. Death is better than dishonour, and the gate of Paradise is open to the warrior.

Krishna then continues by saying that he will expound the Sankhya philosophy, *i.e.*, the system attributed to the above-mentioned Kapila, whose soul was alleged to have been himself, Narayana, &c., in a previous manifestation.

Accomplish works, said Krishna, without considering

their recompense. Seek wisdom as thy refuge. When your reason shall have traversed the dark regions of error, you will arrive at absorption in the Absolute Being. Folly comes of anger. He who is without desires of this world can obtain, in the hour of death, complete separation from matter and union with the Absolute. The world retains us with the chain of works. Those men who, full of faith, continually follow, without murmuring, the opinion which I declare, are freed from the influence of works. Births are many. I know them all, but you know them not. Whenever there is weakness in virtue and accession of vice, then I produce myself. I am born in each age for the preservation of the good and the destruction of the wicked. Whoever knows, in its verity, my birth and my divine office, will return no more to birth. Renouncing anger, fear, desire, many of my faithful, purified by the fire of knowledge, and taking refuge in my bosom, are come to the life in me. Those who desire perfection in works obtain them in this world of men by sacrificing to the deities. But the man to whom I am known is freed from the bondage of works. The man who is without knowledge, without faith, with soul lulled asleep by doubt, perishes. The sage who has renounced the fruit of works arrives at tranquillity. He who is attached to the recompense is enchained by the force of desire. He whose soul is fixed on union sees that the Great Soul is in all creatures, and that all creatures are in the Great Soul.

No one, my son, continues Krishna, if he is the author of good works, can enter into the way of unhappiness. Having become a citizen of worlds reserved for the good actions, when he has there made his abode for a vast period, fallen away from the union, he will pass into the families of those who are happy and pure. He can become united with the thoughts which animated his previous body, and again he may strive to attain perfection. At length, having washed away all his sins in the purification of many births, he is led into the supreme way. I am the principle of living beings, the birth and death of the entire world. Whatever may be the divine person whom one of the faithful desires to honour, it is really me to whom the honour is given. I know all beings, past, present, and future, but I am known by none of them. Those who take refuge in me, know the supreme soul in its plenitude. Those who have learnt, with soul identified with me, that I am before all beings, before all the deities, before all the sacrifices, these know me. Arjouna inquires, How art thou the first sacrifice? Krishna replies that the man-type was before all beings, before the deities; in this essence of the perishable, he is the first of sacrifices. Those who have come to me, he says, entered into the supreme perfection, are no longer condemned to be reborn in the abode of pains. From this earth to the world of Brahmâ men describe the revolution of a circle, and return to animate fresh bodies, but he who seeks his abode in me, endures no new births here below.

"I am the supreme way, Invisible; I have created the world, and all beings repose in me. I am the sacrifice, I am the ceremony, the mother and father, the asylum, immortality and death. I am, Arjouna, that which is and that which is not; and those who sacrifice to other gods in faith, honour me. If any one offers to me with piety water or a flower, I receive it willingly. I am equal towards all creatures: women, the lowest ranks, if they seek refuge in me, they shall enter the supreme way. Attach thy soul to me, and you shall come to me. I am the First-born; before the deities."

"Thy divinity," replies Arjouna, "is supreme; thou art Purity, the eternal Man, the first God, the Lord without birth."

CHAPTER XX.

WHILE two great armies, marshalled in their opposing ranks, are about to commence an internecine strife, this dialogue between one of the principal leaders and his divine charioteer curiously continues. Krishna, to illustrate his supreme divinity, bestows upon Arjouna, for the time, divine eyes. "Behold," he says, "my supreme union with all things." He is then transfigured before Arjouna, who beholds in his body the entire universe, conserving unity in its multiple divisions. Krishna informs him that he, Bhagavat, is Time, which works the destruction of all men, that all the warriors in the two armies shall perish, himself only excepted.

Arjouna then adores him, and addresses him as First Creator, Infinite, Sovereign of the gods, the Habitation of the world, the great Treasure of this universe, the Wind, the Fire, the universal God. He says, "If I have spoken to thee brusquely, if I have not duly honoured thee, forgive me, deign to pardon me as a father a son, a friend his friend, or a lover his mistress." Krishna declares that no other than Arjouna has seen his form. By exclusive devotion he may be known, he may be seen in verity, and even oneness may be obtained with him. "I am," he says, " first object. He who is exempt from enmity towards all beings comes to me. I will lift out of the sea, whose waves overwhelm the world, and save from death, those who place their thoughts on me. If you cannot establish yourself solidly in me by thought, arrive by ascetic process. Knowledge is of more value than religious ceremony, meditation is before knowledge; the renouncing of the fruit of works is above all. When a mortal comes to the time of dissolution, if truth is in all his belief, he enters the pure world of the saints. If he dies, still delivered to passion and desire of action, or still immersed in obscurity of soul, he will be reborn in a foolish or wicked mother. Whoever serves me in constant piety, participates in the essence of Brahma. For I am the habitation of Brahma, the incorruptible food of life, the eternal justice and infinite happiness. There is, it is said, a divine fig-tree imperishable, the branches of which are upon earth, but the roots in heaven. Hymns are its leaves; and to know it is to know the Books of Knowledge. When this tree, with its wide-spreading roots, has been cut down with the axe of indifference to the world, then may that place be sought from which there is no return. Let man, therefore, turn towards this primordial, universal soul, from which came the ancient origin of things." . . . " Under the form of the sun I penetrate all bodies. I am Memory, Science, the Books of Knowledge and Sacred Scriptures. Whoever knows me for the Supreme Spirit, knows all. Courage, constancy, and patience are qualities appertaining to the divine condition; hypocrisy, anger, vanity belong to the nature of demons. Those who give way to their desires, and deny the existence of God, will descend to the impure hell." . . . Krishna continues to Arjouna, "Hearken still to my sublime word; thou art my well-beloved, I will declare to thee that which is for thy good. Fix on me thy heart, address to me thy adoration, offer to me sacrifices (*i.e.*, the bloodless sacrifices or sacraments of offerings of clarified butter, &c. In the morning this and honey seem to have been offered, the holy fire adored, with other ceremonies. Then there was the sacrifice of the moon-plant, &c.). Thou shalt come to me," he continues, "I promise that which is true. . . . Come to me only as thy refuge. I will deliver thee from all sins. Afflict not thyself. Do not repeat these words to the impenitent; but he who will reveal this mystery to my servant will come, without doubt, to me. The man who possesses faith without desire, who has heard these words, shall go to the happy worlds of souls who have done holy works."

He enjoins the observance of caste. He praises the hermits—calm, living on little food, &c., participating in the essence of Brahma. Charity exercised in hopes of return is not good, he declares. He who discerns one single imperishable soul in all beings, realises the Indivisible in all his creatures. Iswara resides in the heart of all beings; he traverses all creatures on the wheel of Time. "Take refuge with all thy soul, O son of Bharata, in this only asylum, and you shall obtain the grace of supreme peace and the eternal Paradise."

CHAPTER XXI.

It had been suggested that this Divine Song, from which these few extracts have been given, is an interpolation. But surely if any author had intruded it into the older poem, he would have selected a more suitable opportunity than this field of battle for his disquisition on the soul and on the adoration of Krishna as the Supreme. It would seem much more probable that the inspiration of genius happened to come to the poet who composed the whole account at this point in his work. He did not pause to consider the unities of the story, but let his ideas flow. It seems reasonable to suppose, from this and other portions of the work, that the story of the war was a mere peg on which to hang religious, moral, didactic, and epigrammatic vesture. It has been thought that the story of the war had been written, and then that later hands interspersed it with these religious and other topics. The gambling incident in the story suggests that there may have been some legend of a family or dynastic feud arising out of that vice. The author may have taken that story as suitable for illustrating one of his morals, viz., the depravity of gambling, which seems to have been very prevalent in ancient India, even in Vedic times, as in modern Europe. But his main design and purpose was evidently to illustrate the divine office of Krishna, and produce, in interesting form, a compendium of profitable exhortations and instruction. Of course there may have been more than one author, and alterations and emendations may probably have occurred, but its mere length need not hinder us from ascribing it to a single author. And if differences of style are discerned, the inequalities of genius may be the cause. So has Shakespeare's real authorship been denied. It is a compilation evidently of all the existing stories with which the author was acquainted. To transcribe these, with all the ancient maxims within his knowledge, adding his own ideas, and bringing the whole to the length of 215,000 lines, is a great but not impossible work for one man. Fifty lines a day, for less than 300 days in the year, would complete it in fifteen years. Hallam has calculated, says a writer in "Temple Bar" of March 1881, that Lope de Vega was author of at least 21,300,000 lines. But Krishna Dwaipâyana, or Krishna of the Island, also styled Vyâsa (collector or arranger), who is said to have composed this poem and to have collected the Vedas and Puranas, seems too miraculous a personage to be the real author. Moreover, he is introduced in the epic; and it would seem that the real author's name has become merged in that of the personage to whom he attributed it. So did Sir Walter Scott introduce the name of Jedediah Cleishbotham in prelude to his Waverley Novels; and Washington Irving attributes his history of New York to Knickerbocker.

The Divine Song of the "Great Bharata" may be a more complete exposition of the doctrines attributed to Krishna than appears elsewhere; but it is in perfect harmony with his aspect throughout the poem, as set forth in deeds, discourses, and descriptions of the popular veneration of him. Again he says, in the Bhishma division of the poem, "Depose thy heart in me, let thy reason dwell in me, and thou shalt be in me, and shalt have no more doubt." "He who honours me, as existing in all beings, arrives at unity."

Brahmâ, creator of the world, adores Krishna as Vishnu or Narayana, and says, "I take refuge in thee. Thy feet are the divine earth, the regions of heaven thy arms; I myself am thy form; the deities are thy body; thou hast for eyes the sun and moon. Strength, patience, and duty are thy daughters. Krishna, destroyer of sorrow, thou art the way, thou art the guide of all beings; the mouth of the world. Filled with faith, in reliance on some one of thy names, saints and deities sing thy praises, as the most sublime of marvels. All beings are in thee, their asylum."

Brahmâ owned himself created of Narayana or Bhagavat. He besought him to take the human form, to destroy the demons, and restore virtue upon the earth. Then the blessed Bhagavat, commander of the lords of the worlds, replied in favourable accents, and descended to be born of Vasudeva. Brahmâ says, "This son of Vasudeva must be propitiated. He is the master of the entire world, the sovereign lord of all the universe, whose son I, Brahma, am. Still he is a man. Behold there the greatest of mysteries. There he is who is the Unknown, the Imperishable, the Eternal; there his praises are sung under the title of Man. Demons and deities, with Indra at their head, must not disdain the son of Vasudeva because he is called man. He who can despise him

—incarnated in human members—is enveloped in darkness." Bhishma, one of the great, pious heroes of the poem, says that he has learnt this sublime, eternal mystery, that the son of Vasudeva is the august Lord of the worlds. Brahmâ, father of the entire universe, is his son. This son of Vasudeva is the eternal God, formed of all beings. He is Shiva himself also. He appointed to the castes their proper duties. When he (Narayana, manifested in Krishna) had created light, wind, and water, he reposed on his couch in the midst of the water, and became absorbed in the Absolute Being. He created the fire and breath, the word, and the Books of Knowledge—the worlds, the deities. He is the bestower of favours, past, present, and future—Infinite. He slew the terrible, malignant demon; he became incarnate as the boar and the man-lion. He is Hari, father and mother of all. "Joy will be the companion of the child of Manu (here again the first created thinking being, the primeval man-type), who shall have the happiness to read this book, who shall bow down before Krishna, falling into no faintness of spirit." "He is the sacrifice of the sacrificers, creator of all beings—the eternal man—the way of the first of all duties." After the leading prince of Krishna's side has conquered, he attributes his success to him. "Victory comes from thy grace, destruction from thine anger. For thou art our asylum, Krishna, thou placest thy faithful where fear cannot reach them."

Again in the Drona division of this "Great Bharata,"

the old blind king, whose sons are striving against the princes with whom Krishna is allied, being himself convinced of the divinity and might of the divine man, inquires, "How can these princes be defeated when they have for their asylum the most eminent of men—the eternal, the spiritual teacher of the worlds, the absolute lord of the universe, the august Narayana?"

"Listen," he says, "to the divine actions of the son of Vasudeva. The magnanimous infant, having taken his birth in a family of shepherds, slew the (demon) king of horses in the forests of Yamouna; he immolated in his infant arms a malignant being in the form of a bull. The monarch Kansa in his splendour, and other monarchs, bit the dust. He vanquished many armies of enemies; and conquering Varuna (deity of the ocean), he became master of the celestial conch shell. What other could repeat that great prodigy which he accomplished in my assembly? Then it was the recompense of my devotion to behold Krishna as the sovereign of the universe."

(In an assembly of princes and chieftains Krishna had displayed a vision of himself as the supreme spirit, and had enabled the blind monarch to see his grandeur.)

"This son of Vasudeva," he continues, "whom the Regenerated invoke as the father of the whole universe, he fights for the Pandu princes. Arjouna is the soul of Cesava (Krishna). Victory is for ever with Arjouna, and eternal glory with the son of Vasudeva."

CHAPTER XXII.

WHILE Krishna is acting as charioteer to Arjouna, he intercepts with his own bosom a dart aimed at him. This dart, in the breast of Cesava, became a bouquet and garland of flowers.

After the death of Arjouna's son, Krishna, much afflicted, repairs to Arjouna's palace to console his sister (Arjouna's wife). "Do not be inconsolable," he says; "there is an hour, supreme in our destinies, which death has appointed for all creatures. Derive happiness from this, that he was a valiant hero; he has conquered those worlds created pure, where all desires are satisfied. Thy son is entered into that way to which those aspire who seek the good—by learning, the Scriptures, purity, and penitence. Do not weep. By the most exalted of ways he has entered Paradise." Before the fighting has again commenced, in which Arjouna craves to revenge his son's death, Krishna conveys him to heaven, where both render homage to Bhava (Shiva), and seek aid of him.

The poet, in describing Krishna's homage to Shiva, the auspicious one, who is a manifestation like himself of the Supreme Spirit, would seem to be desirous of reconciling to his views those who had been accustomed to adore the divine under the name of Shiva and his numerous titles. In fact the Brahminical assertion, that the Almighty may be truly worshipped under different appellations if adored in faith and earnestness, seems here to be illustrated. But happiness in this life, and that to come, seems to be especially and continually throughout the poem held forth by the author as attainable in the utmost perfection by faith in Krishna.

"By thy grace, Govinda, the victory over our enemies is assured," says the chief of Krishna's party. "Those with whom thou art satisfied are assured of conquering the three worlds themselves (heaven, earth, and hell). They can commit no fault, nor can they suffer defeat in war. Entered into immortality, they enjoy the eternal worlds. By thy favour, Lord of the organs of sense, this world of beings, moveable and immoveable, appointed to its course, describes its revolution in the midst of low-voiced prayers and oblations of clarified butter."

"In the beginning there was nothing but sea, wrapped in obscurity. Thanks to thee, the world came into being. The Lord of the organs of sense is the creator of all the worlds, the Eternal, the First Soul, without beginning or end, the everlasting God, the Architect of the world, the primitive Man, the Ancient One celebrated in the Books of Knowledge, lord of the children of Manu. Adoration to thee, greatest of men, Master, Lord, Sovereign, Good Fortune of the universe."

It must be, at all events, evident from the quotations that have been given, that Krishna was regarded as the Supreme Almighty manifested on earth as man, and that faith in him was held to conduct to happiness here and hereafter. It can surely not be denied that such a religion is analogous to Christianity. But the aspect under which it appears seems to be more evidently derived from ideas in the oldest Indian scriptures than from our own Old or New Testaments. In the quotation just given it is claimed that Krishna is in the Vedas. But it seems that he is rather suggested than actually named or described in them; just as we perceive references to Christ in the Old Testament. The Vedas or Books of Knowledge appear to have been composed before the belief in him arose. But passages in these works, referring to the holy fire, &c., and to incarnations of the Divine for man, and, in the Institutes of Manu, to deities incarnate in kings, &c., as has been remarked, seem clearly to lead to the belief in him. The religion of Krishna, though analogous in some of its aspects to Christianity, seems connected indissolubly with the elaborate system of incarnations of deities, religious ritual, faith in the metempsychosis, &c. So many of these fanciful yet usually allegorical conceptions seem undoubtedly Indo-Aryan that it is difficult to conceive that the remainder are borrowed, as they are distinctly akin to the rest in conception and sentiment. And much of the whole can be assigned to astronomical or physical observations. In fact, the whole system seems homogeneous and of unascertained antiquity.

CHAPTER XXIII.

THE story of Krishna's birth, infancy, and youth is given at length in the Harivansa, the last book of or an addendum to the "Great Bharata" epic.

The Harivansa has been translated into French by M. Langlois. "Now learn," it is said in this history of the "Hari Family," "how Vishnu descended on the earth to save beings, whose hope and lord he is; how this god, full of glory and holiness, was born in the house of the sage Vasudeva." A demon had become incarnate in Kansa, the monarch of Madura, which is described as a city beautified with parks and gardens, terraces, open *places*, altogether "brilliant as the smile of beauty." It is full of elephants, chariots, and horses, and surrounded by fertile fields, duly watered by Indra, the regent of the elements.

Curiously, Narada, the sort of Indo-Aryan Mercury, though represented as a divine person, goes to the tyrant Kansa, and warns him that the eighth child of Devaki will be born for his destruction, and that his enemy is "the way of heaven, the grand mystery of the gods, he who is amongst these the greatest, and who only exists of himself." He says that he (Kansa) must respect him; still, if he can attack him when an infant, let him do so. Kansa pretends to fear nothing, though really devoured by disquiet, and he gives orders to destroy Devaki's children. Meanwhile he prays that destiny may be averted; but the prayers of the wicked avail not.

Before descending upon earth Hari goes to the goddess Kali in heaven, who seems to be identified with the divine sun (Savitri) of Vedic hymns. He tells her that in order to deceive Kansa she must be born of the shepherdess Yasoda, wife of Nanda, when he is born of Devaki. After birth Vasudeva will change the children, transferring Kali to the side of Devaki. Kansa, hearing of the birth, will come and seize the new-born infant, and in his rage grasp her by the foot and dash her to pieces on the stones. Then she shall forthwith be relegated to heaven in glory, appearing in a robe of sable silk, with yellow vestment and pearls gleaming like the rays of the moon, &c.

Then follows a hymn in her praise, in which, as in the case of all the deities introduced in the poem, she becomes associated with the Supreme Spirit, appearing to be a personification of certain forms in which the power of life and death becomes manifested.

"Mortals," says Hari to her, "who believe in my virtues and honour thee, shall receive all that they desire, children or riches. Those who fall into evil ways, those who are tossed on the tempest of the ocean, or besieged by their enemies, shall have recourse to thee. Thou shalt be perfection, happiness, glory, modesty," &c.

"Thou shalt be deity of the terrible and barbarous as well as the beautiful. Thou art the night, the first way of all beings; thou art death, and ready to devour the ensanguined flesh; thou art the sacrifice and the supreme light — the object of hunger in all beings. It is in thee that the chief points of the horizon are beheld. Thou art piety in young girls, for the pleaders the object of litigation. Thou sustainest all,—in voyages, in prison, in danger of life: thou art the assured protectress of mortals. O Goddess, my heart is in thee,—my thought, my soul; deliver me from all sin, and bestow on me thy favour."

"Behold," says the author, "the panegyric of the divine Dourga as it has been transmitted to us in ancient traditions."

When the proper hour arrives the wife of the pastor Nanda gives birth to Kali, and Devaki to Krishna. The seas rage, the mountains tremble. The night found itself in the constellation Abhidjit, and the name of Victory was given to that hour in which the divine Hari manifested himself to the world—the powerful Narâyana, the eternal spirit, the first element of the worlds. Music sounded in heaven, with chants of joy, and showers of flowers fell. The entire world was happy in the birth of the Lord of the organs of sense; and Vasudeva beheld on his breast the marks of his divinity. He then took the child and effected the change of infants. Kansa became informed of what had occurred and went to Devaki. Amid the cries of the women about her, she implored compassion for her daughter. "You have slain," she said, "seven of my children; must my poor daughter die also?"

But he ruthlessly seized the infant and dashed it to his feet.

Then Dourga quitted the form, and arose in the air, crowned and magnificent. All her limbs have the gleam of pearls; and she has now become "that divine Virgin, object of the eternal homage of the deities." Her robe is of black and gold. She dissipates the obscurity of night as she appears in the air, holding in her hand an immense goblet, in which she quenches her thirst. She dances and laughs, and announces to Kansa his death.

This "Divine Virgin" protectress of those engaged in voyages, in battle, &c., certainly has a curious prototypical aspect to "Our Lady" of mediæval days, to whom, as the saviour of shipwrecked mariners, we see chapels dedicated on the French coast hung with offerings to the Virgin-Mother. But in her other aspect Kali is a fury, a Hecate, a power of horror and destruction. Kansa craves the pardon of Devaki for destroying her child, saying that destiny was the cause. She says that she forgives him. She accuses only Time, "the first author of evils, who follows the direction which he has received from the moment of the first creation of beings. Death is the necessary consequence of birth."

Then follows a description of the country to which the infant Krishna has been taken. The properties there are duly fenced, and in their centres are the stables. Allusion is made to butter-making. The young shepherdesses are attired in black and yellow vestments; their earrings are formed of wild flowers, their breasts are modestly veiled, and they are carrying jars upon their heads to fetch the water of the Yamouna.

When Narâyana became incarnate in Krishna, he simultaneously became incarnate in Bala-Rama also, who was born of Vasudeva's wife Rohini. But Krishna is always represented as the actual Narâyana on earth, this collateral incarnation merely constituting a companion to him. Bala-Rama is the incarnation of eternity, as has been observed, personified as the serpent Sesha. Bala-Rama is light in colour, while Krishna is dark. Amongst the miracles of Krishna's childhood, it is related that in order to keep him from straying, he is tied to a ponderous car; but he drags it off, and carries away two great trees also in its course. At another time he kicks over a chariot; this being supposed to refer to the passage of a star through the constellation Rohini, which is represented by a chariot. He and his brother Bala-Rama spend seven years in this pastoral region, Krishna being described as attired in yellow, with a garland of wild-flowers and the pastoral flute, the brother in black. He then recommends the pastors to move to another region, as herbage was becoming scanty.

It appears that the cowherds formed a sort of nomadic race in India, dwelling in temporary abodes. The migration is described. There are crowds of cars, files of shepherdesses in black and yellow, with garlands. Then at the new camping-ground they construct huts covered with turf, and cabins consisting of branches of trees. Skins and stuffs are spread for beds; and they have abundance of milk, and are contented.

The charms of the forest are described, where resound the cries of the wild peacocks, where the trees and flowers form arches overhead, and everything breathes of the tender passion.

In this sylvan district is a lake inhabited by a terrible and obnoxious serpent. One day, to the consternation of the cowherds, Krishna tumbles himself into this lake. The monstrous serpent, with his five heads, rises amidst flames, and surrounded by other great serpents, the officers of his court. But Krishna kicks him and stamps upon him, knocks about the serpents in general, and seizes and hurls away one of the serpent-king's heads. Upon this the serpent owns himself vanquished; and Krishna orders him to betake himself to the sea with all of his. And the cowherds raise a song of praise, and congratulate Nanda on having such a son.

The brother, Bala-Rama, having taken some fruit from a forest of date-palms, a sort of monster, corresponding to the giant and enchanter of the old European mediæval romances, comes in the form of a shepherd and seizes him. Bala-Rama cries out to Krishna for advice as to what he is to do in this emergency. And here again occurs one of those episodical interpolations which seem to show that the author cared less for the progress of his story than for the expositions of Krishna's doctrine which it contained.

Krishna replies that the difficulty in which Rama is placed is one of the inconveniences of his human nature.

"But there is another nature in thee," he continues, "spiritual and unalterable. Thou art clad in a terrestrial body, O mysterious form of an incomprehensible being; but thou art also the spirit of Narâyana, the revolution of worlds, the breath of life which animates the universal era, the essence of the antique deities, Brahmâ himself. The heaven is thy head, the world thy body. Who can tell the secrets which thou guardest in thyself? even the gods have no knowledge of them. Thou art surnamed Ananta, Infinite. Thou sustainest the universe, and thou art in the world that which I am myself. We constitute but one body—separated, yet always united. Thou art the eternal, immortal Sesha. That which I am thou art also; that which thou art equally I am. We are two in one body."

Then Bala-Rama recalls to mind his divine existence, and finds himself full of the force "which circulates in the three worlds." He strikes the monster on the head, and a voice from heaven applauds the victory of the Invincible Infant. Bala-deva literally means the deity of force; and here again is a suggestion of Hercules. But the adoration of Bala-Rama seems to have become merged in that of Krishna.

CHAPTER XXIV.

AFTER two months of rain the *fête* of Indra is celebrated amongst these pastoral people. The cows' horns are adorned with peacocks' feathers, bells, and autumnal flowers. Chants of joy resound, cream is abundant, with mountains of rice and viands. Then the great "sacrifice" of the "Hill" is accomplished. Brahmins perform the sacred rites, and are duly presented with various kinds of nourishment. Krishna mystically becomes himself the hill, and rice, milk, and other provisions are offered to him. The cows are crowned with flowers, and are driven in solemn procession around this hill. But while Krishna, as the Universal and Supreme Spirit, enters this mountain, to which the villagers are offering adoration, he is, at the same time, present amongst them as the Goatherd Krishna, and renders homage unto himself in the mountain. This must surely be intended to set forth that the simple, ancient superstition which led the pastoral people to venerate the hill as divine, was still acceptable, if sincerely offered, to the divinity who is of all nature, and who was himself the hill, as, indeed, he was the entire universe. The Church of Christendom has conceived that, in similar significance, Christ laid His hand upon the bread and declared that it was His body though He was there present Himself in the flesh. Indra is angered at the devotion to Krishna, and he pours down a deluge of rain, the clouds being described as resembling elephants. The goatherds have recourse to Krishna, and beseech him to defend them.

He "whose power was founded upon truth" determined to protect them with the mountain; and he raises and sustains it on his finger, while the people with their flocks and herds find shelter beneath. Indra is induced to own the supreme power of Nârâyana in Krishna.

Indra then does homage to him, and says that he will bestow upon him the royal baptism, by emptying on his head certain golden vases filled with divine milk. This he accomplishes according to the proper rite. Flowers fall from heaven, ambrosia drops from the clouds, and heavenly music is also heard as the ceremony is performed. Indra tells him that after the two rainy months his adoration as Govinda shall commence. He recommends him to slay the tyrant

Kansa, and says that an emanation of himself, Arjouna, shall accompany Krishna, and that as he, Indra, lives in Krishna, so shall Arjouna live in him.

The pastoral folk do honour to Krishna, and inquire who he really is that he wields such power. Krishna smiles upon them, and replies, "I am only your kinsman; cease to believe me such as I seem to your souls, now influenced by fear. If there is any mystery in my existence, Time will teach it to you, and then you shall know me when you see me as I am! If I seem to you a deity, it is well for you."

Again Krishna is described as attired in yellow, with garlands of flowers. The shepherdesses fall in love with him, and follow him about, imitating him in dances, &c., their eyes tender as those of the black antelope. Altogether the sylvan delights of Krishna and the "Gopis" lead up to the "pastorals" and "china shepherdesses" of modern Europe.

Meanwhile Kansa has become aware of Krishna's existence and miracles, and designs his death. He has killed a fierce bull, really an incarnate demon, which Kansa has sent against him, and afterwards a savage horse. Kansa now orders that the goatherds shall be summoned to Mathura to pay the annual tribute. Thither Krishna and Bala-Rama proceed; and together they enter the city, and pass along the royal street. Being clad in rustic attire, they demand some rich vestments from a dealer; and as he abuses them grossly, they knock him down, and march off with the coveted garments. They enter a flower-seller's shop, and request a garland; and the flower-seller is so much impressed with them that he immediately presents them with garlands, and Govinda informs him that great wealth shall come to him.

They proceed on their way, and presently meet a hunch-backed woman, who is carrying vases of perfume. Krishna says to her, "Amiable hunch-back, with eyes like the lotus, for whom do you destine these perfumes?" "Do you not know me," she says, "employed as I am in supplying the king with perfumes?"

Krishna asks her to give them some cosmetics in harmony with the colour of their bodies. We are from the provinces, he says, "wrestlers" by profession. The hunch-back expresses delight with Krishna, and says, "Take this marvellous perfume, which is worthy of a king."

Then Krishna lightly touches her back, and she finds herself upright.

"O charming friend!" she cries, "let me follow thee everywhere that thou goest." And she is quite overcome with love for Krishna.

However, he and his brother gaily take leave of her, and march into the palace. There they desire to be shown a mighty bow, the drawing of which is to be one of the feats of strength at a forthcoming tournament or competition of deeds of arms.

Krishna takes it, breaks it in sunder with a terrible

sound, and then he and Bala-Rama disappear from the view of the attendants of the palace.

Kansa is informed of this prodigy, and he is much troubled. He, however, proceeds to visit the great hall which has been prepared for the approaching spectacle.

This is described as situated in the interior of the palace. It contains reserved places for the chiefs of the various corporations; and the elegance of the building is praised, with its graceful columns and cornices, and commodious approaches between the balconies and terraces, &c.

The king orders it to be hung with garlands, flags, and draperies. Large vases filled with drinks are to be placed here and there, golden jugs with acidulated liquors, and eatables. This theatre is described as octagonal in shape, with eight staircases, decorated with paintings and with alcoves, &c.; and the whole interior is resplendent with golden columns, gorgeous chairs, divans glittering with gold, superb carpets, woven to represent trees, flowers, &c. Refreshment-rooms are provided, with golden vases of drinks and basins of fruit. The ladies have "boxes" with light gratings of sugar-cane in front of them. The courtesans have separate places assigned to them, ornamented with magnificent fabrics.

CHAPTER XXV.

The King Kansa, on the day of the spectacle, takes his place upon his throne with all due ceremony. He is described as dressed in two pieces of white, with white turban and gems. The wrestlers come into the arena with fleating vestments, accompanied by strains of music. Then Krishna and Bala-Rama enter; and by the orders of Kansa, a fierce elephant is let loose upon them. But Krishna merely plays with him, deciding, however, to kill him as being an accomplice of Kansa. He and his brother accordingly smite the elephant to death; Krishna remarking that killing in a theatre is brutal.

The two brothers then overthrow Kansa's wrestlers; and when the music of the theatre ceases, heavenly music is heard. The finest diamond in Kansa's diadem ominously falls. After the defeat of the wrestlers, Kansa gives orders for soldiers to attack the two. Krishna then springs to the side of Kansa, and, hurling him into the arena, kills him. The lamentations of his wives resound; but the people in general appear to sympathise with Krishna. He explains that he is touched by the women's lamentations, and that Kansa shall have befitting burial, but that it was necessary that he should be killed on account of his wickedness. And he then proceeds to moralise on death as the common lot of all who are clothed in a perishable body. "Kansa has ceased to live, victim of Time, and his destiny was prepared by his deeds in a preceding birth." He says that he does not want the throne for himself; that he immolated Kansa for the good of the world; and that he will return to the life of the country, "free as a bird."

However, Krishna and Bala-Rama do not return to the pastoral life; but, having set up a king of Mathura, they go to study the art of war. This is contained in the sixty-four parts of the "Dhanour-Veda," one of the later of the sacred "Books of Knowledge." And as their preceptor's son has died, Krishna promises to revive him. Proceeding to the abode of the king of death, he endows this son with a new body, and restores him to his father.

When Krishna and Bala-Rama return to Mathura, the whole population issues forth to greet them. The chiefs of the corporations of the divers orders in the state, the ministers, priests, and old and young, come with all the instruments of a *fête* day, with music, flags, garlands, &c., and chants and benedictions are heard everywhere. "Behold," they cry, "those noble brothers, Rama and Govinda, whose glory fills all the world; peace reigns in your country, O sons of Yadu." Then, in the mansion of their father Vasudeva, they give themselves up to pleasure in gardens, and by cool waters, adorned with the crimson, blue, and white lotus, &c.

But Djarasandha, king of Magadha, puts his army

in motion against Mathura, for his two daughters had been married to Kansa; and many other kings are allied with him.

Krishna and Bala-Rama miraculously overcome the invading armies, and a triumphant entry into Madura, amidst the enthusiasm of the people, is again described. After this Bala-Rama returns to visit the pastoral people, amongst whom he has passed his boyhood. They rejoice to see him, and in the festivities which ensue he becomes decidedly inebriated over good liquor.

It would certainly seem to be an indication of the antiquity of this Harivansa that both Krishna and Bala-Rama, but especially the latter, indulge freely in intoxicating drinks. These are distinctly reprobated in the Brahminical "Institutes of Manu," generally ascribed to between the fifth and tenth centuries B.C. As the "Great Bharata," including the concluding Harivansa, seems to display Brahminical influence with equal distinctness, it is strange, if it is more modern, that the inebriety of a divine incarnation should be introduced. In the archaic Vedas, on the other hand, we find that when the juice of the sacred moon-plant (soma) was discovered to possess intoxicating qualities it became venerated as divine. It was found to impart a sensation of joy which seemed to elevate above this mundane life; so they conceived that it must be heavenly, and they offered it to the deities, in solemn sacrifice, with the rice cake.

I

No reprobation is expressed in Genesis ix. of Noah's drunkenness. It is his son, who accidentally beholds him in an intoxicated condition, who is cursed and punished.

King Djarasandha has fled from the might of Krishna. In a council of chieftains he admits his divinity, and inquires what is to be done, "for Krishna is Narâyana, ancient source of the world, creator of all beings, without beginning, end, or middle."

One king advises peace, but another says, "Why this fear? I know that Krishna is the Eternal,—born to deliver this world, an avatar of Vishnu,—but I also know that we die when our time comes; till then we are assured against harm. This divine Vishnu himself is subject to Fate."

Eventually these inimical monarchs march on Mathura; and Krishna, who has meanwhile been consecrated king with great ceremonies and rejoicings in heaven and earth, announces that they are too powerful. Apparently it is destined that he should found Dwâraka, on the coast of Gujerat. He expatiates to his assembly on the advantages of its site; and he finally conducts the Yadavas, his people, thither in grand procession.

Djarasandha and his ally, the Kala-Yavana king, advance with numerous armies, the latter having under his standard a crowd of barbarians from the mountains. Krishna returns to Mathura and shows himself to the Black Yavana, who chases him. Krishna disappears in the cave. The enchanted monarch, who lies therein, has attached to him the spell of causing by fire the destruction of any one who touches him. The Yavana enters, finds him sleeping, kicks him, and is forthwith consumed by flames.

The sleeper awakes, and inquires of Krishna who he is. Krishna replies that he is the son of Vasudeva, and that he (the slumbering monarch) had fallen to sleep in a former age of the world's history.

The awakened one, like the hero of Washington Irving's story who has slept for years while the Americans have cast off King George, &c., is much astonished at the changed aspect of affairs. He sees men with lessened stature, and he finds that patience, courage, and other virtues are much enfeebled in the world's present (the black) age. Krishna now attacks and destroys the hostile army, and then proceeds to make surveys for his new town, having offered up the usual prayer after sunrise.

By the power of his thought he summons Visvakarman, the All-Architect, and tells him that the city must be the finest in the world — its architecture according to rules, its temples properly provided with places for the Brahmins and assistants at the sacrifices, and for the maintenance of the holy fire, &c. The ocean obeys his demand to cede a large domain. Then magnificent houses, gates, and triumphal arches arise, with ramparts and towers. Elegant pavilions, and delicious gardens, and thousands of streets are constructed, with houses decorated with precious stones, and refreshed by the sea-breezes. Then the Regent of the Winds brings a divine Hall from heaven. In this Sanctuary of Justice, placed in the centre of Dwâraka, the princes of the Yadus are enthroned with the same majesty as the deities in heaven. And Krishna establishes corporations, ministers of state for military and civil affairs, high priests, &c.

Then Krishna falls in love and elopes with Rukmini, vanquishing, but sparing at her intercession, her brother who had followed them. He now solemnly espouses her, and finds great happiness in her love; and they had ten sons and one daughter.

As has been observed, the ancient Indo-Aryans conceived that deity, incarnate in the world, should fulfil to the utmost the obligation inherent upon every one to beget children. Buddhism encouraged the celibate life; but in these books, sacred to Krishna, as in the Brahminical Institutes of Manu, matrimony is inculcated. The Institutes, save in exceptional instances, ordain only one wife. Krishna marries seven other principal wives; and he weds the sixteen thousand secondary spouses, by whom he has thousands of sons.

In our Old Testament (Kings xi.) the fact of Solomon's espousing seven hundred wives does not seem in itself to be mentioned as reprehensible; only in respect to his having "loved many strange women," who "turned away his heart after other gods," so that "his heart was not perfect with the Lord his God, as was the heart of David his father."

Yet the Lord had appeared unto him twice (Kings xi. 2). This prototypical form of Christianity, *i.e.* of deliverance from evil and guidance into bliss, through faith in the Divine incarnate upon earth, naturally appears in archaic form. The unfettered imagination of early civilisation was permitted full play. But it must be remembered that our Song of Solomon has to be interpreted mystically, else its exoteric aspect is certainly that of a mere love-song, and a similar treatment has been bestowed upon Krishna's amours. The general conception seems to have been that, in imagining in the flesh the Supreme and Universal Soul, which sustains all being, animate or inanimate, mere numbers, which rule ourselves, should have no significance.

CHAPTER XXVI.

Thus Krishna became settled in Dwaraka, in which city he remained as its prince till his death, and the destruction of all the race of the Yadus, to which he belonged, under the fated influence of a curse. And the city itself was overwhelmed by the ocean; but to the present day a temple of great sanctity bears asserted testimony to the city's existence on the shores of Gujerat.

It is after he has become settled here that Krishna appears upon the scene in the "Great Bharata," and after vainly striving to act as mediator between the contending hosts, aids by his presence and advice his friends the Pandu princes.

It has been surmised that he was a prince who supported the Brahmins, that they afterwards bestowed upon him his divinity on that account, and set him up as an object for popular adoration. But the opposing warriors equally respect the Brahmins; and their religious crime seems to be their contending against those who are aided by Krishna. There are great religious heroes on the side of the wicked princes, who fight for them because they hold it to be their duty, and there are also Brahmins with them. And altogether the perusal of the poem does not seem to support this view of its purport. The war appears, in fact, to be the mere basis of a magnificent allegory of the contending human emotions, in which Nárâyana, incarnated in Krishna, is declared throughout to be the true way to happiness here and hereafter.

He is repeatedly addressed as the Soul of Nature, the Supreme Intelligence, the Great All, clothed in mortal personifications. And the Harivansa also spiritualises. It is said therein that Rukmini and Krishna's other wives are mere manifestations of this Being, the nature of whose immensity is Vishnu (the all-pervading spirit). Vishnu is at the same time Iswara and also his wife (*i.e.* Shiva and the "glorious Uma"). "There is no difference between Rudra (Shiva as the destroyer) and Vishnu. The powerful Naráyana is the author and substance of all beings. He, with Iswara, has given birth to Brahma, to the ancient universal soul."

As has been observed, it is the continual effort of these works to show that all these modes of addressing the Divine, as Shiva or Vishnu, or as their wives, Lakshmi the goddess of good fortune, or as Uma, Parvati or Dourga, the bride of Shiva, who is also adored as the terrible Kali, and as the divine and beneficent Virgin, —that all these forms of adoration are in reality only expressions of the one Spirit. Originally they may have been conceived as powers of the unseen world in systems of actual polytheism. But undoubtedly in this Indo-Aryan sacred literature, from the period when the Vedas (Books of Knowledge) were compiled, many centuries B.C., these divinities are adopted or continued in veneration only to be associated in divine unity. Even the 16,000 wives of Krishna are regarded as forms of One, who is at the same time one and several, who is wife or energy not only of Vishnu but of Shiva, and also of Brahmâ; for these three and all the deities are still One, who is from everlasting to everlasting, who is all-pervading and infinite.

"To-day," it is said, "for the salvation of the world, Cesava is manifested at Mathura."

"As a meat patty is throughout impregnated with the unctuous dripping, so is the world everywhere penetrated with the presence of Vishnu."

"The sages who know the Books of Knowledge are aware that he is the Sacrifice. His ordinary course is to destroy those who have rejected penitence and complacently abided in ill-doing."

A great saint, Kashyapa, says, "I incline before thee, whose force is infinite, whose firmness is not to be moved. First of beings, Master and Victim of the Sacrifice, thou art the offering of the piety of the world, and the companion of destiny—Divine consoler, who triumphs over death. Thou art the soma (intoxicating juice corresponding to the wine) of the sacrifice, brilliant in thy own light. Preserve me from all ill, efface my sins, O god of gods, O thou who art the enemy of every fault committed in secret, or in thought, the beginning and end of every sacrifice, pastor of pastors. Thou art All."

Again Narada invokes him as, "O you who are the way of the just, be ever favourable to me. Grant me the power to visit ever your abode, and that I may be exempt from being reborn in the flesh. In all my future existences may I still be a divine being."

In the Bhagavata Purana (Ancient Book of the Blessed), Brahmâ, creative agent of the worlds, prostrate before Bhagavat, calls him the abode of happiness, supreme bliss, where the law of regeneration is arrested for those who have taken refuge in him. Even we, the deities, he says, only know him not in his verity, but in the external form which he has created by means of his Illusion (Mayâ). The first

Incarnation was the soul of the Universe (Purusha), that is, the Supreme Essence, called Hari by the first thinking being. Brahmâ imposed upon himself great austerities in order that he might create the worlds; and then Bhagavat was born as the Son of Justice (Dharma). "Adoration," he says, "to Bhagavat, the tree of the world, who divided his proper root into three trunks, forming himself, Shiva and Vishnu."

"He becomes disengaged from attachment to the world who is endowed with faith," says Bhagavat, "who is exercised in the practice of intense devotion towards me, who bestows due attention on my histories, who regards all creatures with perfect equanimity, and who continues in the practice of kindness and chastity—calm, charitable—master of himself. The sage perceives within his personality, which has no real existence, a reflex of the Being, whom he beholds exempt from real attributes. By persistence in duty, devotion, penitence, nature disappears in spirit. When, after numbers of existences, in this world or in that of Brahmâ, he becomes indifferent to personality, devoid of egotism, he who is full of devotion to me, and who knows the truth, thanks to my goodness, obtains that which constitutes his proper nature. That state of happiness which is called absolute deliverance is found in my bosom. Casting aside all doubts he speedily comes, here below, to that state from which there is no more return. Be chaste and pure, lead a life of penitence, read the Books of Knowledge, and adore the Universal Soul."

"Meditate on the smile, so noble, of Hari, which can abate the ocean of tears, which overwhelm, in their profound sorrows, all the worlds."

"I reside perpetually in the bosom of all beings, whose soul I am. The man who cannot recognise me has but the false image of piety.

"Till man, indeed, actually goes to abide in hell, he desires not to abandon his body. He becomes attached to his goods, becomes culpable and violent, and finally degraded. Despair and death come to him, and enclose him in a body destined to the sufferings of hell. Then he has to follow the way of sinners in long and terrible darkness, tormented by hunger and fire, till he reaches the abode of the Monarch of Death (Yama). Then come the pains of hell upon him. His limbs are enveloped in flames, his flesh torn from him; the dogs and vultures of hell devour his entrails before his face. Even in this world, it is said in the Bhagavata, men exclaim, 'This is heaven! This is hell!' for the sufferings of hell are not unknown here, but in hell itself shall the fruits of faults be gathered. Having traversed all the places of pain in the infernal regions, he shall be purified and return to this world. He again has to become a germ, and to re-enter the world helpless and ignorant."

Those who worship the Supreme Being under the material form of Brahmâ, may arrive at his heaven.

But those who take refuge in the Being who dwells in the hearts of all, who is First of all, moveable and immoveable in this universe, who is the Parent of the Scriptures—Bhagavat, son of Vasudeva, who is supreme soul, and knowledge—those may cease from the migrations of their individual souls, and come to him. "Take refuge with him," it is said, "who is at the same time immortality and death. Vowing devotion exclusively for Bhagavat, happiness will be with thee." In finishing an address to his mother, Bhagavat says:

"By continuing in the way which I have indicated, and which you can easily follow, you will come speedily to supreme perfection. Preserve with faith my word, which those love who possess the Books of Knowledge. It will bring thee to me, who am Safety. Those who do not know me fall into death."

The mother then deserted her abode, became an ascetic, practised severe mortifications, with her heart fixed only on the son of Vasudeva, till she arrived at the possession of the Supreme Spirit Bhagavat, who is the final deliverance. Release from transmigrations upon earth and punishments in hell, and an eternal abode above even the heaven of the powers of the elements, &c., is promised to those who, in faithful and exclusive devotion, adore the "blessed," manifested in Krishna.

Chivalrous devotion to woman has been supposed to have emanated from the Christianity of the valiant warriors of Northern Europe. But M. Levêque adduces quotations from the Harivansa to show that the adoration of the fair sex, in terms of humble devotion, is found in the more ancient Aryan poetry. As in a modern romance, the handsome Pradyoumna takes in his the hand of the beautiful Prabhâvati with its glittering ornaments. He feels that it trembles. "Celestial beauty," he says, "object of the most tender hopes, why do you hide your countenance, brilliant as the stars of night? why do you maintain this cruel silence? Do not be envious of my beholding your charming face. O adorable being, disdain not your slave. Accept the homage which he has rendered to you by resigning his liberty. You have no cause for fear; submissive and respectful I address to you my prayer. O incomparable one, let me know that I have touched your heart."

M. Levêque remarks that gallantry of this kind was unknown to the Greeks and Romans. It appears to have passed from India to the romances of the Breton cycle, and thence to modern times. So in Racine Achilles addresses himself to Iphigenia—

> "Princesse mon bonheur ne dépend que de vous,
> Votre père a l'autel vous destine un époux ;
> Venez y recevoir un cœur qui vous adore."

In regard to the story from which this illustration of ancient gallantry has been taken, M. Levêque, in his work entitled " Les Mythes et les Légendes de l'Inde et la Perse, dans Aristophane, Platon, Aristote,

Virgile, Ovide, Tite-Live, Dante, Boccace, Arioste, Rabelais, Perrault, La Fontaine," inquires (p. 68), " Comment se fait-il que nous trouvons la même scène dans *l'Histoire de Pradyoumna* et dans le *Cid*. La chose est moins surprenante qu'elle ne le parait de prime abord. Corneille a puissé dans la pièce de Guillem de Castro, et Guillem de Castro peut avoir en connaissance de la légende ou de la pièce sanscrite par des intermédiaires. Les contes de l'Inde ont pénétré en Espagne, comme on le voit par le livre du Prince Jean Manuel, intitulé *le Livre de Patronio et du comte Lucanor*."

In the late Tom Robinson's play of "Caste," the heroine buckles the sword around the waist of the hero when ordered to the wars. This was forestalled so long ago as to appear in this ancient Sanskrit story of Pradyoumna.

"'Noble hero,' exclaims his beautiful Prabhâvatî, 'arm thyself. Live for thy children, thy wife, and thy venerable parent.' She took the sword, raised her eyes to heaven, and firmly placed it in the hands of Pradyoumna, 'Go,' she said, 'be victorious.' The hero, transported with joy, grasped the sword which his faithful beloved one had presented to him."

CHAPTER XXVII.

The allegorical character of the "Great Bharata" epic is continued throughout. A curious suggestiveness of Bunyan's "Pilgrim's Progress" appears in the conclusion of the lives of the five princes. The eldest, "Firm in Battle," is established on the throne. But he and his brothers, disconsolate at the death of Krishna, and realising the vanity of human hopes, aspire only to the heavenly rest. The king assigns the throne to his nephew. He and his brothers, Bhima the Terrible, Arjouna the special friend of Krishna, and the two heroes who suggest the classical Castor and Pollux, with the Princess Krishnâ or Draupadî, take their departure from Hastinapura, their capital, the modern Delhi, to the deep regret of all its inhabitants. They set forth upon their pilgrimage on foot. The citizens and courtiers follow them for some distance. The princes and princess then wander on through many countries. They come to the site of the old city of Krishna, on the sea coast, now washed over by the waves. Then they turned towards the north, to reach Indra's heaven on Mount Meru, yearning for union with the Infinite; bent on abandonment of worldly things. A translation in verse of this portion of the poem was given by Mr. E. B. Cowell, in the *Westminster Review* of October 1848, from which the following lines are extracted :—

> "With souls well disciplined
> They reached the northern region, and beheld with heaven-aspiring hearts
> The mighty mountain Himavat. Beyond its lofty peak they passed
> Towards the sea of sand, and saw at last the rocky Meru, king
> Of mountains. As with eager steps they hastened on, their souls intent
> On union with the Eternal, Draupadî lost hold of her high hope,
> And, faltering, fell upon the earth."

Then the four princes fall, one by one, and "Firm in Battle" ascribes their inability to continue on their way to worldly thoughts having distracted their souls; and the king continues on his way alone; but a dog has come with them from the city, and he still follows:

> "Suddenly, with a cry that rang through heaven and earth,
> Indra came riding on his chariot, and he cried to the king,
> 'Ascend!'
> Then, indeed, did the Lord of Justice look back to his fallen brothers;
> And thus unto Indra he spoke, with a sorrowful heart:
> 'Let my brothers, who yonder lie fallen, go with me;
> Not even into thy heaven would I enter, if they were not there.
> And yon fair-faced daughter of a king, Draupadî, the All-deserving,
> Let her too enter with us! O Indra, approve my prayer.'
> *Indra.* In heaven thou shalt find thy brothers; they are already there before thee,—
> There are they all, with Draupadî. Weep not, then, O son of Bharata.
> Thither are they entered, prince, having thrown away their mortal weeds.
> But thou alone shalt enter, still wearing thy body of flesh.

The King. O Indra! and what of this dog? It hath faithfully followed me through;
Let it go with me into heaven, for my soul is full of compassion.
Indra. Immortality and friendship with me, and the height of joy and felicity—
All these hast thou reached to-day; leave then the dog behind thee.
The King. The good may oft act an evil part, but never a part like this.
Away, then, with that felicity whose price is to abandon the faithful.
Indra. My heaven hath no place for dogs; they steal away our offerings on earth.
Leave, then, thy dog behind thee, nor think in thy heart that it is cruel.
The King. To abandon the faithful and devoted is an endless crime, like the murder of a Brâhman.
Never therefore, come weal or woe, will I abandon you faithful dog.
You poor creature, in fear and distress, hath trusted in my power to save it;
ot, therefore, for e'en life itself, will I break my plighted word.
To oppress the suppliant, to kill a wife, to spoil a Brâhman, and to betray one's friends—
These are the four great crimes; and to forsake a dependant I count equal unto them."

"Firm in Battle" thus continues in his grand, chivalric refusal to desert the faithful dog for heaven; and he is rewarded for his constancy by finding that the animal was really Yama, monarch of death, in disguise. When he reaches Indra's heaven he is again tried, for instead of seeing there his brothers, he only meets the princes against whom he had been fighting in the great war. And learning that his brothers are in hell, he resolves to abide there with them rather than remain in heaven without them.

But this is a mock scene of heaven, and was intended merely to try his endurance again and constancy of affection, and at length the real heaven is revealed.[1]

CHAPTER XXVIII.

The biblical foundation for Milton's magnificent descriptions of the contest between the powers of righteousness and evil, in the "Paradise Lost," appears to be the text in Revelation xii. 7 and an allusion in the book of Daniel.

It is difficult to conceive that the texts in Revelation suggested the elaborate accounts of the wars between the beings of light and darkness which are found in the "Puranas" or "Ancient Books." Taking these accounts in conjunction with the whole context of the Indo-Aryan system as promulgated in the Vedas, legal treatises, later scriptures, &c., it seems almost impossible to deny that they are equally indigenous with these "Books of Knowledge" (the Vedas)

---

[1] Mr. Edwin Arnold has, in his "Indian Poetry," published by Messrs. Trübner & Co. in 1881, given a version of this portion of the Mahābhārata.

themselves. And, as has been remarked, the battalions of dense clouds, which at the commencement of the rainy season seem to march upwards in gloomy array, seem naturally suggestive of the idea. The rays of the sun, and moon or star beams by night, have filled a serene atmosphere for months. Then come the clouds, weird in aspect, black and awful, accompanied by vivid flashes of lightning and tremendous peals of thunder. And an invasion of the spirits of good by the evil seems an obvious idealisation of the aspect of nature.

It is said in "The Revelation of St. John the Divine," xii. 7-9: "And there was war in heaven: Michael and his angels fought against the dragon; and the dragon fought and his angels, and prevailed not; neither was there place found any more in heaven. And the great dragon was cast out, that old serpent, called the devil, and Satan, which deceiveth the whole world; he was cast out into the earth, and his angels were cast out with him."

In the "Ancient Book of the Blessed" (Bhagavata Purana) it is related that the Asuras (corresponding to demons), "beings full of folly and pride, and loving murder," invade the deities. A terrible demon defeats the divine beings, who seek refuge in Narâyana, whom they address as "Supreme Being, Nature, Spirit, and the universe, from which he is distinct." He promises them succour. A terrific battle ensues, with flaming weapons, &c. The Asuras see the inutility of their efforts, but their chief, "though born amongst this race, characterised by evil passion, has learnt to adore and feel solely dependent on Bhagavat. So the divine beings even cannot prevail against him. And he would have destroyed Indra, the regent of the elements, if he had not been protected by the cuirass of Supreme Universal Soul."

Indra praises the Asura as having escaped from illusion and renounced his nature as a demon. "It is a marvel," he says, "that a heart such as his, of which passion is the nature, should become so firmly attached to the blessed Vasudeva, who is all-goodness." The fight, however, proceeds. The Asura increases in bulk till he occupies all space and swallows Indra, who emerges by the force of his own devotion, and cuts off the Asura's head with his thunderbolt. This clearly signifies that the stormy clouds advance till one black mass seems to overshadow the whole world before they break in the monsoon. They are rent in the first lightning-flash. Then Indra's welcome rainfall descends upon the parched earth.

An elaborately fanciful account is given of the attack of the Asuras; they advance in their ranks to the sound of conch shells, tambourines, kettle-drums, &c., with great variety of weapons. And the devas assume warrior forms to encounter them. Chariots are urged against chariots, cavalry against cavalry, infantry against infantry. There are warriors upon elephants, camels, asses, antelopes, rhinoceroses, bulls, vultures, herons, &c. &c. Standards, umbrellas of honour, and elaborately adorned fans are mentioned. The combatants are resplendent in cuirasses and sparkling ornaments, and their weapons glitter in the sunbeams. Their mantles float in the wind. They have swords, sabres, crescent-shaped arrows, burning projectiles, and arrows shot through tubes. The demons hurl a whole mountain on the deities, with its savage beasts, reptiles, &c. The divine personages were altogether becoming worsted in the encounter, when Indra thought on Bhagavat, creator of the universe. He came, as he had promised, to their assistance. Bhagavat is then described as he may be seen in the ordinary Hindu representations of him. He has many arms, which wield eight weapons, including the discus. Indra, with his thunderbolts, strikes Bali, chief of the Asuras, from his chariot. But the showers of arrows from the demon army for a time conceal him from the view of the deities, who cry out "like merchants whose vessel is wrecked in the midst of the ocean." But the arrows of Hari are irresistible, and the divinities are victorious.

CHAPTER XXIX.

HORACE HAYMAN WILSON, Boden Professor of Sanscrit in Oxford between the years 1832–1860, observes, in the Introduction to his translation of the Vishnu

Purana, that the Purana and epic-poem systems were "extensively, perhaps universally established in India at the time of the Greek invasion. The Hercules of the Greek writers was undoubtedly the Bala-Rama of the Hindus; and their notices of Mathura on the Jumna, and of the kingdom of the Suraseni and the Pandæan country, are evidence of the prior currency of the traditions which constitute the argument of the Mahâbhârata. These are constantly repeated in the Puranas, relating to the Pandava and Yadava races, to Krishna and his contemporary heroes, and to the dynasties of the solar and lunar kings." He says that the "theogony and cosmogony of the Puranas may be traced to the Vedas, and that these last appear occasionally to allude to the incarnations of Vishnu."

He observes that there is a general agreement in the Puranas' scheme of primary creation, taken from the Sankhya philosophy. In them appears pantheism, represented as God, manifested in Vishnu or Siva. He finds a parallel in the Platonic Christians. "Epiphanius (adv. Manichæos) and Eusebius (Hist. Evang.) accuse Scythianus of having imported from India, in the second century, books on magic, and heretical notions leading to Manichæism; and it was at the same period that Ammonius instituted the sect of the New Platonists at Alexandria. The basis of this heresy was that true philosophy derived its origin from the Eastern nations; his doctrine of the identity of God and the universe is that of the Vedas and

Puranas; and the practices he enjoined, as well as their object, were precisely those described in several of the Puranas under the name of Yoga (union). His disciples were taught to extenuate by mortification and contemplation the bodily restraints upon the immortal spirit, so that in this life they might enjoy communion with the Supreme Being, and ascend after death to the Universal Parent" (Mosheim, v. i. p. 173). But Professor Wilson also wrote that "the importation was not perhaps wholly unrequited; the loan may not have been left unpaid." He says that "Anquetil de Perron has given, in the introduction to his translation of the Oupnekhat, several hymns by Synesius, a bishop of the beginning of the fifth century, which may serve as parallels to many of the hymns and prayers addressed to Vishnu in the Vishnu Purana."

Professor Wilson remarks that "the present popular forms assumed their actual state under Sankara Acharya, a great Sáiva reformer, who probably flourished in the eighth or ninth century A.D., and that the Puranas previously existed in more ancient form."

Indian tradition assigns Sankara Acharya to the second century B.C. Whatever may be the date, it is evident that his conceptions are in sequence with those ancient Indo-Aryan books whose antiquity is admitted, rather than with our own Scriptures. His poem entitled the "Atma-Bodha," or "Knowledge of Spirit," seems precisely in accordance with their ideas of the attainment of tranquillity, and overcoming of passion, as the prelude to final emancipation; also of the unreality of the world, and the error of supposing the individual soul to be truly itself, but that in realising Brahma, as I am, is knowledge, &c. &c.

Indeed Professor Wilson says that "it is irrational to dispute the antiquity or authenticity of the greater portion of the contents of the Puranas, in the face of abundant, positive, and circumstantial evidence of the prevalence of the doctrines which they teach, the currency of legends which they narrate, and the integrity of the institutions which they describe, at least in the third century before the Christian era."

"But the origin and development of their doctrines, traditions, and institutions were not the work of a day; and the testimony which establishes their existence in the third century B.C., carries it back to a much more remote antiquity, that is probably not surpassed by any of the prevailing fictions, institutions, or beliefs of the ancient world."

"The metaphysical annihilation of the universe, by the release of the spirit from bodily existence, offers analogies to doctrines and practices taught by Pythagoras and Plato, and by the Platonic Christians of later days."

He places the commencement of the recorded regal dynasties of India at 2600 B.C., *i.e.* 252 years before the date ascribed to the Flood in Archbishop Usher's Chronology, which has been adopted in the Church of

England. He assigns the eastern confines of the Punjab as the "earliest seat of the Hindus."

He thinks that no date can be conjectured for the Vishnu Purana from its contents. But the Mahâbhârata epic is mentioned in it, and allusions are made to both Buddhists and Jains (who possess analogous opinions).

He places its composition at 1045 A.D. As has been observed, however, it appears in his opinion to be irrational to dispute the pre-Christian antiquity of the doctrines, legends, and institutions described in it. He refers them to the period of the Greek invasion, considering them likely to have been then established in growth of antiquity.

The Vishnu Purana (*i.e.*, the Ancient Book of the Pervading One, from *vish*, to pervade), or, as Vishnu is styled the Preserver, the Ancient Book of the Preserver, to quote from Professor Wilson's translation, commences with the usual mystic syllable Om or Aum:

"Aum, glory to Vasudeva! May that Vishnu, who is the existent imperishable Brahma, who is Iswara; who is spirit; who is the cause of creation, preservation, and destruction; who is the parent of nature, intellect, and the other ingredients of the universe, be to us the bestower of understanding, wealth, and final emancipation. Glory to the Supreme Vishnu the cause of the creation, existence, and end of this world; who is the root of the world, and who consists of the world; who exists everywhere, and in whom all things here exist; and who is thence named Vasudeva. He then existed in the forms of Universal Soul and Time." "There was neither day nor night, nor sky, nor any other thing, save only One. The Supreme Brahma, the Supreme Soul, the Supreme Ruler Hari, of his own will entered into matter and spirit. A vast egg, compounded of the elements, and resting upon the waters, became his abode. Then in the form of Brahmâ he engaged in the creation of the universe. Vishnu, with immeasurable goodness and power, preserves created things through successive ages, till the close of a world-period (Kalpa). Then the same mighty deity Janarddana (*i.e.* the object of adoration to mankind) assumes the awful form of Rudra, devours all things, and converts the world into one vast ocean. Then the Supreme reposes upon his mighty serpent (Eternity) amidst the deep, till he awakes after a season, and again, as Brahmâ, becomes the author of creation. Thus the one only God Janarddana takes the designation of Brahmâ, Vishnu, and Siva, as he creates, preserves, or destroys."

The personified Earth (Prithivi) apostrophises him thus: "Hail to thee, who art all creatures! From thee have I proceeded. Those who are desirous of final liberation worship thee as the Supreme Brahma. Thou art my creator, and I fly to thee for refuge! Thou art sacrifice, and the sinless lord of sacrifice! Thou art the oblation!"

"Created beings, although they are destroyed (in

their individual forms) at the periods of dissolution, yet, being affected by the good or evil acts of former existences, they are never exempted from their consequences. When Brahmá creates the world anew, they are the progeny of his will, in the fourfold condition of deities (devas), men, animals, or inanimate things. The demons (Asuras) are born in darkness from Brahmá's thigh. Then, besides the devas, there are heavenly minstrels and nymphs, centaurs with the limbs of horses and human bodies, &c. The four castes are born from his mouth, breast, thighs, and feet respectively. At first these abide in righteousness and perfect faith, and Hari dwells in their sanctified minds. Then through darkness and desire come the seeds of iniquity. As sin gains strength, mortals become afflicted with pain, and they construct places of refuge, protected by trees or water. Villages and cities arise, and from their manual labour come the seventeen useful kinds of grain.

"The sun, moon, and planets shall repeatedly be and cease to be; but those who internally repeat the mystic adoration of the divinity shall never know decay. For those who neglect their duties, who revile the Books of Knowledge, and obstruct religious rites, the places assigned after death are the terrible regions of darkness, of deep gloom, of fear, and of great terror. Sri, bride of Vishnu, mother of the world, is thus exalted and brought into the unity of one all-pervading spirit, here regarded under the double aspect of masculine and feminine. As he is all-pervading so is she. Vishnu is meaning, she is speech. He is polity, she is prudence. He is righteousness, she is devotion. Śrí is the earth, Hari the support of it. He is sacrifice, she is sacrificial donation. Kesava is the sun, and his radiance the goddess. Śrí is the heavens; Vishnu, who is one with all things, is widely extended space. Govinda is the ocean, Lakshmi (her name as the goddess of good fortune) its shore. Lakshmi is the light, and Hari, who is all and lord of all, the lamp. She, the mother of the world, is the creeping vine, and Vishnu the tree round which she clings. Govinda is love, and Lakshmi, his gentle spouse, is pleasure. Hari is all that is called male, Lakshmi is all that is termed female; there is nothing else than they. Śrí seems to be the classic Ceres, as she appears under her more comprehensive character when supposed to be identical with Rhea, Tellus, Cybele, Bona Dea, &c. Identified with Lakshmi, she has the aspect of Venus, even rising, like her, from the ocean. It is said that when Vishnu was Krishna she became incarnate as his wife, Rukmini.

CHAPTER XXX.

In illustration of constancy of faith on the Preserver the following story is given :—

The son of a daitya (the daityas are a demoniacal order of beings, corresponding with the Asuras) becomes devoted to Vishnu, and endures much contumely from his father on account of his still remaining faithful to Janarddana. He is overwhelmed with rocks, but remains unhurt, for his thoughts never swerve from the Preserver, and the recollection of the deity is his armour of proof. He is cast into flames, but it merely occasions the reflection that the dead are born again, that pain is necessary, that only a fool is fond of his body, composed of flesh, blood, &c. He (Prahlada) then preaches to the daityas, and says, "In this ocean of the world, in this sea of many sorrows, Vishnu is your only hope. We are children ; spirit embodied is eternal ; birth, youth, and decay are properties of the body, not of the soul. Even in childhood let the embodied soul acquire discriminative wisdom. Let us lay aside the angry passions of our race, and so strive that we obtain that perfect, pure, and eternal happiness which shall be beyond the power of the elements, or their deities, or the infirmities of human nature. In truth I say unto you, that you will have no satisfaction in various revolutions through this treacherous world, but that you shall obtain eternal calm by propitiating the Preserver whose adoration is perfect peace. Let the whole heart rest on Cesava. Wealth, pleasure, virtue are things of little moment. Precious is the fruit which you shall gather, be assured, from the exhaustless store of the tree of true wisdom. Love for all creatures will be assiduously cherished by all those who are wise in the knowledge that Hari is all things."

The daitya casts his son from the summit of the palace; but he falls, cherishing Hari in his heart, and Earth, the nurse of all creatures, received him gently on her lap, thus entirely devoted to Kesava the protector of the world. And so Prahlada becomes as one with Vishnu. The Preserver, in his yellow robe and glittering splendour, appears to him, and the prince prays to him. "In all the thousand births," he asks, "through which I may be doomed to pass, may my faith in thee never know decay." But Vishnu replies that through his faith he shall obtain liberation.

Analogous traditions certainly seem to have descended to the author of this book and to Dante. An elaborate enumeration of various hells is given, in which certain tortures are assigned to certain crimes. There are hells of red-hot iron, of salt, and of great flame. There is a hell of heated caldrons, another where heads are inverted, another where the condemned feed on worms, another with wells of blood. Besides hells for the great offences of murder and the like, a hell with leaves of sword-blades is reserved for those who wantonly cut down trees. A hell where the flesh is tortured with pincers is ascribed to those who break the vows of their Order.

The inhabitants of the infernal regions, as they move with their heads inverted, see the divine beings in heaven, who look down upon the sufferings of hell. Besides the illustration of this in the parable of Dives and Lazarus, the writings of the Father of the Christian Church, Tertullian of Carthage, who wrote about the year 207 A.D., give a very distinct view of his possibly just but indubitably cruel-seeming ideas upon the topic. Certainly it is absolutely analogous to this Indo-Aryan conception.

In his essay against stage-plays, &c., he writes (as translated in Roberts and Donaldson's "Ante-Nicene Christian Library"):

"But what a spectacle is that fast-approaching advent of the Lord, now owned by all, now highly exalted, now a triumphant one! What that exaltation of the angelic hosts! What the glory of the rising saints! What the kingdom of the just thereafter! What the city, New Jerusalem! Yes, and there are other sights: that last day of judgment with its everlasting issues; that day unlooked-for by the nations, the theme of their derision, when the world, hoary with age, and all its many products, shall be consumed in one great flame! How vast a spectacle then bursts upon the eye! What there excites my admiration! What my derision! Which sight gives me joy? which rouses me to exultation?

as I see so many illustrious monarchs, whose reception into the heavens was publicly announced, groaning now in the lowest darkness with great Jove himself; and those, too, who bore witness of their exaltation; governors of provinces, too, who persecuted the Christian name, in fires more fierce than those with which, in the days of their pride, they raged against the followers of Christ! What world's wise men besides, the very philosophers in fact, who taught their followers that God had no concern in aught that is sublunary, and who were wont to assure them that either they had no souls, or that they would never return to the bodies which at death they had left, now covered with shame before the poor deluded ones, as one fire consumes them! Poets also, trembling, not before the judgment-seat of Minos or Rhadamanthus, but of the unexpected Christ! I shall have a better opportunity, then, of hearing the tragedians, louder voiced in their own calamity; of viewing the play-actors, much more dissolute in the dissolving flame; of looking upon the charioteer, all glowing in his chariot of fire; of witnessing the wrestlers, not in their gymnasia, but tossing in the fiery billows, unless even then I shall not care to attend on such ministers of sin in my eager wish rather to fix a gaze insatiable on those whose fury vented itself against the Lord. 'This'—I shall say—'this is that carpenter's or harlot's son, that Sabbath-breaker, that Samaritan and devil-possessed! This is He whom you purchased from Judas! This is He whom you struck with reed and fist, whom you contemptuously spat upon, to whom you gave gall and vinegar to drink! This is He whom His disciples secretly stole away, that it might be said He had risen again, or the gardener abstracted, that his lettuces might come to no harm from the crowds of visitants! What quæstor or priest, in his munificence, will bestow on you the favour of seeing and exulting in such things as these? And yet, even now, we, in a measure, have them by faith in the picturings of imagination. But what are the things which eye has not seen, and ear has not heard, and which have not so much as dimly dawned upon the human heart? Whatever they are, they are nobler, I believe, than the circus, theatre and amphitheatre, and every race-course."

Tertullian, in these expressions, leads up to the ideas of those English Puritans who have considered the door of a theatre as an entrance to hell. He seems more savage, or, it may be urged by those who believe in eternal punishment, more strictly just than the Indo-Aryan, as he appears to leave no hope for the condemned.

CHAPTER XXXI.

The stages of existence are declared, in this "Ancient Book of the Preserver," to consist of inanimate things, fish, birds, animals, men, holy men, deities, and liberated spirits. Through these states, beings in heaven or hell must proceed till final emancipation. To obtain this end, reliance on Krishna is far better than expiatory acts, such as religious austerity. By addressing his thoughts to Nârâyana, a man becomes quickly cleansed of all guilt. The whole heap of worldly sorrows is dispersed by meditation on Hari; and his worshipper, even looking upon the enjoyment of heaven as an impediment to real happiness, obtains in him final emancipation. "Of what avail is ascent to the summit of heaven if it is necessary to return from thence to earth?" But meditation on Vasudeva is the seed of eternal freedom. The man who thinks of the Preserver day and night goes not to hell after death, for his sins are all atoned. Heaven delights the mind, hell gives it pain; hence virtue is called heaven, and vice, hell. Above Dhruva (the fixed polar star) is the region of saints, above again is the abode of Sanandana, and the other pure minds, sons of Brahma. There are habitations of deities which cannot be consumed by fire. But above all is the sphere of Truth, whose inhabitants will never again know death.

It may be asserted that all these ideas of faith in an incarnate deity of heaven and hell are derived from the teachings of the Apostles; and that the doctrine of the metempsychosis was learnt from Pythagoras, who is related, however, to have himself acquired it in Egypt or the East. It may be conceived that the astronomical notions with which they are conjoined were adopted from the Greeks, after Alexander's invasion. But, as has been observed, the sequence of ideas from the Vedas, through the philosophical books, law treatises, &c., seems so evident, and these points which bear Christian or Greek similitudes are intermingled with such a mass of matter, which appears exclusively indigenous, that it seems contrary to reason not to allow the growth of the whole system in Bharata, or Ancient India, from remote antiquity. The phenomena of Nature in that exuberant region of the earth offer suggestions for the whole of it, from a commencement in adoration of the Sun and Regents of the Elements. If admitted to have been thus apprehended in proto-typical or archaic form in the East, the full development of science, and the complete apprehension of religion, may be held to have been reserved for the western side of our hemisphere.

Professor Weber remarks that "several hymns of speculative purport, in the last book of the songs of the Rig Veda, testify to a great depth and concentration of reflection upon the fundamental causes of things; necessarily implying a long period of philosophical research in a preceding age. This is borne out by the old renown of Indian wisdom, by the reports of the companions of Alexander as to the Indian gymnosophists," &c.

Even in this Vedic period discussions were held upon such a topic of advanced thought as the assumption of matter or spirit for the first cause. "The latter," says Professor Weber, "became gradually the orthodox one, and is therefore the one most frequently, and indeed almost exclusively, represented in the Bráhmanas or essays explaining the sacrificial and devotional hymns and rites, with philosophical speculations," &c.

He remarks that the word *buddha*, awakened or enlightened, was originally a name of honour given to all sages.

Naturally in that region which, for eight months in the year, enjoys uninterrupted brilliance and beauty of starlit or moonlit nights, astronomy commenced with, and continued to be combined with, the theological and scientific systems. The chariot of the Sun is described as drawn by seven horses, which are allegorised as poetical metres. It is said that the glorious Sun darts like an arrow on his southern course, attended by the constellations of the Zodiac.[1]

"While the Sun shines in one continent at mid-day, in the opposite continents it will be midnight."

[1] "Vishnu Purana," translated by H. H. Wilson, p. 218.

"There is in truth neither rising nor setting of the Sun, for he is always; and these terms merely imply his presence and his disappearance. In the commencement of his northern course the Sun passes to Capricornus, thence to Aquarius, thence to Pisces, going successively from one sign of the Zodiac to another. After he has passed through these the Sun attains his equinoctial movement (the vernal equinox), when he makes the day and night of equal duration. The polar star is the centre of the Zodiacal wheel."

It is difficult to conceive that these astronomical ideas, as well as certain Christian doctrines, should have been inserted in the sacred books of a people who, in modern times, have been so self-satisfied with their religions. Even if Christian morality could have been introduced into their Scriptures, with a holier view of the Incarnation than their own, they would scarcely have inserted a foreign system of dividing the constellations in the Sun's path. Their ideas must be assigned to the evolution of antiquity. The Sun is said to be a principal part of the Preserver, and light is his immutable essence; the active manifestation of which is excited by the mystic syllable Aum. The Equinoxes occur at spring and autumn when the Sun enters the signs of Aries and Libra. When the Sun enters Capricorn (the winter solstice), his northern progress commences, and his southern when he enters Cancer (the summer solstice). Liberality, it is said, at the Equinoxes, is advantageous to the donor.

In the "Ancient Book of the Preserver" an enumeration is made of the earlier Indian Scriptures. These comprise the four Books of Knowledge (Vedas), six Angas, or subsidiary portions of the Vedas; which contain rules for reciting the prayers, with accents and tones to be observed; orders on ritual, and on grammar. Then there are Glossarial comments, the rules of metre, astronomy, theology, logic, the institutes of law, medical science, and that of archery; also there are treatises on the arts of music and dancing, and on the science of government.

Death is said to have power over all but the worshippers of the Preserver. He who never deviates from the duties prescribed for his class, who regards with equal indifference friend or enemy, who takes nothing that is not his own, and injures no being, is to be regarded as the worshipper of the Preserver— Janarddana occupies not his thoughts who envies another's prosperity. He who injures living beings injures him, for Hari is all beings; dwelling with their wives for the sake of progeny, tenderness towards all creatures, patience, humility, truth, purity, contentment, decency, adornment, gentleness of speech, friendliness, and freedom from envy and repining, from avarice and from detraction, these are the duties of every condition of life.

"A wise man will never engage in a dispute with those who are his superiors or inferiors; controversy and marriage are only to be permitted between equals."

"A considerate man will always cultivate in act, thought, and speech, that which is good for living beings both in this world and the next."

In such sentences as these which have been quoted the Christian spirit certainly seems present, while the incarnation of the Almighty is continually recounted with some variation of epithet—"The divine Preserver himself, the root of the vast universal tree, inscrutable by the understandings of all deities, demons, sages and men, past, present, or to come; He who is adored by Brahma and all the divine beings, who is without beginning, middle, or end, descended into the womb of Devaki, and was born as her son Vasudeva. At his birth the world was relieved from all iniquity; the sun, moon, and planets shone with unclouded splendour, all fear of calamitous portents was dispelled, and universal happiness prevailed." Again, in this "Ancient Book of the Preserver" it is declared, that "When the practices taught by the Vedas and the Institutes of law shall almost have ceased, and the close of the Black Age shall be near, a portion of that divine Being, who exists of his own spiritual nature in the character of Brahma, who is the Beginning and the End, and who comprehends all things, shall descend upon earth. He will be born as an eminent Brahman, Kalki, endowed with superhuman faculties. By his irresistible might he will destroy all the impure persons and thieves, and all whose minds are devoted to iniquity. He will then re-establish righteousness upon earth, and the minds of those who live at the end of the Black Age shall be awakened, and shall be as pellucid as crystal. The men who are thus changed by virtue of that peculiar time, shall be as the seeds of human beings, and shall give birth to a race which shall follow the laws of the Age of Purity. This age shall return when the Sun and the Moon, and the lunar asterism Tishya, and the planet Jupiter, are in one mansion. The Black Age of the world commenced so soon as the incarnation of the eternal Preserver had departed. And the son of Justice, with his brethren (*i.e.* the princes with whom Krishna had sided in the war), abdicated the sovereignty.

In this "Ancient Book of the Preserver" an account is given of the birth of Krishna, virtually similar to that which has been quoted from the Hari-vansa. The tyrant Kansa, in order to compass the infant Krishna's death, orders: "Let therefore active search be made for whatever young children there may be upon earth, and let every boy in whom there are signs of unusual vigour be slain without remorse."

The father of Krishna goes to Nanda, with whom the child has been deposited, and says: "The yearly tribute has been paid to the king, and men of property should not tarry near the court, when the business that brought them there has been transacted; up, Nanda, and set off to your own pastures."

"Accordingly Nanda and the other cowherds, their

goods being placed in their waggons, and their taxes having been paid to the king, returned to their village."

The story of the childhood is in this book, given in similar form to the narrative in the Hari-vansa; and also the abandonment of Mathura, and construction of Dwáraka.

A curious instance of a false Krishna is related: "A Vasudeva, called Paundraka, flattered by ignorant people, fancies himself *the* Vasudeva, who had descended upon earth. He sends to Krishna to do him homage. But Krishna comes, destroys his army, and with his discus cuts him to pieces. The head of a king who continues to believe in him, by Krishna's power is shot into his own city to the astonishment of the inhabitants. The discus of Krishna, which is described as blazing with the radiance of 100 suns, always returns to his hand, after it has accomplished its sure work. It evidently typifies the power of the Sun, which in India is very suggestive of these ideas. It is destined that all the race of Krishna, the Yadus, shall be exterminated. When the time approaches for the end, the deities send to Krishna to say to him that more than a century has elapsed since he descended. His work is accomplished in the destruction of demons, &c.,—let them behold their monarch in heaven. Krishna replies that the burdens of the earth are not removed until the Yadus are destroyed. "When I have restored the land of Dwáraka to the ocean, and annihilated the race of Yadu, I will proceed to the mansions of the Immortals." Terrible portents now are seen—the Yadus all go to a fête, become drunk, fight and destroy one another, amid supernatural occurrences. The spirit of Bala-Rama issues from his mouth in the form of a great serpent (Eternity) and departs into the ocean, celestial hymns accompanying the proceeding.

Beholding the departure of the spirit of Bala-Rama, Krishna says to the one Yadu remaining: "This must be related by you to Vasudeva and Ugrasena; I shall engage in religious meditation and quit this body; the sea will inundate the town.

"Then the divine Govinda, having concentrated in himself that supreme spirit which is one with Vasudeva, was identified with all beings." "He sat in thought resting his foot upon his knee."

"Then came Jara" (old age or decay), "who mistook the foot for part of a deer, and lodged his arrow in the sole."

Discovering what he has done, he demands forgiveness, and the Blessed One replies, "Fear not thou in the least. Go, hunter, through my favour, to heaven, the abode of the deities." Then a celestial car appeared, and the hunter ascended in it.

"Then the illustrious Krishna, having united himself with his own pure, spiritual, inexhaustible, inconceivable, unborn, undecaying, imperishable, and universal spirit, which is one with Vasudeva, abandoned his mortal body and the condition of the threefold qualities, he became Nirgúna, devoid of all qualities."

The Prince Arjouna found Krishna's body and performed obsequial rites. His eight queens embraced the body and then entered the funeral fire.

Arjouna then conducts the thousands of the other wives of Krishna, and the other women from Dwáraka; and on the same day that Hari departed from the earth, it is said that the powerful, dark-bodied Black Age descended. The ocean submerged Dwáraka, except the dwelling of the deity of the race of Yadu. It was not able to wash that temple away.

"There Cesava constantly abides, even in the present day. Whoever visits that holy shrine, the place where Krishna pursued his sports, is liberated from all his sins."

CHAPTER XXXII.

VARIOUS prophecies are uttered as to the Black Age in which we are supposed to be. Caste shall no longer prevail, money shall be the master of men, and all shall think themselves equal to Brahmins. Food shall be eaten without ablutions, women shall become fickle, princes plunder their subjects, the lowest class will seek a subsistence by begging, and, assuming the outward marks of religious mendicants, these will become the impure followers of impious and heretical doctrines, horrible penances shall be enjoined, and life be shortened. Vishnu, the lord of sacrifice, Creator and Lord of all, shall not be adored. Then shall the rainfall become scanty, and confusion reign in families.

At the end of a thousand periods of four Ages, a total dearth shall occur for one hundred years. "The eternal Vishnu then assumes the character of Rudra, the Destroyer, and descends to reunite all his creatures with himself. The seven solar rays dilate to seven suns. He becomes the scorching breath of the serpent Eternity. The three spheres become like a frying-pan amidst flames. Darkness ensues, and all creation, animate or inanimate, perishes. Then Hari, the Creator, sleeps upon the ocean in the form of Brahma, glorified by the saints in heaven; till he again wakes to re-create the universe.

It is again said in this book that "the term Vasudeva means that all beings abide in that Supreme Being, and that he abides in all beings." "Hence the Lord Vasudeva is the Creator and Preserver of the world. Assuming at will various forms, he bestows benefits upon the whole world, which was his work. He is known by holy study and devout meditation. He may first be contemplated under his manifested forms, but at length he can be realised as the supreme and universal Spirit," "the glorious being, without beginning or end, who destroys all sin; who, though one, became many; who, although pure, became as if impure, by appearing in many and various shapes."

"May that unborn, eternal Hari, whose form is manifold, and whose essence is composed of both nature and spirit, bestow upon all mankind that blessed state which knows neither birth nor decay."

Again, in this book are allusions to Buddhists or Jains. Vishnu is supposed to descend as Buddha, in order to entice certain demons from the truth; for due devotions are supposed to be efficacious, even when offered up by the wicked. He is described as approaching certain heretical ascetics as a naked mendicant, with his head shaven and carrying a bunch of peacocks' feathers. He maintains to them the equal truth of contradictory tenets. These to whom he preached, in their turn, became teachers; and their disciples again taught, till the Vedas became abandoned.

Then the Deluder put on garments of a red colour, assumed a benevolent aspect, and not only converted the Daityas to Jaina and Buddha heresies, but prevailed upon others, who deserted the doctrines and observances inculcated in the three Vedas. Some spoke evil of the sacred books; some treated sacrifices and devotional ceremonies with scorn; others calumniated the Brahmins. "The precepts," they cried, "that lead to the injury of animal life (as in sacrifices) are highly reprehensible;" "to say that casting butter into flame is productive of reward is childishness," &c. The Daityas having thus abandoned the armour of religion are defeated by the Devas (deities). "Men, indeed, fall into hell from only conversing with those who unprofitably assume the twisted hair and shaven crown."

As has been observed, this sort of description seems to suggest the Buddhism of or before the fourth century B.C., rather than the form which it appears to have assumed after the days of Ashoka or Priyadasi, in the third century B.C.

It seems absolutely necessary that we should accept as fact the gradual apprehension in India in long periods of time amongst the Indo-Aryan race, our ethnological cousins, of many spiritual ideas appertaining to our own religious culture. This would seem calculated to enlarge not to destroy our Christian faith.[1] And the gradual apprehension of these ideas, in long periods of time, is in accordance with the views of modern science in regard to the world's history.

CHAPTER XXXIII.

THE Bhagavata Purana, or "Ancient Book of the Blessed One," was translated into French, under the auspices of the French Government, by M. Eugene Burnouf, about the year 1840. In this book the warrior aspect of Krishna appears to be less regarded than in the "Great Bharata" poem. His beneficent character, as the Asylum of all humanity, as the

[1] See Appendix IV.

means of release from all pain, seems to be put forward prominently rather than his princely aspect. He is essentially identified with Purusha, the Soul of the universe, or man soul collectively.

The ideas centered about his personality seem certainly to find their prototypes, or antecedent ideas, in the following hymn from the Rig Veda. This hymn also seems to shadow forth in prophetical, or prototypical strain, the leading ideas of the Christian religion. It is quoted as translated by Coleridge, and published in volume vii., page 251, of "Asiatic Researches:"—

"The embodied Spirit, which hath 1000 heads, 1000 eyes, 1000 feet, stands in the human breast, while he totally pervades the earth. That being is this universe, and all that has been or will be: he is that which grows by nourishment, and he is the distributor of immortality. Such is his greatness, and, therefore, he is the most excellent embodied spirit; the elements of the universe are one portion of him; and three portions of him are immortality in heaven. That threefold being rose above (this world), and the single portion of him remained in this universe, which consists of what does, and what does not taste (the reward of good and bad actions): again he pervaded the universe. From him sprung Viraj (the male power), from which the first man was produced; and he being successively reproduced, peopled the earth. From that single portion, surnamed the universal sacrifice, was the holy oblation of butter and curds produced: and this did frame all cattle, wild or domestic, which are governed by instinct. From that universal sacrifice were produced the strains of the Rig and Saman (Vedas), from him the sacred metres sprung; from him did the Yajur (Veda) proceed; from him were produced all horses and all beasts that have two rows of teeth; from him sprung cows; from him proceed goats and sheep. Him the gods, the demi-gods named Sad'hya, and the holy sages, immolated on the sacred grass, and they performed a solemn act of religion. Into how many portions did they divide this being whom they immolated? His mouth became a priest, his arm was made a soldier, his thigh was transformed into an husbandman, from his feet sprang the servile man. The moon was produced from his mind; the sun sprung from his eye; air and breath proceeded from his ear, and fire rose from his mouth. In that solemn sacrifice, which the gods performed with him as a victim, spring was the butter, summer the fuel, and sultry weather the oblation. Seven were the moats (surrounding the altar), thrice seven were the logs of holy fuel at that sacrifice which the gods performed, immolating this being (Purusha—universal soul) as the victim. By that sacrifice the gods worshipped this victim. Such were primeval duties; and thus did they attain heaven, where former gods and mighty demi-gods abide."

This mystic illustration must surely mean that

spirit can only become realised in the flesh by suffering and self-sacrifice. The active 'soul of passive nature can solely exist, in the body, by means of that pain which, in a greater or less degree, accompanies all earthly life, and alternates to some extent with all human happiness. But from this pain, Bhagavat became manifested to deliver man. The Bhagavata Purana, or Ancient Book of the Blessed or Holy One, commences with:

"Aum, adoration to Bhagavat, son of Vasudeva! let us meditate on the Being, from which is derived the conservation and destruction of this universe. He is united to all things, yet remains distinct from them, powerful, resplendent in his own brilliance; who drew from his intelligence the Veda, for the first inspired singer. Behold a book in which is displayed the Supreme Law, disengaged from all illusion, in which the essence is revealed of that which ought to be known, which can confer happiness, and cause the three sorts of sorrow to disappear."

Like the "Great Bharata Epic," this book is supposed to have been delivered by word of mouth; and the form of dialogue is sustained in it. "Deign to declare to us," say certain sages or hermits, to one who has become versed in it, "the history of him whose incarnation had for its design the protection and happiness of creatures. We have faith. Relate to us the most excellent histories of the incarnations of Hari (Vishnu, &c.),—of the sovereign lord, who of his own free will delivers himself to those sports of his illusive power (Mâyâ); in which he assumes the fallacious appearance of man. Now that Krishna, Master of the Yoga (the uniting of the individual spirit to the Supreme spirit), has entered into his proper substance, in what asylum has Justice taken refuge?"

It does not seem to be intended that the incarnation in Krishna should not be considered real as to the actuality of the flesh; but that he appeared to be man, while he was in reality Almighty Power of the Universe. The Docetes, in the early Christian Church, educated in the Platonic doctrines, conceived that an emanation of the Deity assumed the form and appearance of mortality, and that Christ was really a phantom. Amongst the Indian divines, the incarnations of Deity seem to have been regarded as true in respect to substance, but they are considered as disports of Deity.

Krishna is the manifestation of the Bhagavat, the Blessed or Divine One; but through him it is Bhagavat who is to be adored,—who ought to be the exclusive object of attention, meditation, praise, and respect: "In his compassion for the virtuous of mankind, who give hearing to the narration of his actions, Krishna, whose history equally purifies him who listens to it and him who repeats it, descends to the depths of their hearts, and chases away all evil desires. When once the evil thoughts have lost their empire, the constant worship of Bhagavat produces an unflagging devotion to the god of excellent glory. Then the heart braves the attacks of Desire, Greed, and all the vices born of Passion and of Darkness, and tranquillity reposes in the bosom of Goodness. And the heart which has thus found repose in devoting itself to the worship of the Blessed One, after having sundered the bonds of attachment to the world, arrives at the inward knowledge of Truth, which is the Blessed One himself. All doubts are dissipated, the works of the man are brought to nothing, for then he beholds within himself the Sovereign Lord. Behold therein the reason why the inspired singers, with hearts full of joy, incessantly vow to Bhagavat, the son of Vasudeva, that devotion which brings repose to the soul."

CHAPTER XXXIV.

The aspects in which the adoration of Krishna, under his various immortal and mortal epithets, appear in the "Great Bharata" epic and in the "Ancient Book of the Blessed," afford a parallel to the high and low doctrines of the Church of England. In both faith in the divine manifestation is the way of happiness, and in both there are ceremonial observances; but in the Poems, as in High Churchism, the ceremonial seems to be more closely associated with faith.

In reading this Bhagavata Purana, the sermons

and tracts of Evangelical Protestantism are continually suggested. Of course the local colouring differs with climate and outer aspect of vegetable, animal, and human life; but the essentials of the doctrines seem to be the same.

As has been observed, the word Bhagavata signifies Holy One. As, however, it seems primarily to mean possessing fortune, the term Blessed seems perhaps most fully to render it. *Bhaga* means a liberal or wealthy master, an apportioner of food; and in that sense the expression would seem to bring us to the conception of Christ as the Bread of Life, &c. Purana seems to mean "ancient" in the complete sense of belonging to ancient times. Indeed, it is almost inconceivable that this "Ancient Book of the Blessed One," if written, as has been supposed possible, in about the twelfth century of our era, can have been other than a re-editing of the old stories of the incarnations. In fact, this seems to have been admitted by M. E. Burnouf and Professor H. H. Wilson, the great and acknowledged students of the Puranas. It may, however, have been heightened in its colouring as to the implicit faith and absolute devotion to be bestowed upon Krishna, *i.e.* Bhagavat, in all his manifestations. So in Christendom the evangelical doctrines, which may be supposed to have been preached by all the apostles, appear less earnestly propounded by their more immediate successors. Evangelicalism became speedily overlaid in the Church with ceremonial and priestly assumptions. This intense fervour of Indo-Aryan faith in manifested Deity, as superior to all "works," however late it may be placed, seems to have preceded the Protestant movement of Europe; just as the previous adoration of Hari-Krishna, as the Herakles of Megasthenes, preceded the manifestation of Christ Himself in Judæa. Both equally seem prototypes or previous conceptions. It is said of Bhagavat—"Creator of the worlds,"—he conserves them by the aid of his quality of goodness; loving to assume, in the sports of his incarnations, the forms of a deity, a man, or an animal. Then are enumerated, in the "Book of the Blessed," his principal births:

1st. To create the universe, he took the form of Purusha, composed of Intelligence and other principles (soul of the universe, or man-type, as has been observed).

2d. Then he became the Boar to raise the earth from the abyss.

3d. He became the Instructor of the Deities (Devas).

4th. He manifested himself as Nara and Narāyana.

5th. He became Kapila (to reveal the system of philosophy, afterwards adopted in both Krishnaism and Buddhism).

6th. He came to communicate knowledge to many sages.

7th. He reigned over a former Age, peopled by divine beings.

8th. He showed the just way, revered by men of all the "orders."

9th. He made the most excellent herbage to grow at the solicitation of Holy Sages.

10th. He became a fish, to save the seventh Manu from the flood, and recover the Books of Knowledge which had been carried, by a demon, into the depths.

11th. When a great churning of the ocean took place, by the divine beings, to obtain the drink of immortality, he sustained a mountain on his back as a tortoise.

12th and 13th. He became an enchantress, to deceive the demons, and enable the deities to secure for themselves the drink of immortality.

14th. He became the man-lion, to destroy the chief of a race of demoniacal beings.

15th. He became a dwarf, to deceive the demon Bali, who allowed him to claim as his own all that he could cover in three steps. In his strides he compassed heaven and earth.

16th. Observing that the kings were tyrannising over the Brahmins, he purged, twenty-one times, the earth of the warrior caste.

17th. Seeing that men had insufficient intelligence, he divided the tree of the Vedas (as Vyāsa, reputed author, also, of the "Great Bharata").

18th. As Rama, he invaded Ceylon to recover his bride Sita, and destroy the demon Ravanna, who had become obnoxious to gods and men.

19th and 20th. Born as Krishna and Bala Rama, to relieve the earth of the burden which oppressed it.

21st. At length, in the course of the Black Age, in design of deceiving enemies of the divine beings, it is said that he will be born under the name of Buddha.

22d. Then, towards the end of this Age, when kings will have become no more than brigands, the Master of the World will be born under the name of Kalki.

But the reciter of the Poem is represented as adding: "Oh, wise Brahmins, the incarnations of Hari, Treasure of Goodness, are innumerable—as Deities, Manus, sons of Manu, and patriarchs—brilliant in splendour, but really only manifestations of divers portions of Hari himself. Krishna alone is Bhagavat entirely. So the wise, directing their intelligence exclusively towards the son of Vasudeva, sovereign of the worlds, thus deliver themselves from the terrible law of regeneration (*i.e.* the being re-born in the flesh).

CHAPTER XXXV.

In the most ancient of the Books of Knowledge, the Rig Veda, appears a hymn in which Vishnu, regarded as the Sun, performs the three strides of the fifteenth incarnation, related in the last chapter.

This has been translated by Dr. Muir, in his "Sanskrit Texts."

"Vishnu strode over this (universe); in three places he planted his step; (the world or his step was) enveloped in his dust.

"Vishnu, the unconquerable preserver, strode three steps, bearing from thence fixed observances.

"Behold the acts of Vishnu, through which this fitting (or intimate) friend of Indra perceived religious ceremonies.

"Sages constantly behold that highest position of Vishnu, like an eye fixed in the sky."

The three steps have been surmised to have signified sunrise, mid-day, and sunset; but before the time of the Bhagavata the idea had evidently become further allegorised.

The last incarnation, declared to be yet to come, is suggestive of the appearing of Him whom St. John in his "Revelation" saw on the white horse; out of whose mouth went a sharp sword to smite the nations.

This incarnation is thus described, in the ode of Jayadeva; who has been supposed to have written about the twelfth century of our era—

"For the destruction of all the impure, thou drawest thy cimeter like a blazing comet (how tremendous). O Cesava, assuming the body of Kalki; be victorious, O Heri, lord of the Universe."

This final incarnation has also been thus versified—

"When Kalki mounts his milk-white steed,
Heaven, earth, and all will then recede."

In this "Ancient Book of the Blessed One," as in the other works of a similar character, this future incarnation in Kalki is associated with descriptions of disorders of various kinds, prevailing before his coming. These are certainly very analogous to those foretold in the New Testament, as about to happen before the Second Coming of Christ.

The one before the last of these incarnations of Bhagavat, that of Buddha, is introduced as if prophetically written. The author ascribed the work to Vyāsa, who belonged to the epoch of Krishna, at about 1300 B.C., according to views of European scholars, or 3000 B.C., according to the notions of the Indians themselves. This introduction of Buddha either shows an interpolation, or it probably assigns the book, at least, to a later date than 500 B.C. But, as has been remarked, Professor Wilson, and others, have ascribed it, in its present form, to so recent a period as the 12th century. Some learned Hindus have agreed with them; though, in India, the work is generally believed to have been inspired in the remote past.

Considering the prominent position occupied by Buddhism, in the time of Ashoka, who assembled a Buddhist Council, B.C. 258, at Pataliputra, the modern Patna, and the number of monastic establishments, in which the Buddhistic canons of scripture were studied in the Age of the Chinese pilgrims, about the 4th and 6th century, A.D., it is again difficult to conceive that a writer, 1500 years after its rise, *i.e.* in about the 10th or 12th centuries of our era, could treat it as something still in the future.

It is more reasonable to suppose that such an idea might have occurred to a Brahminical author on observing the rise of Buddhistic teaching. He saw ascetics promulgating principles opposed to the Brahminical views, and reprobated them accordingly. He was assigning his rescript of old legends, with heightened Krishnaism for doctrine, to the holy sage Vyāsa, of ancient days. He wished to check these rising errors, and had perhaps found that Buddha had been asserted to be an incarnation of Vishnu or Bhagavat. He therefore stated, prophetically, as if from Vyāsa, that it was merely an incarnation to effect benefit by deceiving the enemies of the good. If he had lived at a period when Buddhism, for some 1200 or 1500 years, had been extensively triumphant throughout the land, he must, surely, have indicated its system more distinctly. Indeed, at the time when Amara-Sinha compiled the oldest Sanskrit dictionary, which has descended to us, attempts seem to have been made to reconcile Krishnaism and Buddhism.

With regard to the date of this dictionary-compiler, various periods, from 56 B.C. to 1050 A.D., seem to have been assigned to him. At all events, the ideas prevailing at any epoch between these limits must be reasonably supposed to have had influence upon the views which a Brahminical writer, at the later date, would have taken of Buddhism. He may have disapproved of them, but he must surely have recognised their existence, and combated them more definitely, if he introduced them at all. This is not a mere sketchy author, hurrying over his delineations.

CHAPTER XXXVI.

M. Levêque observes on page 95 of his work, which has been quoted, that the orphic theology is of Indian origin. It has two characteristic features.

1. Zeus is the universal soul.
2. All things are contained in the body of Zeus.

Now the fragments in which these two conceptions are displayed, are merely a free translation of the "Vision of Márkandéya," as related in the Mahábhárata.[1]

Zeus, lord of the thunder-bolt, is the first-born; he is the last; he is the head and the middle. He has produced all things. He is the male, he is also the immortal nymph. There is but one master, one God, chief of all beings. There is but one royal body, in which move all things. After that Zeus has absorbed all beings into himself he again brings them forth, and by ineffable deed returns them to the light.

M. Levêque exhibits the Indian doctrine of the

[1] This has been narrated in Chapter XVIII. of this book.

metempsychosis in juxtaposition with that of Plato, as expounded in the Phædo, &c.

He remarks that the theory of the *transmigration* rests upon two principles; the one metaphysical, the other moral.

1. Souls are eternal, as motive forces—the living are born from the dead, the dead from the living.

2. Justice demands that the soul should be punished for its vices and recompensed for its virtues. This principle is realised by transmigration; for the conduct which has characterised a soul in one life determines the corporal form with which it will be united in another life.

Reminiscence is the consequence of the pre-existence and transmigrations of the soul.

Our idiosyncrasies, according to this doctrine, are really owing to unconscious reminiscences of the desires and influences, mental and bodily characteristics, tastes, habits, and deeds of previous existences.

"Not only is this Indian doctrine to be found in the writings of the Platonic school, it distinctly existed in those numerous sects of Christians which are denounced by the *orthodox* Irenæus and others in their writings against heresies.

There is certainly nothing immoral or contrary to the wellbeing of humanity in a doctrine which teaches that every act of our lives, good, evil, or indifferent, must have its necessary sequences in this life and in life to come. Every wrongful deed will eventually react upon the doer; and punishment, or consequences of the nature of punishment, if escaped in this life, will inevitably arrive hereafter.

Buddha in the East, Pythagoras on the Mediterranean, the Brahmins and sects of early Christians have taught or held this doctrine as a spiritual fact. Many uncivilised races appear to have entertained crude ideas concerning some sort of analogous belief. The ancient Germans, Druids, &c., seem to have entertained it; and, as Josephus informs us, it was a tenet of the Pharisees. We have abandoned it as a doctrine in Christianity; but Christianity now seems to be abandoning the conception of hell, if not of heaven. Certainly, in so-called Christian nations, numbers are lapsing into Agnosticism or positive Materialism. As has been shown in Chapter V., a "Materialist" appears, with a pupil, in the ancient Hindu drama of the "Rising of the Moon of Awakened Intellect."

In fact, the contest between the two schools of Thought, which may be classed as the Platonist and Aristotelian, extends backwards far beyond the periods of the Greek supremacy.

Gautauma Buddha narrated past existences. Pythagoras affirmed that he had been present at the siege of Troy. He asserted that he had been Euphorbus, slain by Menelaus. He also claimed to have been Æthalides, son of Mercury.

In the Mahábhárata, the Deity of Deities said to Arjouna, "In a former existence thou wast Nara, companion of Narāyana (Krishna)." Ovid has said in the Metamorphoses—

> "O genus attonitum, gelida formidine mortis
> Quid Styga, quid tenebras et nomina vana timetis
> Materiem vatum, falsique pericula mundi?
> Corpora sive rogus flamma, seu tabe vetustas
> Abstulerit, mala posse pati non ulla putetis.
> Morte carent animae, semperque priore relicta
> Sede, novis domibus vivunt habitantque receptae."
> —(xv. 153.)

O race terrified by cold death, why do ye dread the Styx, the darkness and pains of an imaginary world, vain names and fictions of the poets? Your body, which the flame of the pyre or decay can destroy, can suffer no further ill. Souls are immortal, and they leave their first abodes only to live in others.

This certainly agrees with the Mahábhárata, in which it is said that the soul is not born, neither does it die. It is eternal, ancient. It is not slain with the body. The sages have said that the bodies of mortals are as houses; they are destroyed by time, only the soul is eternal.

M. Levêque writes of the Pythagorean and Orphic verses that—

"Les vers dorés ont été composés par un Pythagoricien. Ils contiennent des idées empruntés au Brahminism, au Bouddhism, au Mazdéism. En voici deux examples."

1. "Si ayant quitté ton corps, tu t'élèves dans

l'éther libre, tu seras immortel, tu seras un dieu à l'abri du trépas, tu ne seras plus un mortel."

2. "N'accueille pas le sommeil sur tes yeux appesantis avant d'avoir examiné trois fois chacun des actes de ta journeé. l'ar ou ai-je péché ? qu'ai je fait ? quel devoir ai-je negligé d'accomplir. Reprends ainsi tous les actes l'un après l'autre ; puis, si tu as fait quelque chose de honteux, gourmande toi, toi-même ; si quelque chose de bon, réjouis toi" (Vers dorés 40-44).

This last precept, he says, is borrowed from Mazdéism, in which the faithful are enjoined, in retiring to rest, to examine the acts of the day.

He continues, "Aux Pythagoriciens se rattachent les Orphiques dont la théologie est d'origine indienne."

The recognised antiquity of the most ancient Indian and Persian Scriptures negatives the assertion that in Greece, in comparatively modern times, these ideas had their birth. It was not claimed that Pythagoras taught, but that he learnt in or from the East.

The doctrine of faith in the "Blessed One," in this "Ancient Book," is entirely connected with this belief in the transmigration of souls. But Bhagavat, incarnate in Krishna, saves not only from recurring ills in transmigrations but from immense periods of torments in hell. And by faith in him not merely an absorption of self in the divine soul of the universe seems inculcated ; but an actual consciousness of eternal bliss. In constancy of devotion to the Blessed or Holy One, as manifested in multitudinous forms, but especially in Krishna, happiness as well as rest is to be found.

CHAPTER XXXVII.

THE divine personage named Narada appears to hold, in the Indian Olympus, a position somewhat analogous to that of the classic Mercury. He is one of the ten Lords of Creation (Prajapatis), sons of Brahma. He relates that, in a previous birth, he had served certain Yogins, or saints united to Bhagavat, who appear to be prototypes of our evangelical "converted." These saints instructed him in the pure glory of Hari. They informed him that works were the cause of return to this world; but that works could themselves destroy their influence, if only they were entirely directed towards the Supreme Being. When men deliver themselves to works, solely in the spirit of submission to Bhagavat, they repeat the names and attributes of Krishna, and meditate on him; saying, "Adoration to thee, Bhagavat, son of Vasudeva. He who thus addresses his devotion to the male of the sacrifice, to this incorporeal one, whose spiritual form is a prayer, this man possesses the true knowledge."

"Adoration to Krishna, son of Vasudeva, cherished child of Devaki, to Govinda, the young shepherd of the Pastor Nanda. He was born of the wife of Vasudeva, for the happiness of this universe."

Such is the constant style of invocation or praise addressed to this incarnation of the divine in this work of doubtful age; which certainly seems to be the sequence of ideas which appeared many centuries before the commencement of the Christian era.

When Krishna returns to his own city of Dwarka, on the sea coast of Gujerat, all the inhabitants came forth to meet him. Joyfully they cry, "We prostrate ourselves, O Lord, before the lotus of thy feet—O thou who art worshipped by Brahmâ, by the chiefs of the divinities, who art in this world the asylum of those who desire the supreme happiness—O thou who causest the universe to exist, grant to us existence—thou who art for us mother, father, spouse, friend—in your absence each instant seems ages to your faithful servants."

The city is again described in the usual fashion, as ornamented with woods, gardens, orchards, groves. At the gates and in the streets, arches of triumph had been erected—flags and standards of various colours enlivened it, and it was sprinkled throughout with perfumed waters. He is greeted with flowers, fruits, roasted grain, baskets of fruits and provisions set forth at the doors of houses, the general uprising of the people from couches, chairs, or repasts. A procession of Brahmins brings offerings of good augury, with sacred prayers from the Vedas, and accompanied by elephants, instruments of music, &c.

With them come on chariots, that they may behold Krishna, hundreds of dancing girls, brilliant in jewellery, and troops of actors, dancers, singers—of men who recite the sacred histories, genealogists and panegyrists, repeating the history and marvels of him whose glory is excelling.

Bhagavat, seeing his relations and servants, salutes them, bowing, smiling, &c. He embraces some and takes the hands of others, and he distributes valuable presents. As he advances up the royal street, the women ascend to the housetops, and would apparently have overwhelmed him with showers of flowers but for the fans and white umbrella held over him. He is brilliant in yellow garments, with garlands of woodland flowers (which may be as large and gorgeous in colour in India as our choicest products of the conservatory). He prostrates himself before the seven wives of his father, Vasudeva, of whom his mother, Devaki, was the chief. Then he entered his own palace, with its 16,000 pavilions for his wives, who eagerly embrace their husband, shedding tears of joy.

"So Bhagavat descended into the world of men under the veil of the illusion which he wields, and delivered himself to pleasure amidst his numbers of incomparable spouses like a simple mortal."

Even Shiva, it is said, the enemy of love, would have forgotten himself amidst Krishna's spouses. Their charms, however, could not really affect the soul of him whom men believed to have been a mere mortal, slave to passions like themselves. The Supreme Spirit, even in the bosom of Nature, is not enchained by its qualities. Intelligence reposes in the various envelopes of the soul without being attached to them. But the wives, deceived, ignorant of the real grandeur of their husband, thought him enslaved by their charms.

Brahmâ is represented as instructing his son, Narada, that it is to Bhagavat that we must address our adorations—"to Narâyana the Vedas are really addressed." "When," says Brahmâ, "I was born from the lotus (which came from the navel of Narâyana), I found only the members of the Soul of the Universe for sacrifice—the prayers, the utensils were all of him (Purusha=Narâyana). Then I celebrated the sacrifice in honour of Purusha, the Sovereign Lord, who had himself become the sacrifice. Then," continues Brahmâ, addressing Narada, "thy nine brothers, the lords of creation, celebrated the sacrifice of Purusha considered under his forms visible and invisible. And divine beings, saints and men, addressed their sacrifices to him who pervades the universe."

CHAPTER XXXVIII.

This "ancient book of the blessed or holy one," like the other Puranas, is alleged to have been indited in order to set the truths of religion before the masses. As Sanscrit, the language in which it is written, had become corrupted into various dialects after the commencement of our era, and was only understood by the learned classes, it seems curious that this should have been composed in Sanscrit at the late date attributed to it. M. Eugène Burnouf, translator of the Bhagavata Purana, seems to have agreed with H. H. Wilson in attributing it to Vopadeva, a grammarian of the thirteenth century A.D., resident at Dowlutabad. But it certainly is difficult to conceive how he can have made the slight allusions to Buddhism which the book contains without pursuing the topic further, if he wrote it at this period. As has been shown from the Chinese Pilgrims, corroborated by recent archæological explorations, &c., what may be styled multitudes of Buddhist monasteries had been established in India before this epoch. Buddhism had become systematised, and its canons of scripture, defined in general councils, were elaborately studied in these monasteries. The allusions in the Puranas undoubtedly suggest the period when Buddhism was first making its appearance in a form of asceticism differing from that of the

Brahminical sects, or in a rejection of the Brahminical caste system.

Considering the invasion of Alexander, the subsequent establishments of the Greeks in the North-West, and the Mohammedan inroads of the eleventh century A.D., it certainly seems more reasonable to suppose that the epic poems and Puranas, in forms approximating to their present, were composed between the tenth and fourth centuries B.C. rather than the fourth and tenth centuries A.D. Supposing the Greek and Scythic invasions of the North-West before the time of Christ to have been ignored, surely the Priyadasi of the edicts must have been mentioned in connection with Buddhism, also Vicramaditya and his exploits. The general contents of the Bhagavata and Vishnu "Ancient Books," suggest their composition at a period preceding the invasion of Alexander the Great, and before the extensive promulgation of Buddhism under Aśoka or Priyadasi, about the third century B.C.

But let us admit these books to have been re-edited, or compiled, or altogether composed at a period corresponding to our Mediæval Ages. Even then those vast storehouses of legends, myths founded on observations of the heavens, moral and didactic discourses, &c., would seem to have required two or three thousand years for their development, judging from the developments which have taken place in our own culture. Portions of them might seem to have been adopted from our New Testament. But these portions are intertwined with such a mass of matter distinctly Indian or old Bharatan. The doctrine of the Incarnation seems to be so elaborately conceived, in progress of growth to be traced from the oldest to the most modern of the existing sacred literature in the Sanscrit. It is accompanied by such an enormous accumulation of astronomical allusions, sun-myths, speculations as to the origin of things, and metaphysical and moral reflections, that it is difficult to imagine that the aspect of the doctrine which resembles the Christian idea is an interpolation.

If we consider the elaboration of the system with which these incarnation ideas are connected, and the association of the whole with astronomical observations, and conceptions suggested by the sunshine and rainy seasons, &c., the remote antiquity seems demonstrated. Taking the ramifications of the idea and exuberant fancies into consideration, together with the mass of literary evidence, it seems absolutely certain that they exhibit the legitimate growth of spiritual ideas. The Vedas afford us earliest existing exposition of these ideas. But the ideas themselves must have been gradually evolved before the poet was inspired to chant them.

CHAPTER XXXIX.

HORACE HAYMAN WILSON observes that the chief *dramatis personæ* of the Indian epics are impersonations of gods, demi-gods, and celestial spirits, and that the ritual appears to be that of the Vedas. "The Puranas repeat the theoretical cosmogony of the two great poems, they expand and systematise the chronological computations, and they give a more definite and connected representation of the mythological fictions and historical traditions." Of these eighteen "Ancient Books," twelve seem more particularly devoted to the adoration of deity manifested in Krishna or in some of his forms. The others hold up Shiva to veneration. But as the trinity of Brahma, Vishnu, and Shiva, and indeed all the deities, are continually asserted to be only forms of the one Supreme Spirit, the difference between the sects appears to amount to no more than the diversities between the great branches of the Christian Church.

Evangelical Protestantism asserts that the Church of Rome does not do proper honour to the Son while it permits images of the Virgin to be set up and litanies to be hymned to her. The Church of Rome has held those to be outside the pale of salvation who have denied the viceregency on earth of the supposed successors to St. Peter in the possession of the keys of heaven. Certainly these are differences equal to those which are maintained by the Hindu sects. And there appears to be no evidence of their waging such sanguinary wars over their tenets as have agitated Christendom.

The Puranas are said by him to have contained, in the aggregate, 400,000 *slokas*, or 1,600,000 lines. These do not appear to be all forthcoming now. But they extend to a length which is great (or even stupendous) in comparison with the New Testament of Christianity. Their numerous legends seem to demand long periods for their evolution.

The epics and "Ancient Books" seem to be recounting current legends. These they adapted to Brahminism. But although mighty powers, and the most exalted position, are attributed to Brahmins, the actual, fervent desire to urge the adoration of the Supreme Spirit, on earth in Krishna, seems to have been the most absorbing motive of the authors. Then there are other books called Upa-Puranas, and later works in pursuance of the same topic.

While the All-pervading or Preserving Spirit is more especially to be worshipped in the incarnations, the deity, contemplated as Shiva, is adored in the Lingam (a point), which is a dome-shaped emblem of Creative Power, or of the Universe. Shiva is represented as the Ascetic; and in the performance of severe penances and mortifications of the flesh, the Hindu votary of Shiva seems only to follow his divine example.

It appears to be evident, although these Puranas describe Buddha as a deceptive incarnation of Vishnu, that Buddha came to be regarded under a very similar aspect to Krishna. In fact, both Krishnaism and Buddhism arose out of the ancient philosophical systems; but the former became venerated in Brahminism and amongst the military aristocracy of the north-west of India. In the case of the latter the monastic and celibate life was enjoined, and caste taught to be of no religious consequence. It seems to have arisen amongst the more peaceful populations of the east of Hindustan.

Various dates have been assigned to Gautauma Buddha, or Sakya Muni (*i.e.* Gautauma the Enlightened, or the Ascetic of the Race of Sakya). These range from B.C. 2422 to B.C. 546. European scholarship assigns him to the latter period. Professor Weber states the possibility of his having died so late as 370 B.C. On the other hand, doubts have been raised as to whether he ever existed. His story is connected with superhuman events. Tradition ascribes his birthplace to Kapila-vastu, *i.e.* the abode of Kapila. As his mother's name is Mâyâ-dêvî (the divine Mâyâ), and as his miraculous birth occurs at a place named after the founder of a philosophical system, these considerations, conjoined with his father's nomenclature of "clean-food," and other points in his history, have raised suspicions that he is but the embodiment of a school of religious thought. These have been put forward by M. Senart in his work on Buddhism. Krishna, in his expositions in the "Divine Song" of the "Great Bharata," seems equally connected with Kapila. In fact, it appears that in the period when the Sanscrit dictionary of Amara-Sinha was compiled at the court of Vicramaditya, Krishna and Buddha had equally come to be regarded as forms of the One Supreme Being. Sir William Jones, writing towards the close of the last century, has recorded his observation in the "Asiatic Researches," that "in the principal Sanscrit dictionary, compiled about two thousand years ago, Krishna, Vasudeva, Govinda, and other names of the Shepherd God are intermixed with epithets of Narayan or the Divine Spirit." Again, however, we are upon debatable ground as to whether this Vicramaditya, emperor of India, lived at the time of the commencement of the era (Samvat), which is supposed to date from his reign, or at some subsequent epoch.

This Samvat, the era of northern India, commences B.C. 56. But Vicramaditya and Amara-Sinha, the author of the "principal Sanscrit Dictionary," are together enveloped in doubt by our modern Anglo-Indian chronologists.

It appears, at all events, to be evident that the system delivered under the name of Krishna, and that attributed to Buddha, both of which present many points of close contact with Christianity, are developments in somewhat different directions of the ideas expounded under the name of Kapila, which name appertains to an age centuries B.C. An exposition of undoubtedly pre-Christian religion is associated with the name of Kapila, who became himself elevated to divine rank, and regarded as an incarnation of the Preserver.

As in the Institutes of Manu, usually attributed to about the same period, it is taught in Kapila's system that the soul transmigrates into semi-divine, human, or animal bodies, according to its deeds and desires. By the study and practice of the highest philosophy the soul may achieve reunion with the Divine Spirit of All, from which it originally proceeded. To this end it must throw off its desire of individuality. It is taught that sentient soul experiences pain, arising from decay and death, until it be relieved of its personality. By attainment of perfect knowledge, the separation of the soul from the corporeal frame at length becomes complete. In *Yoga*, *i.e.* in junction or union, the individual soul becomes united with the Supreme Soul. Man's liberation is to be obtained by concentrating his attention on Iswara, who is God, on whom reliance is to be obtained by knowledge. This comes in meditation, and the highest happiness is to be secured in this union with the Supreme Spirit.

By delivering the body to a life of asceticism and entire abnegation of self, in constant consideration of Nature (both of the material and immaterial universe) in God, the bliss of union with God is to be attained. The systems of both Krishna and Buddha, in holding forth the perfections of Krishna or Buddha for imitation, and in affording these material persons as objects of devotion by faith, seem to have been a natural sequence to the more abstruse philosophies. They offered a tangible manifestation of God upon earth in the first case, and of highest human perfection in the second, to enable the soul to grasp the divine idea. While in Krishna the actual divine spirit of the universe enters the human flesh, Buddha seems to be rather a man, who in successive transmigrations has attained complete enlightenment and become divine or equivalent to the divine. In Krishnaism release from earthly woes appears to be achieved essentially by faith. Buddhism seems to teach reliance upon continued good works, or abnegations of self-indulgence, and increase of knowledge in study. But again the ideas are interchanged in the two religions.

CHAPTER XL.

In vol. i. "Asiatic Researches," the following inscription from Buddha-Gaya is given, as translated by Charles Wilkins towards the close of the last century. It seems distinctly to show an intermingling of Buddhist and Krishnaist ideas:—

"In the midst of a wild and dreadful forest, flourishing with trees of sweet-scented flowers, and abounding in fruits and roots, infested with lions and tigers, destitute of human society, and frequented by the Munis (saints), resided Buddha, the author of happiness, and a portion of Narâyana. The deity Hari, who is the Lord of Hari-sa, the possessor of all, appeared in this ocean of natural beings at the close of the Dwaipara and beginning of the Kali Age. He who is Omnipresent and everlastingly to be contemplated, the Supreme Being, the Eternal One, the Divinity, worthy to be adored by the most praiseworthy of mankind, appeared here with a portion of his divine nature. Once upon a time the illustrious Amara, renowned amongst men, coming here, discovered the place of the Supreme Being, Buddha, in the great forest. The wise Amara endeavoured to render the god Buddha propitious by superior service, and he remained in the forest for the space of twelve years, feeding upon roots and fruits, and sleeping upon the bare earth; and he performed the vow of a Muni, and was without transgression. He performed acts of severe mortification, for he was a man of infinite resolution, with a compassionate heart. One night he had a vision, and heard a voice, saying, 'Name whatever boon thou wantest.' Amara Deva having heard this, was astonished, and with due reverence replied, 'First give me a visitation and then grant me such a boon.' He had another dream in the night, and the voice said, 'How can there be an apparition in the Kali Yug (Black Age)? The same reward may be obtained from the sight of an image as may be derived from the immediate visitation of a deity.' Having heard this he caused an image of the Supreme Spirit, Buddha, to be made, and he worshipped it according to the law, with perfumes, incense, and the like; and he thus glorified the name of that Supreme Being, the incarnation of a portion of Vishnu, ' Reverence be unto thee in the form of Buddha, reverence be unto the Lord of the Earth, reverence be unto thee, an incarnation of the Deity and the Eternal One. Reverence be unto thee, O God! in the form of the god of mercy, the dispeller of pain and trouble, the Lord of all things, the Deity who overcomest the sins of the Black Age, the Guardian of the Universe, the emblem of mercy towards those who serve thee. Aum, the possessor of all things in vital form! Thou art Brahma, Vishnu, and Mahesa! Thou art Lord of the Universe! Thou art, under the proper form of all things, moveable and immoveable, the possessor of the whole! And thus I adore thee; reverence be unto the bestower of salvation; and Hrishikesa, the ruler of the faculties! Reverence be unto thee (Kesava), the destroyer of the evil spirit Kasi! O Damodara, show me favour. Thou art he who resteth upon the face of the milky ocean, and who lieth upon the serpent Sesha. Thou art Trivikrama (who at three strides encompassed the earth); I adore thee, who art celebrated by a thousand names, and under various forms, in the shape of Buddha, the god of mercy! Be propitious, O most high God!' Having thus worshipped the guardian of mankind, he became like one of the just. He joyfully caused a holy temple to be built of a wonderful construction, and therein were set up the divine foot of Vishnu, and in like manner of Brahma and the rest of the divinities. This place is renowned and is celebrated by the name of Buddha-Gaya. The forefathers of him who shall perform the ceremony of the Sraddha (funereal ceremony) at this place shall obtain salvation. The great virtue of the Sraddha to be performed here is to be found in the book called Vayu Purana, an epitome of which hath by me been engraved upon stone.

"Vicramaditya was certainly a king renowned in the world. So in his court there were nine learned men, celebrated under the epithet of the Navaratnani, or nine jewels; one of whom was Amaradeva, who was the king's chief counsellor, a man of great genius and profound learning, and the greatest favourite of his prince. He it certainly was who built the holy temple which destroyeth sin, in a place called Jambudwipa, where, the mind being steady, it obtains its wishes, and in a place where it may obtain salvation, reputation, and enjoyment, even in the country of Bharata and the province of Kikata, where the place of Buddha, purifier of the sinful, is renowned. A crime of an hundredfold shall undoubtedly be expiated from a sight thereof, of a thousandfold from a touch thereof. But where is the use of saying so much of the great virtues of this place? even the hosts of heaven worship with joyful service both day and night. That it may be known to learned men that he verily erected the house of Buddha, I have recorded upon a stone the authority of the place, as a self-evident testimony, on Friday, the fourth day of the new moon, in the month of Madhu, when in the seventh or mansion of Ganisa, and in the year of the era of Vicramaditya 1005, *i.e.* A.D. 949."

This inscription would seem to indicate that at all events in this part of India Krishna had become merged in Buddha.[1] The Supreme Spirit which had been specially venerated under the form of Krishna, came to be adored in the Enlightened (Buddha). He (the Enlightened) became regarded as Brahma, Vishnu, and Mahesa (Shiva), *i.e.* as the Indian Trinity. Now it must be remembered that Buddhism was not a mere contention against caste. It was a great systematised organisation of monastic institutions, for the worship of the Enlightened and the study of the voluminous Scriptures which had been pronounced orthodox in Buddhistic councils before the time of Christ. This inscription displays the superstitions which had been fostered in the religion. It has been represented as an atheistic system; and doubtless atheism, nihilism, or agnosticism are in it as in Christianity (*i.e.* among those who are born and baptized in Christianity). But the Nirvana, or extinction of the soul, seems to mean the abandonment of all desires and the obtaining of

[1] See Appendix V.

perfect calm — not of absolute nothingness in the Supreme Spirit — through the Enlightened One.

Here are the last words of the great Chinese Buddhist Pilgrim, Hiouen Thsang, of the seventh century, as quoted from Professor Max Müller's "Chips from a German Workship." "I desire," said the Chinese Pilgrim before his death, "that whatever merits I have gained by good works may fall upon other people. May I be born with them again in the heaven of the blessed, be admitted to the family of Mi-le, and serve the Buddha of the future, who is full of kindness and affection. When I descend again upon earth, to pass through other forms of existence, I desire, at every new birth, to fulfil my duties towards Buddha, and arrive at last at the highest and most perfect intelligence."

This adds the Roman Catholic doctrine of works of supererogation, in which the good works of the saints in excess of those required for their own salvation are imputed to others, to the numerous similitudes existing between the practices of Buddhism and the Church of Rome. We find in the former, as in the latter, monks with conventual dress and shaven crown, nuns, the adoration of relics, the use of bells and rosaries, a high Pontiff corresponding to the Pope, altars and choirs, &c. &c. From what Protestants consider the erroneous adoration of Christ in Romanism, mingled with vows to the Blessed Virgin and saints, and the obedience to a celibate priesthood, emerged the Protestant faith, in which reliance only on Jesus was inculcated. Buddhism, after the time of Ashoka, seems to have widely abrogated the Brahminical system of caste, sacrificial or sacramental ordinances, &c., and substituted for faith in Krishna the belief in Buddha. A celibate monastic order took the place of the hereditary Brahminical priesthood to a great extent. Strict morality appears to have been required in Buddhism, and the practices of asceticism seem to have differed from those of Brahminism in kind, though not in virtual effect. It would seem probable that the religion became in some way effete in India. Perhaps, on the one hand, it was gradually overlaid with too many superstitions. On the other hand, it may have become too lax in the estimation of certain zealous religionists of deep and earnest convictions. At all events, between about the twelfth and fifteenth centuries of our era arose a great revival of the adoration of the Supreme Spirit in Krishna. Kabir, Ramanuja, and Chaitanya appear, in the Indian religion, as curious forerunners of the Protestant opponents of the Papacy in Europe. Here the change was effected in return from the worship of Christ as overlaid with Mariolatry, &c., to what seems to have been its pristine simplicity. In India, the adoration of the Supreme and Universal Spirit was similarly brought back from Buddhism. This seems to have become a system of most ritualistic character, strikingly analogous to that of the Roman Church, as has been observed. These reformers desired to return to a pure and simple religion of the heart—of faith in Krishna as the incarnation of the Supreme, to be worshipped on earth to secure the bliss of hereafter. Brahminism had existed through all changes. But Brahminism is really independent of all these faiths. It is a system of hereditary class sanctity, of which the Vedas are the great, holy, rallying point. And the system of incarnations is considered divine as connected with the revelation of religion in these " Books of Knowledge."

After this reformation, from the twelfth to the fifteenth centuries A.D., superstitions and ritual again seem to have overspread the Indian faiths, just as the Protestantism of the Church of England has witnessed a revival of the last. Never, of course, entirely extinct, it would seem that, in all religions, the tendency to ceremonial worship, and to venerate tangible images, may be repressed for a time, but that it is a natural bias in humanity to resort to it. This is especially shown in our Old Testament. These Indian reformers might have appeared to have been led to their ideas by our great European movement, but the periods of their careers can be accurately estimated. They seem distinctly to have preceded Luther, Calvin, and John Knox. In vol. xvi. of " Asiatic Researches," Professor H. H. Wilson has left an essay on the various sects of the Hindus. Before showing from this essay the efforts at establishing a sort of Protestantism in India, an illustration of Buddhistic worship is given in the next chapter.

CHAPTER XLI.

In volume xvi. of "Asiatic Researches," Professor H. H. Wilson gives an extract, in illustration of Buddhist ritual, from Nepaulese tracts. The following rite is directed to be performed on the eighth lunar day of each half month; upon which day, in the Vedas also, fasting and oblations were enjoined. In the Puranas it was made sacred to Vishnu.

The rite seems analogous to "confession" in the Christian Church.

The worshipper, accompanied by his wife and family, presents water and flowers, incense, lights, and rice to Tathagata Sakya Sinha (Buddha). He then says:

"I ever offer my salutation with my head declined, to the holy Benefactor of the world—to the Lord of the saints, the Remover of the ills of the Black Age. I adore Sakya Sinha (the Lion of the Race of Sakia), the ruler of all, propitious, the asylum of clemency, the all-wise, lotus-eyed, comprehensive Enlightened. Whatever sin may have been committed by me, child and fool that I am, whether originating in natural weakness, or done in conscious wickedness, I confess all, thus standing in the presence of the lords of the world, joining my hands, afflicted with sorrow and fear, and prostrating myself repeatedly before them. May the holy sages conceive the past as the past, and then the evil I have done shall never be repeated."

Then the disciple, before his spiritual adviser (Guru), places his right knee on the ground and continues: "I, such an one, having uttered my confession, take refuge with the Enlightened from this time forward, until the ferment of ignorance shall have subsided, for he is my protector, the lord of exalted glory. Of an imperishable and irresumable form, merciful, omniscient, all-seeing, and free from the dread of all terrors. I do this in the presence of men." To this the Guru replies, "Well done, well done, my son! perform the Niryátana." Then the worshipper takes flowers, rice, and water, places them on a consecrated place, and says, "This consecrated place is the Lord, the comprehensive 'Enlightened,' replete with divine knowledge, the Supreme, the Curber of the wild steeds of human faults. To him, gem of the 'Enlightened,' I address the rites performed in this consecrated place."

He then makes offerings, a portion of ground having been marked off as consecrated, and exclaims: "Om, namah to the gem of the Enlightened, whose heart is laden with the burden of compassion, the Supreme Spirit, the universal Intellect, the triple essence, the endurer of all ills for the benefit of existing beings, accept this offering, savoury and fragrant, and confirm me and all men to the supreme, all-comprehending wisdom." Then the devas, demons, regents of the planets, spirits of the earth, &c., are invoked; spirits of lakes, villages, and deserted temples, existing where cross-roads meet, and in cemeteries, &c.,—all are invited to receive the lights, incense, and food, and render the act of worship propitious. Indra, Agni, Yama, the progenitors of mankind, &c., are prayed to accept, eat, drink, and render the act propitious. In fact, Buddhism has continued to be a highly ritualistic religion. While its ceremonials have been considered analogous to those of the Roman Church, the classical rites which have been revived in a London theatre for the Laureate's drama of the "Cup" have been pronounced similar to Chinese Buddhistic ceremonies. Images, the adoration of relics, the celibacy of monks, vestments, incense, the chanting of religious services by choirs, right and left of the altars, and various instruments of music employed, with the institution of a high pontiff in Thibet—certainly these all combine to impart an outer aspect to the religion absolutely analogous to that of the Church of Rome.[1]

Altogether our mediæval days are suggested, when various orders of monks and begging friars existed in England; for the Buddhist monk usually lives upon alms. In India, as in England, these orders seem to have been abolished or become extinct in about the fifteenth century of our era. No evidence seems to exist of their being extirpated by war, except, perhaps, in occasional instances. As has been shown, the dramas exhibit them co-existing with the Brahmins without any apparent antagonism to suggest civil war, or persecution such as the hierarchy of Rome has

---

[1] See Appendix III.

inflicted. It would seem that there was a great revival of faith in the Supreme as manifested in the Pastor Krishna. Reformers arose who preached zealously the adoration only of Vishnu, the pervading Spirit or Preserver.

"The chief religious tenet of the followers of Ramanuja, who arose in the twelfth century," says H. H. Wilson, "is that Vishnu is Brahme, before all worlds, cause and creator of all. He and the universe are one, but, in opposition to old philosophies, they deny that the Deity is void of form or quality, and regard Him as endowed with all good qualities, and of twofold form, viz., the Supreme Spirit, Paramatma, or cause, and the gross one, the universe or matter. Creation originated with Vishnu, who was alone. He willed to become embodied as visible and ethereal light, and became manifest in the elements. Narãyana, after having created men and animals, through the subordinate angels which he willed into existence, still remained the supreme authority of the universe. He has assumed at different times particular forms and appearances for the benefit of his creatures, of which four are especially to be revered, viz., Vasudeva or Krishna, Balarama, Pradyumna, and Aniruddha. He is to be worshipped in temples with offerings of flowers, perfumes, &c., and prayers to be repeated with the aid of the rosary. Union with the Divine is to be sought. And perpetual residence in Vishnu's heaven, in condition of pure ecstasy and eternal rapture, is the goal."

CHAPTER XLII.

It may have been the re-writing or re-editing of the "Ancient Books," Vishnu and Bhagavata Puranas, &c., which occasioned a wider dissemination of these conceptions of the Divine. As has been observed, it seems impossible that they can have originated at this epoch. Probably philosophisings had abrogated the fervour of the Buddhistic faith. The monks had, perhaps, become generally regarded as idlers rather than zealous religionists. An aversion to the celibate system is likely to have arisen; and the devotion to the all-pervading spirit in Vishnu infected men with the ardour of a fresh impulse. Monastic establishments, however, remained in the revived Hinduism, with their superiors, monks, attendants, and scholars, their chapels and accommodation for travellers, &c., but not, apparently, established upon so extensive a scale as in Buddhism. Professor Wilson (who had an actual acquaintance with India) mentions from thirty to forty monks in a monastery, whereas Hiouen Thsang has informed us that there were often 1000 or more in a single Buddhistic establishment. The ideas promulgated in the "Ancient Books" at this revival do not appear, during the period of the Buddhist supremacy, to have actually sunk into abeyance, but to have continuously existed side by side with the religion of Buddha. They seem to have continued in their stages of successive growth, from the time when they emerged, as the natural sequence of certain doctrines, from the Vedas at 1000 B.C. or 1500 B.C. There seems to be much religious fervour in both the Puranas and the Buddhistic books; and while the latter are still revered in Nepaul, China, Tibet, Burmah, Siam, &c., the former have made the more lasting impression in India.

War may in places have overthrown the Buddhists, but in general Brahmins and Buddhists seem to have co-existed with, possibly, wordy warfare, but no more recourse to bloodshed than exists amongst Romanists and Protestants in England in the present day. Kabir was one of the twelve disciples of Ramanand the weaver. He attacked the whole system of idolatrous worship, and ridiculed the learning of the Pandits. He is related to have been born of the virgin widow of a Brahmin, having been in the world, according to his followers, from 1149 A.D. to 1449 A.D. And he is said to have vindicated his doctrine by miracles, having been thrown into flames without harm, &c. Outward signs of religion, according to him, were of no importance, and attention was especially to be paid to the inward man. The worship of his followers was largely expressed in chanting hymns, and after his death he was claimed as a saint by both Hindus and Mohammedans.

Chaitanya was born in 1485 A.D., and became regarded as an incarnation of Krishna or Bhagavat.

At the age of twenty-four he shook off the obligations of society, and commenced preaching between Mathura and Jaganath; and after a course of asceticism beheld beatific visions of Krishna, Raddha, his shepherdess love, and the other shepherdesses. He disappeared about A.D. 1527. Although admitting other incarnations, he held that the principal, the actual, sensible manifestation of the Supreme Spirit was as Krishna. But when identified with the Supreme Spirit, Krishna possessed real attributes, in opposition to the old philosophising belief in the negative properties of God. The whole moral code of his sect is comprised in the word *Bhakti*, a term which signifies an union of implicit faith with incessant devotion. Caste is of no account in these systems of intense devotion to Krishna, though Brahmins always seem to have been held in respect, even under Buddhism, as Mr. Rhys Davids has shown in his work on that religion.

The higher form of this Bhakti, says H. H. Wilson, is a tender affection for the divinity, of the same nature as the love of parents for their children; the highest is such passionate attachment as the shepherdesses (Gopis) felt towards their beloved Krishna.

In Chaitanya's system, homage was to be performed in Krishna's temples twice daily; but the ritual and sacrifice were only repetitions of his name. Singing and dancing in his honour were allowed. Fasting is to be practised every eleventh day. Anger, avarice, and lust are to be suppressed, and the Guru or spiritual teacher venerated. The teachers, as a rule, were married; but there have been amongst them hermits or begging ascetics.

The adoration of Radha, bride of Krishna, seems to have been introduced at this period. She is regarded as the incarnate *will* of the deity, and she is styled the Mother of the Universe. She appears to correspond with Durga or Parvati. Besides numerous sects who worship Krishna, others are enumerated by Professor Wilson who adore the Supreme Spirit in Shiva, who seems to be a manifestation of deity in a superhuman rather than human form, though there are also incarnations of him. The bull which seems to connect him with Osiris and the Apis of Egypt is associated with his worship, and placed before his shrines.

CHAPTER XLIII.

It must be remembered that Buddha-Gaya, the chief centre of Buddhist history, is situated at about 450 miles distance from Mathura or Muttra, the centre of the legendary lore of Krishna. This is about equivalent to the distance between Rome and Geneva. As each of these centres has been surrounded by a flourishing and extensive region of cultivated territory, there is ample space for two religions to have arisen. The adoration of the Divine as Brahma, and the promulgation of the system of Brahminism, with the legal Institutes of Manu, seem to appertain to the northwest of Mathura, while the adoration of Mahadeva or Shiva was probably more prevalent in the district about Bahar. Shiva became regarded as Rudra, then as forming part of a trinity with Brahmâ and Vishnu. It would seem that a mass of stories and legends became centred round two persons associated with these respective centres. At Mathura, amongst a warlike and aristocratic race, deity was regarded as manifested in the brilliant Prince Krishna. In the district of Bahar, where the adoration of Mahadeva seems to have encouraged excess of asceticism, and to have laid little stress upon caste considerations as connected with religion, a prince also became worshipped. But it was a prince who abandoned his rank and wandered forth in poverty and self-abnegation. The soul of each is held to have been often incarnate in previous terrestrial existences for the sake of mankind. While their lives as Krishna and Buddha are different, many similar stories are connected with them in the histories of their previous incarnations. It has been asserted that Shivaism as well as Krishnaism merely succeeded Buddhism. But the evidence seems to demonstrate that Buddhism arose out of Brahminism and Shivaism. This is shown by the Buddhist legends containing frequent allusions to

Indra and other personifications of the Hindu Pantheon, including Rudra or Shiva.

The doctrine of previous incarnations of the Supreme Spirit is not inconsistent with the Christianity revealed to us in our Old and New Testaments. To this testimony is afforded by the statements in both concerning Melchizedek. Return will be made to this topic in a subsequent chapter.

Gautamma Buddha or Sakya Muni seems invariably to be represented as a successor of previous Buddhas. The institution of celibate monks and nuns may have been due to him. It would certainly seem that the conception of a Buddha, the Enlightened, in India, may have arisen out of the worship of Shiva (the auspicious one) as the ascetic, in which incarnation or manifestation he is often represented.

Some of the eighteen "Ancient Books" advocate his supremacy; but as all declare the real unity of deity, though adored under different forms, the differences are not more important than those which divide Christian sects. The universality of deity, its personification for the sake of humanity, the necessity of self-sacrifice and universal love and charity,—these seem to be essential points of Christianity, which have been leading doctrines of the allied religions of our race, prototypes seemingly in the ancient civilisations of our own religion.

M. Emile Burnouf, in his "Science des Religions," observes (p. 4) that "il est certain que les dieux ont été adorés, par des peuples qui, à bien des égards, nous égalaient en civilisation." (P. 8.) "La lecture des livres Indiens et l'histoire qui commence à s'éclaircir, de la propagation des idées indiennes prouvent que ni la philosophie antique, ni les lettres grecques, ni les croyances anciennes ou modernes ne peuvent être suffisamment comprises, si l'on ne remonte vers l'ancien Orient. Or, l'Inde est la contrée religieuse par excellence ; on n'y peut pas séparer la litérature des rites sacrés, ni la philosophie des dogmes religieux."

(P. 183.) "Tandis que les religions affirment leur propre originalité, les recherches scientifiques, poursuivies, sans parti pris d'avance, et avec la seule pensée de découvrir les lois de la nature, font que l'homme d'étude se demande à lui même s'il n'y a eu en effet aucune filiation réelle entre les religions. Les faits constatés sont aujourd'hui si nombreux et tellement d'accord entre eux que toute illusion à cette égard est scientifiquement impossible. Les religions ont procédés les unes des autres. Non seulement les formes du culte ne sont originales chez aucune d'elles, non seulement les symboles ont passés des unes aux autres et l'appareil extérieur dont elles se sont servies s'est transmis à travers les siècles, ne subissant que des altérations superficielles ; mais encore la doctrine mystique ou, si l'on veut, métaphysique, qui se cache sous ces voiles, ce que nous pouvons appeler l'élément divin des religions, est demeuré le même depuis les temps les plus anciens jusqu'à nos jours, animant tour à tour ces figures symboliques, ces rites et ces formules qui en sont l'élément sensible."

CHAPTER XLIV.

The other great Indian epic, the Rāmāyana, is also rich in descriptions which indicate elaborate systems of cultivation of the various æsthetics of life. In the *Gentleman's Magazine* of October 1880, Sylvanus Urban observes, in commenting upon " Cradleland of Arts and Creeds," that " we hear of watering the roads, of public gardens, curtained screens, folding doors, golden statues and inlaid floors; of music, palaces, terraces, ramparts, and warlike instruments which slay an hundred men; all sorts of inventions indeed, which are supposed to be altogether modern discoveries. What, however, is from a literary standpoint even more remarkable, is that modern poetry is anticipated by the constant celebration throughout the epic (the Rāmāyana) of the grandeur and beauties of nature, especial praise being bestowed upon the charms of forests and flowers. What then became of this taste? Nothing is more remarkable in European literature, or has furnished subject of more frequent comment, than the insensibility to the beauties of landscape which seems to have prevailed until times altogether recent."

This poetical history of Rama, who is held to have

been an earlier incarnation of the Divine than Krishna, has been ascribed by its translator, Mr. Griffiths, Head of the College of Benares, to about the twelfth century B.C., with the exception of certain possible interpolations, which do not affect the illustrations of civilisation contained in it.

Certainly the people of ancient India possessed a spiritual culture in philosophy, literature, art, and science before the epoch of Pythagoras, viz., the sixth century B.C. That philosopher is related to have been educated in Eastern knowledge, and the whole tradition of his life and teaching points not merely to Egypt or Babylon having been his *Almæ Matres* in science, but to his having been fostered by the learning of the great realms further to the east.

Undoubtedly since the epochs of these epics there have been changes in India. But the alterations have so slightly affected the pictures of its general aspect of life that the description of the daughters of Zion in Isaiah iii. 16–23 might apply to Hindu women in the streets of the commercial Bombay in the present day. Still as they walk do they "make a tinkling with their feet," *i.e.*, with the bunches of silver bells upon their anklets. Their bracelets and spangled ornaments (as the New Version renders the words which have been translated as chains and mufflers), their headbands, earrings, nose-jewels; their mantles, fine linen, hoods, and veils,—all these still appear on the figures of the wealthier Hindu women in forms apparently corresponding closely to the fashions of the days of Isaiah, amongst our English feminine *modes*. And their aspects are true outward signs of their inward manner of life—of their spirituality. The pictures of old civilisation, therefore, which we behold in these ancient poems cannot be reasonably supposed to have been of rapid growth. If borrowed from Babylonians, Greeks, or others, it would seem that Portuguese and British would, in their turn, have been imitated. Of course a few of the natives have adopted our costume, language, and customs; but as a people the inhabitants of British India remain unaffected by our settlements in the country. We have overcome the land in war, but not conquered it socially or spiritually. Indeed, we are still strangers there, in no sympathy with the mass of its inhabitants. And there appears to be no evidence of our being nearer the winning of the people to our religion and our manner of life, though a few more Hindus may be seen in London, studying our legal system, &c., and doubtless the efforts of our missionaries have made some impression in Hindustan.

At about the epoch of the Ramayana epic, some 300 to 1000 or more years B.C., appertains the earliest Indian code of laws, the Institutes of Manu. This is still held to be an authority in our Anglo-Indian courts of law when adjudicating upon Hindu matters. The word Manu is derived from the Sanskrit verb *man*, to think; and it is considered by the Hindus to represent the first grand existing man-type, to whom these laws were delivered by the Divine.

Like the laws of Moses, these Institutes contain rules for moral as well as legal obligations, and for the duty of man to the Divine as well as to his neighbour. And the spiritual conception of one Supreme Deity is distinctly set forth. The laws are thus prefaced: "Manu sat reclined, with his attention fixed upon one object, the Supreme God, when the divine sages approached him, and, after mutual salutations in due form, delivered the following address: 'Deign, sovereign ruler, to apprize us of the sacred laws in their order, as they must be followed by all the four classes in their several degrees. For thou, the Lord, and thou only amongst mortals, knowest true sense, the first principle, and the prescribed ceremonies of this universal, supernatural Book of Knowledge.'"

After prescribing the laws in questions of inheritance, merchandise, contracts, wrongs, &c. &c., and assigning penalties for criminal transgressions, these laws proceed to describe penalties in purgatorial hells. They even lay down the rule as to the future transmigrations of the soul in accordance with its deeds.

Chapter xii. of the Institutes of Manu is headed "On transmigration and final beatitude." In ver. 3 it is said that "action either mental, verbal, or corporeal, bears good or evil fruit as itself is good or evil, and from the actions of men proceed their various transmigrations, in the highest, the middle, and the lowest degree."

And as to the purgatorial hells of punishment it is declared: "By the vital souls of those men who have committed sins in the body which has been reduced to ashes, another body composed of nerves with five sensations, in order to be susceptible of torment, shall certainly be assumed after death. They shall feel in that new body the pangs inflicted in each case by the sentence of Yama (the deity of the dead), having endured torments according to his sentence; and the taint having been removed, the soul may reach the five pure elements, &c.

"The three qualities of the rational soul are a tendency to goodness, to passion, and to darkness. Goodness is true knowledge. Darkness is gross ignorance. Passion is an emotion of desire or aversion. In the transmigrations, souls endowed with goodness can attain the state of deities (devas = shining beings); those who cherish ambitious passions will return to the state of men; those involved in darkness may descend to the state of beasts."

Each of these has a threefold division, and the dark quality may even bring the individual down to the condition of minerals, vegetables, worms, fish, &c., to elephants and lions, &c., or to contemptible barbarians in the middle division; or to dancers, singers, birds, and bloodthirsty savages in the highest division of the states entered by the souls of those imbued with the quality of darkness.

From the lowest division of the passionate quality, boxers and wrestlers, cudgel-players, actors, gamesters, &c., may result; kings, domestic priests, warriors, controversialists, &c., are allotted to the middle division; while the condition of heavenly nymphs may even be attained by the highest of those who have the quality of passion.

Hermits, Brahmins, demi-gods, genii of the signs and lunar mansions, are the lowest states reserved for those distinguished by the quality of goodness. Sacrificers, holy sages, deities of the lower heavens, regents of stars not in the paths of the sun and moon come from the middle divisions; while even to be Brahmâs with four faces, creators of worlds under him, the genius of virtue, &c., may be the destiny of those endowed in the highest degree with the quality of goodness.

A priest who has drunk spirituous liquor may become an insect or fly feeding on ordure.

Those who do injury to sentient beings may be born cats and eaters of raw flesh.

More than once it is said that the wicked shall have agonising births, lives afflicted with diseases, and terrible deaths. "With whatever disposition of mind a man shall perform in this life any act, religious or moral, in a future body endued with the same quality shall he receive his retribution." Hells are described for the wicked as in the Puranas, which forestall the horrors of Dante, except that the agony of hopelessness was not considered to appertain to the just punishments of the old Aryan Deity. There are hells of utter darkness, with forests of sword leaves, with burning sands, &c. On the other hand "Studying and comprehending the Veda, practising pious austerities, acquiring divine knowledge of law and philosophy, command over the organs of sense and action, avoiding all injury to sentient creatures, and showing reverence to a natural or spiritual father,—these are the chief branches of duty which ensure final happiness."

In this life, indeed, as well as the next, the study of the *Veda*, to acquire a knowledge of God, is held the most efficacious of duties in procuring felicity to man. For in the knowledge and adoration of one God, which the Veda teaches, all the rules of good conduct, before mentioned in order (*i.e.* in these Institutes), are fully comprised." "The ceremonial duty prescribed by the Veda is of two kinds,—one connected with this world and causing prosperity on earth, the other abstracted from it and procuring bliss in heaven." "He who frequently performs interested rites obtains an equal station with the regents of the lower heaven; but he who frequently performs disinterested acts of religion becomes for ever exempt from a body composed of the five elements." "Equally perceiving the Supreme Soul in all beings, and all beings in the Supreme Soul, he sacrifices his own spirit by fixing it on the spirit of

God, and approaches the nature of that sole divinity who shines of his own effulgence."

In this and other texts in these Institutes, the numerous gods of what has been called the Hindu Pantheon are declared to be only emanations from or expressions of the One Supreme Spirit. And the sacred scriptures, the Vedas or Books of Knowledge, and works founded upon them, are repeatedly held up to veneration: "To patriarchs, to deities, and to mankind the scripture is an eye giving constant light." "Nor could the Veda Shastra have been made by human faculties." "All systems which are repugnant to the Veda must have been composed by mortals and shall soon perish; their modern date proves them vain and false." "He alone comprehends the system of duties, religious and civil, who can reason by rules of logic, agreeable to the Veda, on the general heads of that system as revealed by the holy sages." "Let every Brahmin, with fixed attention, consider all nature, both visible and invisible, as existing in the Divine Spirit; for when he contemplates the boundless (universe existing in the Divine Spirit) he cannot give his heart to iniquity." "It is He (the Supreme Omnipresent Intelligence) who, pervading all beings in five elemental forms, causes them, by the gradations of birth, growth, and dissolution, to revolve in this world until they deserve beatitude."

It must, at all events, be evident, on the evidence of a few texts which have been quoted out of many to the same effect, that great veneration was paid to scripture as the word of God. Our Aryan cousins in India at about 500 B.C. certainly regarded their Bible with reverence equal to that which Protestants have bestowed upon the Christian Scriptures. It might have been urged that this veneration for the written word was suggested by the Jewish devotion to their sacred writings. But the systematic reverence for the Books of Knowledge (Vedas) seems too deeply implanted in the Indo-Aryan mind to be a merely borrowed idea, considering the religious conservatism now displayed by them.

CHAPTER XLV.

ARRIAN in his "Indica," of the second century of our era, observes that "none of the Indian kings ever lead an army out of India to attempt the conquest of any other country, lest they should be deemed guilty of injustice," which certainly seems a Christian sentiment, though it has rarely been acted upon by so-called Christian monarchs. He says that the Indians allow no monuments to their dead, but have odes in their praise. He thinks the Indian cities too numerous to be reckoned, stating that those which are situated near the sea or upon any river are constructed of wood, because no buildings of brick would long withstand the violence of the rains and the overflow of the rivers. But the cities seated on any eminence are frequently built with brick and mortar. He states that Megasthenes assures us that the capital Palimbothra (Pataliputra, argued to be the modern Patna by General Cunningham in his "Ancient Geography of India"), situated at the confluence of the rivers Erannoboas and Ganges, measured in length ten miles, in breadth two miles, that it was surrounded by a wide and deep moat, and that its walls were adorned with 570 towers and 64 gates. "All the Indians are free, being neither slaves themselves nor suffering any others to be slaves in their country."

Arrian then bears testimony to the civilised nature of the warfare waged in old India, by saying that in the event of intestine war it is deemed a heinous crime either to seize the husbandmen or to spoil the harvest. He says that the soldiers who during the time of war were obliged to serve their country, in peace lived merrily and pleasantly. "They had as much stipend allowed them from the public as was sufficient to maintain them with their dependants."

Here then we find the archaic "standing army" duly supported at the public expense, with this difference, that instead of being composed of volunteers from the general body of the public, as in modern England, it was drawn from a caste devoted from birth to warfare. In fact, Arrian shows elsewhere the strict maintenance of caste, and observes that only the

Sophists could exercise what employments they pleased. The remainder had to continue in the craft in which they were born. But their religion, as set forth amongst the Institutes of Manu, taught them that in another birth they might enter a higher or lower caste, according to their life or aspirations in the present life. They might also be exalted to heaven or debased to temporary hell. But even then they would return to this or some other world, unless in absolute purity, perfection, and faith, union with the Supreme Spirit had been obtained.

He remarks that the lives of the Sophists in general were not easy but vastly laborious.

He speaks of the hunting of elephants and wild beasts and the taming of elephants. He says, "I myself have seen an elephant beat upon a cymbal whilst others danced to his music. Two cymbals hung upon his forelegs, and one was tied to his trunk; the other elephants moved around him and danced justly."

He tells us that the foot-soldiers were usually bowmen; that their bow was of the same length as the bearer, and that it was placed upon the ground and drawn with their left foot upon it. The arrows were shot with such force that no shield or breastplate could withstand them. They wore swords of great breadth, &c. &c.

Altogether the whole picture seems to present a race highly civilised according to our modern ideas in civil government, arts, and arms. Their long-bows recall our British yeoman's famous yew-tree bow, six feet in length; while the arrows, described as three cubits long, seem the forerunners of our old "cloth-yard shafts." We are informed that the people wore shirts of white cotton reaching to the middle of the leg, with veils which covered the head, and shoes of white leather, curiously stitched, sometimes having high soles. The richer persons were adorned with ivory earrings, and had umbrellas carried over them. Beards were dyed white, black, red, purple, or green. The richer rode upon elephants; horses, camels, and asses being also employed. Both bricks and wood were employed for the walls of towns. Alexander had been informed that the country beyond the Hyphasis was rich, that the inhabitants were good husbandmen and also excellent soldiers, that they were governed by the nobility and lived peaceably, their rulers imposing nothing harsh or unjust upon them.

Megasthenes, Greek ambassador in India in about the third century B.C., in addition to his descriptions of the civilisation, has afforded us direct extraneous evidence upon the antiquity of Krishna (Strabo xv. 3). He states that the inhabitants of the plains of Hindustan are addicted to the worship of Hercules (or Heracles, as it should be written, 'Ηράκλεα). He thinks that this Heracles had, in ancient times, conquered India. But Arrian (second century A.D.) informs us (Arrian, Ind. Hist. chap. viii.) that the Indians say that the Heracles who had penetrated so far was a native of their country. Arrian further states that he was particularly worshipped by the Suraseni, who have two great cities belonging to them, viz., Methoras and Clisoboras, and that the navigable Iobares passes through their territories.

There appears to be no doubt that the Methoras refers to Mathura, or Muttra, on the Jumna, related to have been the birthplace of Krishna, and where his adoration was especially established.

Arrian continues: " This Herakles, as Megasthenes asserts and the Indians themselves assure us, used the same habits with the Theban Hercules. He took many wives, and begot a great number of sons, though but one daughter, whom he named Pandœa. Other Indians tell this story of Hercules, namely, that when he had travelled through all the earth, and purged it of every vice, he found a pearl in the sea, such as the merchants at this day in India buy up at a great price and bring to us. And he commanded pearls to be searched for. His daughter ruled over his realm: in this the women were marriageable at seven, the men not till forty."

Is the Krishna of a period corresponding with mediæval Europe one and the same with the Herakles mentioned by Megasthenes, the Greek ambassador in India, as adored in the region of Mathura three centuries B.C. ? It seems to be so, because Krishna is constantly called Hari in the "Great Bharata" poem, and Mathura is still traditionally assigned for his birthplace. And it is difficult to say what other divine being in the Hindu Pantheon can have been indicated. In some points, indeed, Krishna's brother, Bala-Rama, appears rather to afford attributes akin to the Greek Heracles; but Bala-Rama is mystically one with Krishna. In fact, the analogy seems completed by Iphiclus, the twin brother of Hercules. The club with which Hercules is represented is amongst the weapons of Krishna.

CHAPTER XLVI.

JUST as the first Roman Catholic missionaries in the East saw in the Buddhist ritual suggestions of their own, so the early Spanish invaders of the Central American civilisations seem to have observed what they conceived to have been a wicked imitation of their Christian rites at the instigation of the devil. Instead, however, of the Mexicans acknowledging one human-divine sacrifice for mankind, they offered many human sacrifices with great solemnity to the Deity. The sun was adored by them with magnificent ceremonial and implicit reverence; and ideas seem to have existed concerning regents of the elements, corresponding to those of the Vedic religion. But as an expiatory sacrifice they continued, what had been abandoned in India in what we call the Vedic period, actual human sacrifice. This was, at all events, equivalent to the idea of vicarious satisfaction, the doctrine of Christianity, though only one human sacrifice of Deity as man is proclaimed to be sufficient for all time. The Gauls are also related to have immolated human victims. In fact, it seems to have been a frequent conception that the Divine wrath was to be appeased by the sufferings of some sort of "scapegoat." This was a natural prototype of the Divine and universal Victim.

In the ancient American civilisations appear very curious analogies to Christian beliefs, also to the Krishnaism and Buddhism of India. It has been considered that the apostolic preaching not only extended to India, but even reached America. If the apostles or their disciples can be conceived to have travelled thus far, the Divine blessing may be held to have especially accompanied their work and rapidly accomplished conversion. The human sacrifices, however, seem to render it apparent that the converts rapidly forgot the apostolic lessons.

"It is a remarkable fact," says Prescott in his "History of the Conquest of Peru," "that many if not most of the rude tribes inhabiting the vast American continent, however disfigured their creeds may have been in other respects by a childish superstition, had attained to the sublime conception of one Great Spirit, the Creator of the Universe, who immaterial in His own nature, was not to be dishonoured by an attempt at visible representation, and who, pervading all space, was not to be circumscribed within the walls of a temple. They admitted the existence of the soul hereafter, and connected with this a belief in the resurrection of the body. They assigned two distinct places for the residence of the good and of the wicked, the latter of which they fixed in the centre of the earth. The good were supposed to pass a luxurious life of tranquillity and ease, which comprehended their highest notions of happiness. The wicked were to expiate their crimes by ages of wearisome labour. They associated with these ideas a belief in an evil principle or spirit, bearing the name of Cupay, whom they did not attempt to propitiate by sacrifices, and who seems to have been only a shadowy personification of sin that exercised little influence upon their conduct. It was this belief in the resurrection of the body which led them to preserve the body with so much solicitude — by a simple process, not of the elaborate embalming of the Egyptians, but by exposing it to the cold, dry, highly rarefied atmosphere of the mountains."

The Peruvians adored the Supreme Being under the names of Pachacamac and Viracocha. The first of these signifies He who sustains or gives life to the universe. The second has been thought to mean the Foam of the sea, suggesting a foreign origin.

Only one temple has been dedicated to this being,

to which numerous pilgrimages were made by the Indians from remote parts.

The sun was the chief representation of Deity. In honour of the sun were consecrated temples in every city, with numerous altars smoking with burnt-offerings. The moon, the stars, thunder and lightning, also had their shrines; and deities of the elements, mountains, rivers, &c., were invoked. Everything had its mother, or spiritual essence, which seems to correspond to the notions of the Hindus, who assigned to each deity a wife or energy.

"The ritual of the Incas involved a routine of observances as complex and elaborate as ever distinguished that of any nation whether Pagan or Christian. The sacrifice with the Peruvians consisted of animals, grain, flowers, and sweet-scented gums, sometimes of human beings, on which occasions a child or beautiful maiden was usually selected."

"In the distribution of bread and wine at the high festival the orthodox Spaniards, who first came into the country, saw a striking resemblance to the Christian communion, and also in the practice of confession and penance." "The good fathers were fond of tracing such coincidences, which they considered as the contrivance of Satan, who thus endeavoured to delude his victims by counterfeiting the blessed rites of Christianity." "Others, in a different vein, imagined that they saw in such analogies the evidence that some of the primitive teachers of Christianity, perhaps an apostle himself, had paid a visit to these distant regions, and scattered over them the seeds of religious truth."

In similitude with their own nuns, they found Virgins of the Sun, who were to be buried alive if caught in the offence of intrigue.

The Peruvians were divided into castes, which seems to associate their civilisation with that of India; and they were acquainted with husbandry, like the Hindus.

The Mexicans had the terrible Huitzilopotchli at the head of their deities, under the Supreme. He was a sort of Mars, whose "altars smoked with the blood of human hecatombs in every city of the empire."

"A far more interesting personage in their mythology," continues Prescott, "was Quetzalcoatl, god of the air, who, during his residence on earth, instructed the natives in the use of metals, in agriculture, and in the arts of government." He was doubtless one of those benefactors of their species, observes Prescott, who have been deified by the gratitude of posterity. "Under him there were halcyon days, when the earth teemed with fruits and flowers, without the pain of culture. He was compelled by the wrath of the principal deity to abandon the country. On the shores of the Mexican Gulf he took leave of his followers, promising that he and his descendants would revisit them hereafter." Then, "entering his wizard skiff, made of serpents' skins, he embarked on the great ocean for the fabled land of Tlapallan. He was said to have been tall in stature, with a white skin, long dark hair, and a flowing beard." "The Mexicans looked confidently to the return of this benevolent deity."

The Mexicans held that there were three states in the future. The wicked, which were the greater part of mankind, would have to expiate their sins in a place of everlasting darkness. Others, who had died of certain diseases, were to have a negative existence of indolent contentment. The highest class, heroes who fell in battle or in sacrifice, passed at once into the presence of the sun, whom they accompanied with songs and choral dances in his bright progress through the heavens. After some years their spirits went to animate the clouds and singing birds of beautiful plumage, and to revel amidst the rich blossoms and odours of the gardens of Paradise.

An "extraordinary coincidence may be traced with Christian rites in the ceremony of naming their children. The lips and bosom of the infant were sprinkled with water, and the Lord was implored to permit the holy drops to wash away the sin that was given it before the foundation of the world, so that the child might be born anew."

"We are reminded," remarks Prescott, "of Christian morals in more than one of their prayers, in which they used regular forms." "Wilt Thou blot us out, O Lord, for ever?" "Impart unto us, out of Thy great mercy, the gifts which we are not worthy to receive through our own merits." "Keep peace with all; bear injuries with humility. God, who sees, will avenge you."

The most striking parallel with Scripture, says Prescott, is in the remarkable declaration that "he who looks too curiously on a woman commits adultery with his eyes." "These pure and elevated maxims," he adds, "are mixed with others of a puerile or even brutal character."

Numerous priests who superintended education besides filling the sacerdotal office, choirs, oral traditions, the ordinances of confession and absolution, hieroglyphic paintings in the temples, continue the affinities presented to the Catholic Church. The priests were married, but they lived in the stern severity of conventual discipline, suggestive of the asceticism enjoined to the Brahmins, who were not, like the Buddhist monks, ordered to celibacy. Thrice during the day, and once at night, they attended at prayers. They endured frequent vigils, fastings, penances, flagellations in which blood was drawn, and piercing the body with the thorns of the aloe. Ablutions were ordained as in India. There was a sort of parochial clergy. Priestly absolution was even received in place of the legal punishment of offences, suggesting our mediæval privilege of sanctuary and benefit of clergy. There were priestesses, to whom the education of the girls was entrusted. The boys were drilled in monastic discipline and great decorum. The temples were endowed with lands. There were religious processions, some of which were bright and cheerful fêtes, in which garlands were carried and offerings of fruits were made. The temples seem to have assumed a form suggestive of our old pictures of the Tower of Babel, in which an ascent wound upwards, encircling the tower to the flat summit. On this were the sanctuaries with images, and altars " with fires inextinguishable as those in the Temple of Vesta," or, it may be added, upon the old Aryan and modern Parsi altars. They had calendars of their sacred days.

Altogether there appear to be suggestions of both Brahminism and Christianity. The human sacrifices are in accord with those practised, probably, in very ancient times in India, and amongst the ruder Aryans of Europe till the spread of Christianity and the substitution of the belief in the One Human and Divine Sacrifice.

It must be remembered that the sacrificed were supposed to obtain immediate entrance upon the realms of bliss. For some time before the sacrifice the victim was permitted to live in the most indulgent luxury, and perhaps a consciousness of the dignity of the destiny consoled for the deprivation of life.

According to Prescott, the Mexicans seem to have fastened upon this horrible rite with extraordinary avidity. In Christianity the flesh of the sacrificed Redeemer is figuratively eaten in commemoration. They actually fed upon their victims as a part of the ceremony, not in any barbarous fashion, but in the course of an elaborate and delicious banquet. He says that human sacrifices were adopted by the Azteks early in the fourteenth century of our era, about two hundred years before their conquest. They even sacrificed as many as 20,000 victims in a year—men, women, and children. They are described as luxuriantly treated for a time; and, as has been observed, this death, like the Christian martyrdom, opened Paradise.

Perhaps the Mexicans would have been as much horrified at being informed of the burnings and tortures of the Inquisition, and the martyrdoms in our own land for refusing to receive all the dogmas of the Church, as ourselves at discovering their religious bloodshed.

The inhabitants of India and China, Brahmins and Buddhists, seem to have been far superior in toleration, and what we now consider the Christian quality of gentleness, to the inhabitants of Europe, till the last few centuries, and to those of the old "New World." There may have been local wars between the followers of the Prayerful and the Enlightened; but there seems to be no evidence of any general persecution, and the principles and edicts of both religions enjoin respect for the religious professions of others. Only in the worship of the benign Dourga or Parvati, under the destroying aspect of Kali, does bloodshedding seem to be offered to Deity. As has been shown by

Dr. Hunter in his work on Orissa, there may have been religious suicides at Jaganatha as there are in the Ganges, but the religion of the "Lord of the world" absolutely forbids any shedding of blood before him.

CHAPTER XLVII.

A SERPENT typifies Time with the Azteks, which corresponds with the Hindu serpent of Eternity. They venerated a goddess, whom they called "Our Lady and Mother," "who had bequeathed the sufferings of childbirth to women as the tribute of death, by whom sin came into the world." She was usually represented with a serpent near her, and her name (Cioacoatl) signified the "serpent-woman." It was the good deity, mentioned in the last chapter (Quetzalcoatl), who had established ecclesiastical communities, the rules of confession and penance, &c., and who had disseminated knowledge of the Trinity and Incarnation, according to the curious antiquaries of Mexico, says Prescott. Some of the orthodox have identified him with the Apostle Thomas; others have seen in him a type of the Founder of Christianity. Even the cross was found on the temples of Anahuac; and the Christians were astonished at beholding in the religious service an image of the tutelary deity, compounded of maize mixed with blood, distributed amongst the people. As they ate it, they exhibited signs of humiliation and sorrow, and declared that it was the flesh of the Deity.

Prescott remarks that Mr. Stephens considered that the celebrated Cozumel cross, which claims the credit of having been originally worshipped by the natives themselves, was a mere Spanish cross, but that the existence of the worship does not depend upon such spurious monuments. "The existence of the cross as an object of worship in the New World rests on the unequivocal testimony of the Spanish discoverers themselves."

In the word from which Mexico is derived, another analogy with Christianity appears. The word from which is derived the epithet anointed, is thought to be nearly identical with Mesi or Mexi, which was the name of the chief who was said to have led the Azteks on the plains of Anahuac.

The tradition of the Deluge existed amongst the old Americans. Coxcox and his wife survived the general destruction of beings, and are depicted in a boat floating at the foot of a mountain, with a dove holding in his mouth the hieroglyphic emblem of languages. In one account the boat is described as filled with animals. A vulture is sent forth to look for the land, but does not return. The little humming-bird comes back with a twig in his mouth.

Between Vera Cruz and the capital, says Prescott,

stands the venerable relic called the Temple of Cholula. It is a pyramidal mound, built or rather cased with unburnt brick, rising to the height of nearly 180 feet. The popular tradition of the natives is that it was erected by a family of giants who had escaped the great inundation, and designed to raise the building to the clouds; but the gods, offended with their presumption, sent fires from heaven on the pyramid, and compelled them to abandon the attempt. Prescott observes that the partial coincidence of this legend with the Hebrew account of the Tower of Babel, received also by other nations of the East, cannot be denied.

There seems sufficient evidence for supposing that these ancient American civilisations had emanated from or been in communication with Asia. It does not appear to have been asserted that they can have come from the Roman Empire, or any previous European civilisation westwards.

Prescott observes that the coincidences are sufficiently strong to authorise a belief that the civilisation of Anahuac was in some degree influenced by that of Eastern Asia. And, secondly, that the discrepancies are such as to carry back the communication to a very remote period, so that a peculiar and indigenous civilisation had time to grow. Dr. Zerffi observes, in his "Manual of the Historical Development of Art," that there are analogies between East and West which are too striking to be attributed to mere chance.

CHAPTER XLVIII.

In more or less spiritual or material forms the Divine seems to have been worshipped as present to man in the human form throughout the great old civilisations. Noble prototypes of the Revelation in Judæa seem to have been afforded. The termination of the allegories of the "Great Bharata" poem, in the illustration of the unsatisfactory nature of all earthly aspirations even when crowned with success, seems in perfect consonance with much of Christian teaching. From the period of this poem in the classical Sanscrit, the march of spiritual thought may be reviewed nearer to its apparent starting-point.

In the "Aitareya Aranyaca" or "Forest" portion of the addenda to the hymns of the "Praise" Veda, so called because intended to be studied by hermits in the forest, we have an incarnation of Nârâyana presented to us. He descends in Mahidása during a solemn religious ceremony at which both divine beings and priests are present. The whole assemblage, alarmed or astounded at his sudden appearance, faints, but is revived at the intercession of Brahma, and instructed in holy science. It must be remembered that in the climate of India, amid the bounty of nature in the plantains, roots, hot peppers, &c., hermit life could be easily sustained. The meditative life has been pursued under most favourable conditions.

In the Yajurveda, according to Colebrooke's translation, in vol. vii. of "Asiatic Researches," "Bhrigu, the offspring of Varuna (Regent of the Ocean), approached his father, saying, 'Venerable (father), make known to me Brahme.' Varuna replied, 'That whence all beings are produced, that by which they live when born, that towards which they tend, and that into which they pass, do thou seek (for), that is Brahme.' He meditated in devout contemplation, and having thought profoundly, he recognised food (or body) to be Brahme; for all, when born, live by food. Then, having deeply meditated, he discovered breath (or life) to be Brahme; for all these beings are indeed produced from breath; when born they live by breath. Then he discovered intellect to be Brahme; for all these beings are produced from intellect, they live by intellect, &c. Then he thought deeply, and knew Ananda (felicity) to be Brahme; for all these things are produced from pleasure; when born they live by joy, they tend towards happiness, they pass into felicity."

In the Yajur Veda, also, "Fire is that (original cause); the sun is that, so is air, so is the moon; such, too, is that pure Brahme, and those waters, and that Lord of creatures. Moments (and other measures of time) proceeded from the effulgent person, whom none can apprehend (as an object of perception) above, around, or in the midst. Of him whose glory is so great there is no image; he it is who is celebrated in various holy strains. Even he is the god who pervades all regions: he is the first-born; it is he who is in the womb, he who is born, and he who will be produced; he, severally and universally with all persons. He, prior to whom nothing was born, and who became all beings; himself the Lord of creatures, with (a body composed of) sixteen members, being delighted by creation, produced the three luminaries (the sun, the moon, and fire). To what God should we offer oblations but to him who made the fluid sky and solid earth, who fixed the solar orb and celestial abode, and who formed drops (of rain) in the atmosphere? To what God should we offer oblations but to him whom heaven and earth mentally contemplate, while they are strengthened and embellished by offerings, and illuminated by the sun risen above them? The wise man views that mysterious (being), in whom the universe perpetually exists, resting on that sole support. In him this (world) is absorbed, from him it issues; in creatures he is twined and wove, with various forms of existence. Let the wise man who is conversant with the import of revelation promptly celebrate that immortal being, the mysterious, existing, and various abode; he who knows its three states (its creation, continuance, and destruction), which are involved in mystery, is father of the father. That (Brahme), in whom the gods attain immortality, while they abide in the third (or celestial) region, is our venerable parent, and the providence which governs all worlds—knowing the elements, discovering the worlds, recognising all regions and quarters (to be him), and worshipping (speech or revelation who is) the first-born, the votary pervades the animating spirit of solemn sacrifice by means of (his own) soul. Recognising heaven, earth, and sky (to be the same), he views that being; he becomes that being, and is identified with him on completing the broad web of the solemn sacrifice."

Colebrooke observes, "The Aswa-médha and Purus-hamed'ha, celebrated in the manner directed in this Veda, are not really sacrifices of horses and men. In the first of these ceremonies 609 animals of prescribed kinds, wild and domestic, including birds, fish, and reptiles, are made fast, the tame ones to twenty-one posts, and the wild in the intervals between the pillars. After certain prayers have been recited the victims are let loose without injury. In the other, 185 men of various specified tribes, characters, and professions are bound to eleven posts, and after the hymn concerning the allegorical immolation of Nárâyana has been recited, these human victims are liberated unhurt, and oblations of butter are made to the sacrificial fire."

CHAPTER XLIX.

COLEBROOKE remarks that "the practice of reading the principal Vedas in superstitious modes tends to preserve the text. Copies prepared for such modes of recital are dispersed throughout India. Interpolations and forgeries have become impracticable since this usage was introduced. The explanatory table of contents, belonging to the several Vedas, also tends to ensure the purity of the text, since the subject and length of each passage are therein specified. The index again is itself secured from alteration by more than one exposition of its meaning. It is a received and well-grounded opinion of the learned in India that no book is altogether safe from changes and interpolations till it has been commented. When once a gloss has been published no fabrication can succeed, because the perpetual commentary notices every passage and, in general, explains every word. Commentaries exist whose genuineness is secured by a crowd of annotators, whose works expound every passage in the original gloss, and whose annotations are again interpreted by others. The Nirukta, with its copious commentaries on the obsolete words and passages of Scripture, further authenticates the accuracy of the text. The grammar of the Sanscrit language contained rules applicable to the anomalies of the ancient dialect. Philosophical works illustrate and support every position advanced in them by ample quotations from the Vedas. Numerous collections of aphorisms by ancient authors on religious ceremonies contain, in every line, references to passages of the Vedas. Rituals are extant, not only for ceremonies which are constantly observed, but for others which are rarely practised, and even for such as have been long disused. In all, the passages taken from the Vedas agree with the text of the general compilation. The Indian legislators frequently refer to the Vedas, especially on those points of law which concern religion. So writers on ethics draw illustrations from them. In astronomy, so far as it relates to the calendar, in medicine, in the writings of the heretical sects, the Vedas still appear, in fact, in numerous citations, in thousands of volumes, dispersed through Hindustan and the Deccan."

In the first of the four, the Rig Veda or "Praise Book of Knowledge," Agni, the Fire of the Altar, as personified, is said to have been born as the Saint or Patriarch Angiras; also as Manu, or the personified, first self-existent Man. He is constantly styled the sacrificer, who is to arouse the deities to the due reception of the offerings. He is young and wise, the guardian of the domestic hearth. He is the purifier, who is spiritually to protect his votaries, just as the material fire in actual fact warms, comforts, and defends from numerous ills.

M. S. A. Langlois, who has been mentioned as the translator of the Harivansa, or history of the family of Hari Krishna, has also translated the hymns of the Rig Veda. They fill the greater part of four octavo volumes of about 500 pages each. And as Professor Weber has remarked, the songs dedicated to Agni are the most numerous therein. They seem to suggest an archaic or prototypical Christianity, in which a mediatorial divine being, present with humanity, is besought to protect and aid in the acquisition of material blessings, which may be spiritualised like the prayers in our psalms. He is the light of the world, realised and possessed by man for communication with the great light of the universe. And he not only is of that light, but he seems to be, in the accretion of ideas, held to be the omnipotent light. It is not merely once incidentally or accidentally that this idea appears, but it is urged and repeated with the fervour of Indian religious zeal, which may be too superstitious, but which is certainly in earnest.

In hymn after hymn expressions appear, which would certainly have been considered most holy and essentially prototypical of Christ if they had been found amongst our Hebrew Scriptures. It is altogether very difficult to conceive that this fervent, beautiful, and apparently pure adoration of Agni can have had no effect upon the Western Aryan world, with which we know that there was much commercial intercourse by at least the commencement of our era. And what do we find? Dr. Schliemann has exhumed from fifty feet below the ground of what he held to be the site of ancient Troy, a number of relics marked with the old fire cross, the *suastika*. This *suastika* (or in Greek εὖ ἔστι, Let it be well with you) assumes the shape of a sort of Maltese cross (amongst numerous cruciform figures), and it is a common symbol in ancient India. Combined with the whole evidence of the question, it may be assumed as an historical fact that the religion of the Agni (or Holy Fire upon earth) was in existence in Asia Minor long before the beginning of our era. Hence has come the assertion of M. Emile Burnouf in his "Sciences des Religions," that the Agni-deva of the Indo-Aryan altars is connected with the *Agnus-Dei*, the light of the New Jerusalem in the Revelation of St. John. This may have come through interchange of ideas, or by word-derivation. It is curious that when, in his "Industrial Arts of India," Sir George Birdwood gives an illustration of Agni, he appears to be depicted as riding on a ram, which also seems to be connected with Buddha the Enlightened. We have become familiar with the Lamb, as expressed in St. John i. 29, and associated with Isaiah liii. 7. It is perhaps safer to suppose that the similarity existing in sound between the Sanscrit Agni and the Latin Agnus is merely accidental. But there are indubitably links between the sacrifice on the cross of the Agnus Dei and the symbolism of the Agni. It is curious that the latter is constantly styled in the Vedas the sacrificer, and that he also seems to become the sacrificed. The symbol of the Agni, in the form of a cross, had marks of nails in it to represent the nailing down of the woodwork to constitute a firm platform. In its centre was a hollow to signify the hole in which the churning-stick was inserted to engender the divine spark. This newly born fire is called, in the Veda, the Child of Force. The officiating priest is styled his Father, and the two pieces of wood, out of which the fire is engendered by friction, are addressed as the two mothers of the infant.

CHAPTER L.

As the sacrificial books of these Vedas adapt much of the hymnal portion of the " Praise " Veda to their ceremonials, the hymns of that book form the main portion in existence of the ancient devotional outpourings of our Indo-European or Aryan race. Though the material blessings seem to be more frequently the object of the devout prayers than spiritual satisfyings, still the aspiration of heavenly happiness does appear. With this is associated the merging of all the deities (devas) in one Supreme Spirit of the universe, as inculcated in the later religious books. It must be remembered that many of the prayers in our Liturgy are for temporal benefits. And certainly in the Old Testament temporal advantages are prominently the objects for which devotion is paid to the Almighty.

The hymns of the "Praise Veda" in which ideas emblematical or prototypical of Christianity especially appear are those addressed to this Divine Fire of the Altar. The first hymn in the collection is subjoined from M. Langlois' translation. Hymns translated by Professor H. H. Wilson will be found in Appendix VI.:—

A AGNI.

1. Je chante Agni, le dieu, prêtre et pontife, le magnifique (Agni) hérant du sacrifice.
2. Qu'Agni, digne d'être chanté par les Richis, anciens et nouveaux, rassemble ici les dieux.
3. Que par Agni (l'homme) obtient une fortune sans cesse, croissante (une fortune) glorieuse, et soutenue par une nombreuse lignée.
4. Agni, l'offrande pure tu enveloppes de toute part, s'élève jusqu'aux dieux.
5. Qu'avec les autres dieux vienne vers nous Agni, le dieu sacrificateur, qui jouit à la sagesse des œuvres, la verité et l'éclat si varié de la gloire.
6. Agni, toi qui portes le nom d'Angiras,[1] bien que tu feras à ton serviteur (par le fruit de sa reconnaissance), tourner à son avantage.
7. Agni, chaque jour, soir et matin nous venons vers toi, apportant l'hommage de notre prière.
8. (A toi), gardien brillant de nos offrandes, splendeur du sacrifice ; à toi qui grandis au sein du foyer que tu habites.
9. Viens à nous, Agni, avec la bonté qu'un père a pour son enfant ; sois notre ami, notre bienfaiteur.

As the collection commences, so it concludes with a hymn to this Holy Fire or Light.

---

[1] Here appears the incarnation as Angiras, first of sages. The name is of the same derivation as Agni, from *Ag*, to shine.

A Agni.

1. O Agni, maître généreux, tu te mêles à tout ce qui existe. Dans la demeure de l'offrande tu allumes tes feux. Apporte nous la richesse.

2. Venez, rassemblez vous pour vous entendre. Que vos âmes se comprennent. C'est en unissant que les antiques devas ont obtenu leur part (de l'immortalité).

3. Les (mortels) ici assemblés n'ont qu'une prière, un vœu, une pensée, une âme. J'offre dans ce sacrifice votre prière et votre holocauste presentés par une intention commune.

4. Que vos volontés et vos cœurs soient d'accord, que vos âmes s'entendent, et le bonheur est à vous.

In the following hymn the incarnation idea seems again distinctly apparent:

A Agni.

Section 1, Lecture 2, Hymn 12.

1. Agni, tu as été l'antique Richi Angiras, dieu, tu es l'heureux ami des autres dieux. . . .

10. Agni, tu es pour nous un défenseur prudent et un père; à toi nous devons la victoire, nous sommes ta famille. En toi sont les pieux par centaines, par milliers, (Dieu) invincible, tu es la force des héros et le gardien des sacrifices.

11. Agni, alors que tu pris une forme humaine, pour le bien de l'humanité, les dévas te donnèrent comme général à Nahoucha. Quand le fils de notre (premier) père naquit, ce sont eux aussi qui choisirent Ilâ pour commander aux enfants de Manou. . . .

16. Agni, si nous avons commis une faute, si nous avons marché loin de toi, pardonne nous. Tu es un parent, un père, un défenseur prévoyant. En faveur des mortels qui offrent le *soma* tu apparais pour accomplir le sacrifice.

17. Agni, toi qui fus Angiras, (dieu), saint, viens en ces lieux avec ces sentiments qu'avaient autrefois Manou, Angiras, Yayâti et les anciens.

Agni is addressed as Djatavêdas (him in whom

wisdom is inborn). He is said to be honoured, the divine messenger, our refuge, the friend of men. He is styled the treasure of light, the master of the prayer, the author of the sacrifice, the wise and victorious high priest, a divine being in the midst of mortals, priest of humanity, a friend amongst the pious, to be honoured in hymn and sacrifice. He is said to save by the sacrifice, and to be the wonderful king of nations, and supreme sustainer of the world.

A Agni.

Section 2, Lecture 1, Hymn 7.

1. Il nait sous la forme de Manou, le premier des pontifes, Agni, sacrificateur de l'ordre des Ouvidjs (a family of saints), oui, sacrificateur d'un ordre qui nous appartient (*i.e.*, which is in our nature). Agissant partout avec empressement, il est pour celui qu'il aime comme un seigneur opulent. Pontife invincible, il s'assoit au foyer du sacrifice; ou il s'entoure d'un cordon (lumineux) au foyer du sacrifice.

6. (Dieu) universel, immense, infatigable, et protecteur, il tient (tous les biens) dans sa main droite.

7. Le fortuné Agni, placé dans sa demeure humaine, est au milieu des sacrifices comme un monarque désirable; il est au milieu des sacrifices comme un monarque chéri. Ame de tous les êtres, connaissant la nature entière, sacrificateur digne lui même des sacrifices.

Section 2, Lecture 2, Hymn 5.

1. Le Dieu, en prenant une forme apparente, se distingue par sa substance lumineuse, qu'il doit à la Force, dont il est né. Une fois produit il est fortifié par la prière, et les voix du sacrifice, le soutiennent et l'accompagnent.

Hymn 9.—1. Priez le: il vient, il (nous) entend, il s'avance, plein de sollicitude, il s'avance rapidement. Pour lui sont les bénédictions, pour lui les offrandes. Il est le maître d'abondance, de la force, de la splendeur.

3. Il nous donne un secours infaillible, il nous aime de l'amour d'un nourrisson.

A Agni.
Section 7, Lecture 8, Hymn 13.

1. Agni, (surnommé) Djâtavedas, né une première fois dans le ciel, une seconde fois dans (l'air) qui nous environne, une troisième au milieu des ondes, d'où il enchante les mortels. L'homme pieux allume ses feux perpétuels et le chante.

2. O Agni, nous savons que tu es triple, et placé en trois demeures. Nous savons aussi que tu habites en beaucoup de lieux.

5. Père de la richesse, gardien de l'opulence, roi magnifique, enfant de la Force, dépositaire de nos prières, il conserve les trésors de Soma (the intoxicating juice of the moon-plant, offered as a sacrifice or sacrament), il s'allume et resplendit devant l'Aurore. O Agni, toujours jeune.

A Agni.
Section 8, Lecture 1, Hymn 1.

1. Il est né le grand sacrificateur; il soutient tout.

2. Les prêtres par leur saintes pratiques, ont fait et amené, parmi les enfants de Manou, cet adorable et fortuné sacrificateur, qui vient à nous pour diriger nos cérémonies, cet hôte des mortels qui purifie (la terre) et porte nos holocaustes.

5. Les insensés ont amené le (dieu) sensé, le vainqueur des mondes, le maître qui soutient le sage, et brise les villes (célestes). Ils ont établi (dans le sacrifice) l'enfant (de l'Arani) pour être un riche trésor d'hymnes et de prières : (ils l'ont lancé) comme un coursier aux poils dorés. Il veut le bien de la terre.

He is said to be above us in one of his forms, here below in another, and in a third in the luminous star. Generous and brilliant, by his rays he kills the demons.

He is the only refuge. He is represented under one name as dead in the Aranî, and reviving to life by means of the rubbing together of the two pieces of wood; and he returns to life with each new sacrifice. He is both Master and Way of the People. His way is black, white, and red. Brahmâ, Vishnu, and Shiva are represented as red, black, and white respectively. Straight is his advance, grand, brilliant, glorious. His father (*i.e.* the sacrificing priest) has given him a golden car. His cuirasse defends humanity. He is the first-born amongst the deities, surnamed the Lord of Increase, and presiding over speech. He opens to us great pastures, abounding in cattle. He is Varuna (lord of the ocean), Mitra (who seems to have become the Persian Mithras, incarnation or embodiment of the sun). He, the antique Agni, is son of heaven and son of earth.

A AGNI.

Section 3, Lecture 1, Hymn 23.

1. Voici le moment d'agiter (l'Aranî), le moment d'enfanter (Agni). Apporte la reine du people (l'Aranî, the wood of the sacred fig-tree or banian).

2. Le (dieu) qui possède tous les biens est dans les deux pièces de l'Aranî : il est comme l'embryon au sein de la mère. Cet Agni que chaque jour les enfants de Manou, en s'éveillant, doivent honorer avec l'hymne et l'holocauste.

3. (Prêtre) intelligent, pouse (la pièce supérieure) dans la pièce inférieure ; et qu'à l'instant (l'Aranî) fécondée enfante (le dieu) qui remplit tous les vœux. (Cependant) reçue sur une poignée (de feuilles) l'étincelle rougeâtre a brillé, et le fils d'Ilâ (the earth) a paru sur le foyer.

4. O Agni, possesseur de tous les biens, nous te plaçons sur

le sein d'Ilâ, sur ton trône de terre, pour te charger de nos holocaustes.

5. Prêtres pieux, travaillez à produire (le dieu) sage, prudent, véridique, immortel et charmant. Enfantez Agni, le héraut du sacrifice, le premier des êtres adorables.

So the priest, in the sacrifice of the Mass, in his prayer of consecration, brings Christ into the elements on the altar, according to the Church of Rome.

7. Agni est né ; ses feux s'animent ; fort, sage, bienveillant. Il est chanté par les poètes ; et les devas ont établis pour le sacrifice ce (dieu) adorable, qui connait tout, et qui porte l'holocauste.

10. Voila le berceau (yoni), où, dans le moment favorable, tu brilles après ta naissance. Reconnais le, O Agni, et viens t'y placer, pour te montrer sensible à nos vœux. Les immortels ont enfanté un mortel invincible, un sauveur, vigoureux, redoutable.

It is said that, under the name of Vishnu, Agni becomes the great Pastor; he is then born for the happiness of the world. Adorable author of life, guardian of the seasons, he triumphs over the demons. He reigns in heaven and on the earth, known as its pastor.

CHAPTER LI.

COLEBROOKE observes, in his article on the Vedas in vol. viii. of "Asiatic Researches:"

"In the last part of the Nirueta (of Yaska), which entirely relates to the deities, it is twice asserted that there are but three gods; and many passages in the Vedas support that these intend but one deity, personifying the elements and planets, and peopling heaven and the world below with various orders of beings." He quotes from the Nirueta, which appears, without doubt, to have been composed many centuries B.C., as follows:

"The deities are only three, whose places are earth, the intermediate region, and heaven, viz., Fire, Earth, and the Sun. They are pronounced to be (the deities) of the mysterious names severally of *bhur*, *bhurah*, and *swar*, called the Vyâhritis; and Prajâpati, the Lord of creatures, is the (deity) of them collectively. The syllable Om intends every deity: it belongs to (Paramesthi), him who dwells in the supreme abode; it appertains to (Brahme) the vast one, to (Deva) god, to (Adhyatma) the superintending soul. Other deities belonging to those several regions are portions of the (three) gods; for they are variously named or described on account of their different occupations; but (in fact) there is only one deity, the Great Soul (Mahamatma). He is called the Sun, for he is the soul of all beings; (and) that is declared by the Sage—the soul of (jagat) what moves, and of that which is fixed." "The wise call fire, Indra, Mitra, and Varuna, &c."

The Gayatri, or sacred Brahminical confession of faith, is subjoined, with its context, in which the sun is regarded as the emblem of the divine.

"This new and excellent praise of thee, O splendid, playful sun (Pushan), is offered by us to thee. Be gratified by this my speech; approach this crawling mind as a fond man seeks a woman. May that sun (Pushan) who contemplates and looks into all worlds be our protector.

"*Let us meditate on the adorable light of the Divine Ruler (Savitrī); may it guide our intellects.* Desirous of food, we solicit the gift of the splendid sun (Savitrī), who should be studiously worshipped. Venerable men, guided by the understanding, salute the divine sun with oblations and praise."

Speech declares, according to Colebrooke's literal translation: "I range with the Rudras, the Vasus, the Adityas, and the Visvadevas. I uphold both the sun and the ocean (Mitra and Varuna), the firmament (Indra) and fire, and both the Aswins (sunbeams). I support the moon (soma), destroyer (of foes) and (the sun entitled) Twashtri (divine carpenter), Pushan or Bhaga (food-giver). I grant wealth to the honest votary who performs sacrifices, offers oblations, and satisfies (the deities). Me, who am the queen, the conferer of wealth, the possessor of knowledge, and first of such as merit worship, the gods render universally present everywhere, and pervader of all beings. He who eats food through me, as he who sees, who breathes, or who hears through me, yet knows me not, is lost; hear, then, the faith which I pronounce. Even I declare this self, which is worshipped by gods and men. I make strong whom I choose; I make him Brahmâ, holy and wise. For Rudra I bend the bow, to slay the demon foe of Brahmâ; for the people I make war (on their foes), and I pervade the heaven and earth. I bore the father on the head of this (universal mind); and my origin is in the midst of the ocean; and therefore do I pervade all beings, and touch this heaven with my form. Originating all beings, I pass like the breeze; I am above this heaven, beyond this earth; and what is the great one, that am I." In the Aitareya Aranya of the Veda it is said—"Originally this universe was indeed soul only, nothing else whatsoever existed, active (or inactive). He thought, 'I will create worlds,' thus He created these various worlds; water, light, mortal (beings) and the waters. That 'water' is the (region) above the heaven which heaven upholds; the atmosphere comprises light, the earth is mortal, and the region below is the waters. He thought, 'These indeed are worlds. I will create guardians of worlds.' Then he drew from the waters, and framed an embodied being. He viewed him; and of that being, so contemplated, the mouth opened as an egg; from the mouth speech issued; from speech fire proceeded. The nostrils spread; from the nostrils breath passed; from breath air was propagated."

CHAPTER LII.

Hari or Krishna is apparently the Heracles of the Raseni, whose adoration seems to have been introduced into Etruria in about the twelfth century B.C. Mrs. Hamilton Gray observes, in her work on Etruria, that Hercules, the deified man, was the first of the series of forty-five Hercules. To him were anciently erected altars, but no images. In Tyre he was styled Melek-karta, the king of the city. His image became represented with four wings; and he held a bow in one hand, and a club in the other. Mrs. Gray remarks that "he was worshipped in Tartary as the introducer of agriculture, and that he was one of the gods of India." No image was so common as his upon the Etruscan terra-cotta or bronzes. He became, in Etruscan mythology, the husband of Minerva, thus constituting the union of wisdom and strength. To Saturn, or Time, who may have been equivalent to the destroying and terrible deity of the Mexicans, and to Shiva, as Rudra or Kali of the Hindus, human victims were offered. These were afterwards replaced by figures made of clay. Altogether it seems reasonable to suppose that the great populous territories of Asia sent forth their superfluous populations in emigrations which extended eastwards into Central America, and westwards to the Italian peninsula, and that this accounts for the affinities. Language and religion alike accompanied them. Amongst these ancient people in Hari-Krishna, Heracles or Quetzalcoatl was presented the idea of the Divine incarnate for the benefit of humanity, suffering that our sufferings might be alleviated. The way was thus prepared for the development of Christianity and the general knowledge of our advanced civilisation of the last three centuries.

The cross[1] seems to demonstrate the connection between the three great cultured centres of the ancient world, viz., the tropical and subtropical Asia, Central America, and the shores of the Mediterranean. In the three prevailed the custom of maintaining the perpetual fire. The cross, which has been found in Old America, and in Dr. Schliemann's excavations beneath the site of Troy, is probably the symbol of the Agni in both. It is the sign of devotion to the benign and mediatorial personification of Deity, hymned in the most ancient books of our race. Our collateral Indo-Aryan ancestors are now allowed by the science of the age to have had a language more regular and perfect than the Greek or Latin. Their voluminous literature is gradually being revealed to us, with habits of life akin to those of our actual ancestors. Surely we may be permitted to recognise in their faiths prototypes of Christian doctrines, the truths of all time, without indignity to our religion. With the sacred fire of the Vedas Krishna is associated as being

[1] See Appendix VII.

on earth Supreme Being, Agni of the altar, Indra of the atmosphere, Nârâyana, who moves upon the waters.

As has been observed, the actual name of Krishna may have come into greater prominence since the fourteenth century of our era. But Krishna is distinctly Hari, who seems to have become the Hercules of the West. Language and mythology will be found to be in evident accordance between ancient India and the settlements on the Mediterranean. Phœbus Apollo would seem to have been derived from Vishnu, considered as the Sun, or Surya, whom Sir G. Birdwood represents in the plates of his "Industrial Arts of India" in a chariot drawn by a horse with seven heads. The materialistic story of Apollo, exiled from heaven and employed as one of the shepherds of Admetus, seems suggested in a Vedic hymn which has been quoted, in which Vishnu as Agni becomes the Great Pastor, born for the happiness of the world.[1] Parts of his history certainly suggest a derivation from the same legends which appertain to Hari-Krishna; as, for instance, the destruction of the serpent Python, and his employment amongst the shepherds when incarnate upon earth. In Heracles the same story appeared under another form. His mother was mortal, but he claimed the chief of the Olympian deities as his father. He had a twin brother, Iphiclus, as has been observed, just as Krishna was accompanied by Bala-Rama. Hercules

[1] See Appendix VIII.

was adored as a model of piety and virtue, and as spending his whole life in the benefit of humanity; and after his painful death, his immortal self is said to have been carried to heaven in a chariot, saluted by peals of thunder. The stories related concerning him also seem suggestive, not of those actually narrated of Krishna, but of those from which these latter were derived.

CHAPTER LIII.

In his introduction to Vol. I. of "Sacred Books of the East," Professor Max Müller observes that "it has been stated that the religious notion of sin is wanting altogether in the hymns of the Rig-Veda. Yet the gradual growth of the conception of guilt is one of the most interesting lessons which certain passages in the ancient hymns teach us."

Also he remarks that "it has been asserted that in the Rig Veda Agni, fire, was adored essentially as earthly sacrificial fire, and not as an elemental force. How greatly such an assertion has to be qualified may be seen from a more careful translation of the Vedic hymns."

In this volume he gives translations of treatises connected with the Vedas, and styled Upanishads. These are considered by the Hindus to be revealed scriptures, and there appears to be no doubt that those which are quoted must be assigned to a period earlier than the time of Plato in the West. The appellation Upanishad is considered to have been derived from a root signifying to destroy, as these writings are intended to destroy passion and ignorance.

In the Khândogya Upanishad it is said, "All this universe has the Supreme Deity for its life. That Deity is truth. He is the Universal Soul." "The path of the deities is the path that leads to Brahma. Those who proceed on that path do not return to the life of man." In this book allusion is made to the contest between the divine beings and demons, which is so evidently the foundation of the Christian legend which Milton has adopted in the "Paradise Lost." The eye, the ear, speech, mind, and air are said to be the five men of Brahma, who are the door-keepers of the heaven-world. "The chest which has the sky for its circumference and the earth for its bottom, does not decay, for the quarters are its sides, and heaven its lid above. That chest is a treasury, and all things are within it." In the Aitareya Aranyaka it is said that water was the root-cause, the world the effect. The Supreme Being is the father, and earth, fire, &c., are the sons. Whatever there is belonging to the son, it belongs to the father also. Whatever belongs to the father belongs to the son.

In the Kanshîtaki Upanishad the spirit is described

as going after death to heaven, where is the river called Ageless, and the tree which showers down the sacred soma-juice, &c. There is also the palace styled Unconquerable, and the hall of Brahma, named Egoism. Herein are the throne Perception, the couch Endless Splendour, &c. Five hundred celestial nymphs come with garlands, ointments, perfumes, garments and fruits, and adorn the soul entering heaven with the adornment of Brahma. The soul arrives at the lake Ara, and crosses it by the mind alone; while those who come to it without knowing the truth are drowned. Then he crosses also the river Ageless by the mind alone, and there shakes off his good and evil deeds. His beloved relatives obtain the good, and his unbeloved relatives the evil, which he has done. And as a man, driving in a chariot, might look at the two wheels without being touched by them, thus will he look at day and night, thus at good and evil deeds, and at all pairs such as heat and cold, &c. He approaches the hall of Egoism, and the glory of Brahma reaches him, and he thinks, as he approaches the throne, "I am Brahma." Verses of the Vedas are the feet of that throne, and the throne itself is knowledge. Brahma says to him, "Who am I?" and he shall answer, "That which is true."

It has been remarked that the doctrine of the metempsychosis does not appear in the actual hymns of the Vedas; but in this literature associated with the Vedas, and also esteemed as revealed from the

Almighty, we find it. Three classes of people are said, for instance, to have transgressed and to have been born again as birds, trees, herbs, and serpents.

As has been shown, the Institutes of Manu declare re-birth in animal or vegetable life, instead of human, to be the consequence of very dark or debased life.

It is declared in the Khândogya that there are three branches of the law. Sacrifice, study, and charity are the first.

The offering of the sacred soma juice, the libation of clarified butter to the holy fire—these are the sacrifices enjoined, with the self-sacrifice of the desires of the flesh. The Books of Knowledge are lauded as nectar, and hymns as spiritual food. Worshippers are said to approach Agni slowly when his name does not stand at the beginning of the hymn. But here it is written (where Agni's name appears early in the hymn); the worshipper obtains his proper food at once; he strikes down evil at once.

Five Upanishads are combined in one, called the Atharva shiras. Two of these are especially interesting, as displaying the continued effort of the old Bharatan divines to set forth the unity of deity under the apparent polytheism. The sectaries of the two principal forms of deity, Vishnu and Shiva, have been styled antagonistic; but really they seem to have been constantly endeavouring, or at all events their teachers have endeavoured, to demonstrate that the two are one. Here, side by side in one collection, are the Naráyan and Rudra (Shiva) Upanishads, which distinctly affirm this equality of the two deities, otherwise called Vishnu and Shiva—in fact, their absolute unity. They again appear as links in the chain of connection between the Vedas and the accounts of the incarnation of the Almighty in Krishna. They are taken from Professor Max Müller's "Sacred Books of the East."

The Naráyana Upanishad.

"The primeval male Naráyana loves the beings that he has created. From Naráyana were produced the vital breath, the mind, the senses and their organs, ether, fire, air, water, and earth. From Naráyana were produced Brahma, Rudra, the Prajapatis" (Patriarchs virtually), "the twelve suns" (? the passage through the twelve signs of the Zodiac), "the Rudras and Vasavas; and from Naráyana were produced the Vedas and all sacred learning. By Naráyana are all things created, preserved, and destroyed, and again produced. Thus Naráyana is Rudra, Naráyana is Brahma, and all Rishis. He is Kala" (time), "and all that is above or below, external or internal: Naráyana is all that was or shall be, without parts, without passion, incomprehensible, unnamable and immaculate. Naráyana is the one God, and there is not a second. He is certainly Vishnu. Let *Aum* be first said, then *nama*, and afterwards *Naráyanaya*. *Aum* is one syllable, *nama* is two syllables, and Naráyana is five syllables; thus *Aum Naráyanaya nama* is the eight-syllabled invocation from the repetition of which are obtained long life, wealth, and progeny, and finally immortality, by participating in the bliss ineffable of God. The syllable *Aum* is composed of the letters A, U, and M, and he who repeats these letters thus joined together shall be delivered from the miseries of transitory existence. Hence *Aum Nárâyanaya nama* is that invocation which whoever repeats, he shall ascend to Vaikuntha, *he shall ascend to Vaikuntha*" (heaven). "Of divine nature is the son of Devaki" (Krishna). "Of divine nature is Madhusudana; for Nârâyana, who dwelleth in all things, the uncaused cause of all that exists, is Parabrahm. Aum, He who meditates on this portion of the Atharvashiras at night, the sins which he has committed during the day shall be remitted; if in the morning, all nocturnal sin shall be destroyed; and if at mid-day, seated opposite the sun, the five great sins, and all lesser ones, shall be forgiven to him: his virtue shall become equal to that acquired by a thorough knowledge and observance of the Vedas, and he shall obtain identification with Nârâyana."

The Rudra Upanishad.

The deities proceeded to the celestial abode of Rudra, and inquired, "Who art thou?" He replied, "I am the first and sole essence; I am and shall be, and there is not anything which is distinct from me." Having thus spoken he disappeared, *and then an unseen voice was heard saying,* "I am he who causeth transitoriness, and yet endureth for ever; I am Brahm; I am the east and the west, the north and the south; I am space and *vacuum;* I am masculine, feminine, and neuter; I am Savitri, the Gayatri, and all sacred verse; I am the three fires; I am the most ancient, the most excellent, the most venerable, and the mightiest; I am the splendour of the four Vedas, and the mystic syllable; I am imperishable and mysterious, but the revealer of mysteries; I am all that is, and all space is pervaded by my essence." This heard, the deities meditated on Rudra, though unseen, and then with uplifted hands thus adored him: "Praise be unto thee, who art Brahma, Vishnu, and Maheswara" (that is, who hast manifested thyself under all these different forms); "praise be unto thee who art Uma, Ganesha, and Skanda; praise be unto thee who art Indra and Agni; praise be to thee who art the earth, the sky, and heaven; praise be to thee who art the sun and moon, the stars and planets; praise be to thee who art Time, Death, and Yama (king of hell), who art immortal, the past, the present, and the future; praise be to thee who art all that is, the sole and universal essence; praise be to thee, O Rudra and Ishana, O Maheswara, O Mahadeva, O Lord, for thou art Parabrahm, the one and only God."[1]

The Rev. K. M. Banerjea, in his "Occasional Papers on Missionary Subjects," observes that "The funda-

---
[1] See Appendix IX.

mental principles of Christian doctrine in relation to the salvation of the world find a remarkable counterpart in the Vedic principles of primitive Hinduism in relation to the destruction of sin, and the redemption of the sinner by the efficacy of sacrifice, itself a figure of Prajápati, the Lord and Saviour of the creation, who had given Himself up as an offering for that purpose." He holds that " the meaning of Prajápati, an appellative variously described as a Purusha begotten in the beginning, as Viswakarma, the Creator of all, singularly coincides with the meaning of the name and offices of the historical reality Jesus Christ." He remarks that " sacrifice offered according to the three ways—the right path—has been held in the Rik, Yajus, and Saman (Vedas), to be the good ferrying-boat or raft by which we may escape from sin," and that " the idea of a sacrifice of a Divine Person is not found merely in a single isolated passage, in which case it might have been explained away, but in various passages; in the different Vedas it finds expression in different ways." He quotes an obscure passage in the Rig Veda which Yaska, the author of the Nirukta, thus expounds: "Viswakarma had, in a universal sacrifice, offered all creatures, and then eventually offered himself also;" and then from the Brihadaranyaka Upanishad: "Priests solemnise the sacrifice (Asvamedha) as if it were an offering of Prajápati himself, or the universal Godhead." He observes that Prajápati or Purusha is spoken of as

Atmadá (giver of self), whose shadow, whose death is immortality;" that Prajápati not only means the lord of creatures, but also "the supporter, feeder, and deliverer of his creatures; and that the name Jesus, in the Hebrew, means the same."

CHAPTER LIV.

The writings of the Fathers of the Church testify very completely to the extensive prevalence of the doctrine of the metempsychosis, for they frequently allude to and condemn it as a heresy. The sects who held this ancient Aryan doctrine appear to have asserted themselves to be true followers of Christ with ardour equal to that of their opponents, though the doctrine of the resurrection of the actual body for reward or punishment became the acknowledged doctrine of the Church. Origen, however, who flourished in the 3d century A.D., avowed distinctly his acquiescence with this doctrine of the transmigration of souls. He is esteemed, in a general way, as an orthodox Father of the Church, his admirable defence of Christianity having probably condoned his heterodoxy upon this point. The statements of his belief certainly seem to reveal ideas approximating to those of the Buddhists in the East and Platonists in the West.

In the preface to Roberts and Donaldson's translation of Origen in the "Ante-Nicene Christian Library," it is said :

"Origen's work, 'De Principiis,' exposed him to more animadversion in the ancient Church than any other. The points in which he had plainly departed from the orthodox faith were the four—

"1st. That the souls of men had existed in a previous state, and that their imprisonment in material bodies was a punishment for sins which they had then committed.

"2nd. That the human soul of Christ had also previously existed and been united to the Divine nature before that incarnation of the Son of God which is related in the Gospels.

"3rd. That our material bodies shall be transformed into absolutely ethereal ones at the resurrection.

"4th. That all men, and even devils, shall be finally restored through the mediation of Christ."

The Rev. Messrs. Roberts and Donaldson continue: "There seems no adequate reason to doubt his substantial orthodoxy, though the bent of his mind and the nature of his studies led him to indulge in many vain and unauthorised speculations." Origen, however, quotes scriptural authority for his contentions; and he was undoubtedly a man of learning and talent. Of course he was intrinsically not less qualified to comprehend the truth of Christian doctrine than the zealous Tertullian, whose anticipations of satisfaction in beholding the torments of the condemned players, &c., have been quoted.

"How could his soul or its images," inquires Origen, referring to John the Baptist, "be formed along with his body who, while lying in his mother's womb, was filled with the Holy Ghost? I allude to John leaping in his mother's womb, and exulting because of the voice of the salutation of Mary which had come to the ears of his mother Elizabeth. How could his soul and its images be formed along with his body who, before he was created, is said to be known to God? Some, perhaps, may think that God fills individuals with His Holy Spirit, and bestows upon them sanctification, not on grounds of justice and according to their deserts, but undeservedly. And how shall we escape that declaration, 'Is there unrighteousness with God?' God forbid! Or this, 'Is there respect of persons with God?' For such is the defence of those who maintain that souls come into existence with bodies. . . . Those who have been made the sons of God or children of the resurrection; who have abandoned the darkness and loved the light; who have become sons of peace; who, mortifying their members upon earth, and rising above not only their corporeal nature, but even the uncertain and fragile movements of the soul itself,—these have united themselves to the Lord, being made altogether spiritual, that they may be for ever one spirit with Him."

This certainly resembles closely the doctrine of the Bhagavata Purana, &c.

Origen thinks that human souls cannot fall so as to

become animals. "Angels may sink to be men or demons, and the latter may rise to be men or angels."

He holds those to be wrong who have quoted the speaking of Balaam's ass in proof of the soul which inhabited it having been human.

He writes that "the necessity of logical reasoning compels us to understand that rational creatures were created at the beginning, but that material substance was separated from them only in thought or understanding, and that they never were without it—an incorporeal life being a prerogative of the Trinity alone—but that when the soul becomes the servant of blessed beings, it shines in the splendour of celestial bodies, with the clothing of a spiritual body such as adorns the angels of God, or sons of the resurrection." The soul may be dragged down to beings of a lower order, "moulded into the crasser and more solid conditions of a body." In rising to the divine, it may obtain an immortal and incorruptible body. At length, in progress from the more refined bodies, death is swallowed up in the gradual disappearance of the material nature. But rational natures, with free will, may again be subjected to movement through the act of the Lord Himself. These movements may again be attended by variety and diversity of bodies, by which the world is always adorned. He holds that there may be worlds not exactly similar to our own.

Theophilus of Antioch, bishop in A.D. 168, exhibits acquaintance with this doctrine of the metempsychosis.

In book iii. chap. vii. he says, "And Plato, who spoke so much of the unity of God and of the soul of man, asserting that the soul is immortal, is afterwards found, inconsistently with himself, to maintain that some souls pass into other men, and that others take their departure into irrational animals." And he observes that Pythagoras, too, is found venting "similar nonsense." Irenæus strongly reprobates it also. He (Bishop of Lyons in the last quarter of the second century) says that "our bodies must rise again in the flesh to confess the power of Him that raises them from the dead." In his Book against Heresies, he observes that some heretics declare themselves similar to Jesus, maintaining "that things are evil and good simply in virtue of human opinion. They deem it necessary, therefore, that by means of transmigration from body to body, souls should have experience of every kind of life as well as every kind of action (unless indeed by a single incarnation one should be able to prevent any need for others), and some one thing being wanting for their deliverance, they should be compelled once more to become incarnate. They quote this text, 'While thou art with thy adversary in the way, give all diligence that thou mayest be delivered from him, lest he give thee up to the judge, and the judge surrender thee to the officer, and he cast thee into prison. Verily I say unto you, thou shalt not go out thence until thou pay the very last farthing.' The adversary is equivalent to the devil, an angel in the world who may shut up souls in another body. Souls may be saved by participating in all actions in one incarnation; or by passing from body to body, at length accomplish what is requisite. They declare that Jesus spoke in a mystery to His disciples and apostles privately, and that they requested to hand down the things which He taught them. We are saved, indeed (they say), by means of faith and love; but all other things, while in their nature indifferent, are reckoned by the opinion of men—some good and some evil, there being nothing really evil by nature."

Now this demonstrates that there were followers of what they asserted to be Christian doctrine, who held views absolutely in correspondence with those of the "Divine Song," &c. of the Indian epic. And their assertion that Christ spoke in a mystery to his disciples about these matters, certainly is corroborated by no word of His having been recorded against this doctrine; which must have certainly been sufficiently prevalent to suggest His reprobation if He disapproved of it.

As his own opinion, Irenæus declares that "God gives each soul its special character. And therefore when the number (fixed upon) is completed, which He had predetermined in His own counsel, all those who have been enrolled for life (eternal) shall rise again, having their own bodies, and having also their own souls and their own spirits, in which they had pleased God. Those, on the other hand, who are worthy of punishment, shall go away into it; they, too, having their own souls and their own bodies, in which they stood apart from the grace of God. They shall cease from marrying and giving in marriage; so that the number of mankind, according to the foreordination of God, being completed, may fully realise the scheme formed of the Father." St. Paul seems to have taught that, if not entirely a spiritual body without form, it was at all events spiritualised in the resurrection. But Irenæus seems to have held the actual material resurrection for good or evil. This doctrine seems to have had its prototype in Egypt. The idea must undoubtedly have existed, in the making of mummies, that the body would be resuscitated for the soul's residence, if we consider this practice in conjunction with the Egyptian conception of the judgment of the soul, &c.

Irenæus is undoubtedly one of the greatest links between Christ upon earth and the Church founded on His life and doctrine. It is Irenæus who first quotes the four Gospels by the names of the authors to whom they have since been attributed. He was personally acquainted with Polycarp, who related his conversation with St. John the Apostle and others who had seen the Lord. Irenæus says that Polycarp "related their sayings, and what he had heard concerning the Lord, both concerning His miracles and His doctrine."

Irenæus, therefore, ought to be reliable authority;

but as the Church accepts his testimony in respect to the doctrine of Christ on the strength of this acquaintance with Polycarp, &c., it certainly ought equally to receive his account of the lifetime and period of the death of Christ. He is very strangely at variance with our accepted traditions upon those points. The account given by Irenæus of the duration of the preaching of our Lord shows that the account which we now accept was by no means universally established in his time. In fact, this great pillar of the early Church, St. Irenæus, Christian Father of the second century, held that Christ had continued to preach till a comparatively advanced period of life, till long after the age at which we have doctrinally alleged that He quitted the earth. The acquaintance of Irenæus with St. John the Apostle, through only one intervening person, St. Polycarp, ought, it might be supposed, to have rendered the Church more disposed to take his words into earnest consideration. It must be observed, however, that Keim, in his "Jesus of Nazara," argues that the John with whom Polycarp was personally acquainted was the Presbyter of Asia Minor, not the Apostle. Irenæus himself seems to have absolutely believed that it was the beloved Apostle of the Lord.

CHAPTER LV.

In chapter xxii., sections 4, 5, and 6, of the translation of the works of St. Irenæus by the Revs. A. Roberts and W. H. Rambaut, in Roberts and Donaldson's "Ante-Nicene Christian Library," Irenæus recounts various miracles as we have received them. He relates how Jesus had made the water wine, conversed with the Samaritan woman, cured the paralytic at the pool, fed the multitude with five loaves, and raised Lazarus from the dead. He also alludes to Christ's coming to Bethany six days before the Passover, then to His proceeding to Jerusalem, eating the Passover, and suffering on the next day. He then gives the account of the preaching life of our Lord, to which allusion has been made in the last chapter. "Being thirty years old when He came to be baptized, and then possessing the full age of a master, He came to Jerusalem so that He might be properly acknowledged by all as a master. For He did not seem one thing while He was another, as those affirm who describe Him as being man only in appearance; but what He was that also He appeared to be. Being a master, therefore, He also possessed the age of a master, not despising nor evading any condition of humanity; not setting aside in Himself that law which He had appointed for the human race, but sanctifying every age by that period corresponding to it which belonged to Himself. For He came to save all through means of Himself — all, I say, who, through Him, are born again to God — infants and children, boys, youths, and old men. He therefore passed through every age, becoming an infant for infants, a child for children, thus sanctifying those who are of this age; being, at the same time, made to them an example of piety, righteousness, and submission; a youth for youths, becoming an example to youths, and thus sanctifying them for the Lord. So likewise was He an old man for old men, that He might be a perfect master for all, not merely as respects the setting forth of the truth, but also as regards age, sanctifying at the same time the aged also, and becoming an example to them likewise. Then, at last, He came on to death itself, that He might be the first-born from the dead, that in all things He might have the pre-eminence, the Prince of Life, existing before all, and going before all.

"They, however (*i.e.* the heretics), that they might establish their false opinions regarding that which is written, 'to proclaim the acceptable year of the Lord,' maintain that He preached for one year only, and then suffered in the twelfth month. (In speaking thus) They are forgetful to their own disadvantage, destroying His whole work, and robbing Him of that age which is both more necessary and more honourable than any other; that more advanced age, I mean, during which also, as a teacher, He excelled all others.

For how could He have had disciples if He did not teach? And how could He have taught unless He had reached the age of a master? For when He came to be baptized, He had not yet completed His thirtieth year, but was beginning to be about thirty years of age (for thus Luke, who had mentioned His years, had expressed it, 'Now Jesus, as it were, beginning to be thirty years old, when He came to receive baptism'), and according to these men He preached only one year, reckoning from His baptism; completing His thirtieth year He suffered, being in fact still a young man, and who had by no means attained to advanced age.

Now that the first stage of early life embraces thirty years, and that this extends onwards to the fortieth year, every one will admit; but from the fortieth and fiftieth year a man begins to decline towards old age, which our Lord possessed while He still fulfilled the office of a teacher, even as the Gospel and all the elders testify; those who were conversant in Asia with John the disciple of the Lord (affirming) that John conveyed to them that information. And that He remained among them up to the time of Trajan. Some of them, moreover, saw not only John but the other apostles also, and heard the very same account from them, and bear testimony as to (the validity) of the statement. Whom, then, should we rather believe; whether such men as these, or Ptolemæus, who never saw the apostles, and who never, even in his dreams, attained to the slightest trace of an apostle? But, besides this, those very Jews who then disputed with the Lord Jesus Christ have most clearly indicated the same thing. For when the Lord said to them, "Your father Abraham rejoiced to see My day; and he saw it and was glad," they answered Him, "Thou art not yet fifty years old, and hast Thou seen Abraham?" Now such language is fittingly applied to one who is already past the age of forty, without having as yet reached his fiftieth year, yet is not far from this latter period. But to one who is only thirty years old it would unquestionably be said, "Thou art not yet forty years old." For those who wished to convict Him of falsehood would certainly not extend the number of His years far beyond the age which they saw He had attained, but they mentioned a period near His real age.

Whether they had truly ascertained this out of the public register, or simply made a conjecture, from which they observed that He was about forty years old, He certainly was not one of only thirty years of age. For it is altogether unreasonable to suppose that they were mistaken by twenty years when they wished to prove Him younger than the times of Abraham. For what they saw that they also expressed; and He whom they beheld was not a mere phantasm, but an actual being of flesh and blood. He did not then want much of being fifty years old, and, in accordance with that fact, they said to Him, "Thou art not yet fifty years old (St. John viii. 57), and hast Thou seen Abraham?" He did not, therefore, preach only for one year, nor did He suffer in the twelfth month of the year; for the period included between the thirtieth and fiftieth years can never be regarded as one year." Irenæus then proceeds to argue against an heretical idea that the woman afflicted by the issue of blood was a type of the "suffering Æon," and against the folly of heretical arguments from letters and numbers, &c. Messrs. Roberts and Donaldson say, with respect to this "extraordinary assertion of Irenæus," that "Harvey remarks that the reader may here perceive the unsatisfactory character of tradition where a mere fact is concerned. From reasonings founded upon the evangelical history, as well as from a preponderance of external testimony, it is most certain that our Lord's ministry extended but little over three years; yet here Irenæus states that it included more than ten years, and appeals to a tradition derived, so he says, from those who had conversed with an apostle."

Paley observes in his "Evidences of Christianity," chap. ix., when he comes to Irenæus: "The evidence now opens upon us full and clear. In his youth he had been a disciple of Polycarp, who was a disciple of John. In the time in which he lived he was distant not much more than a century from the publication of the Gospels; in his instruction, only by one step separated from the persons of the apostles . . .

the testimony which this writer affords to the historical books of the New Testament, to their authority and to the titles which they bear, is express, positive, and exclusive." Yet we have utterly ignored his statements as to the duration of Christ's ministry.

CHAPTER LVI.

EAST and West had been long in communication eighteen hundred years ago. The early Christians of eminence did not neglect to study the spiritual tone of the age in East as well as West. That they were impressed with the merits of the Brahminical religion is evidenced by the following quotation from the "Recognitions" of the Roman Clement, chap. xx. (taken also from the Rev. Messrs. Roberts and Donaldson, "Ante-Nicene Christian Library"): "There are likewise, amongst the Bactrians in the Indian country, immense multitudes of Brahmans, who also themselves, from the tradition of their ancestors and peaceful customs and laws, neither commit murder nor adultery, nor worship idols, nor have the practice of eating animal food; are never drunk, never do anything maliciously, but always fear God. And these things, indeed, they do, though the rest of the Indians commit both murders and adulteries, and worship idols, and are drunken, and practise other wickednesses of this sort."

Hippolytus also, the disciple of Irenæus, alludes to the Brahmans—to their philosophical pursuits, their content, their temperance. He states that they despise death, and affirm that God is light, and that he who triumphs over sensuality—which holds all men captive—goes to God.

In the "Miscellanies" of Clement of Alexandria it is written: "Numa, the king of the Romans, was a Pythagorean, and aided by the precepts of Moses, prohibited from making an image of God in human form, as the best of kings could not be comprehended but by the mind alone. Thus philosophy flourished in antiquity among the barbarians, shedding its light over the nations. Afterwards it came to Greece. First in its ranks were the prophets of the Egyptians, and the Chaldeans among the Assyrians, and the Druids amongst the Gauls, and the Samanæans amongst the Bactrians, and the philosophers of the Celts; and the Magi of the Persians who foretold the Saviour's birth, and came into the land of Judea guided by a star. The Indian gymnosophists are also in the number, and the other barbarian philosophers. And of these there are two classes, some of them called Sarmanæ, and others Brahmans. And those of the Sarmanæ who are called Hylobii neither inhabit cities nor have roofs over them, but are clothed in the bark of trees, feed on nuts, and drink water in their hands. Like those called Eucratides in the present day, they know not marriage nor begetting of children. Some, too, of the Indians obey the precepts of Buddha (Βούττα), whom, on account of his extraordinary sagacity, they have raised to divine honours."[1]

Mr. Arthur Lillie, in his work on "Buddha and Early Buddhism,"[2] remarks that in the "Clementines" we have a theory about Christ which is quite the mysticism of esoteric Vedism and Buddhism. Christ, it is said, "has changed His forms and names from the beginning of the world, and so reappeared again and again in the world" (Roman Clement, *Homilies*, chap. 20).

He also quotes St. Augustine, in reference to the connection between Buddhism and Christianity, when that saint says, "For the thing itself which is now called the Christian religion really was known to the ancients, nor was wanting at any time from the beginning of the human race until the time that Christ came in the flesh, from whence the true religion which had previously existed began to be called 'Christian;' and this in our day is the Christian religion, not as having been wanting in former times, but as having in later times received this name" (*Opera*, vol. i. p. 12).

The links in the chain of connection between the earliest Indian Scriptures and the later books narrating the incarnation of Krishna, seem too succinct to have been mended by any interpolation from a foreign source. If we accept the theory of Clement, Krishna,

---

[1] See Appendix X.
[2] "Buddha and Early Buddhism," by Arthur Lillie, late Regiment of Lucknow. Messrs. Trübner & Co.

Buddha, and previous incarnations were manifestations, suggestions, or prototypes of Christ, with distinct foreshadowings of His life and of the Roman Catholic doctrine of the immaculate conception of His mother.

The name of the father of Krishna, as shown in a previous chapter, has a divine significance. Devaki, the mother, also is divine. She is held to have been an incarnation of Aditi, who, in the Vedic hymns, seems identified with the sky, or equivalent to heaven and earth, and yet distinct from them. She is mother of Mitra, Varuna, and other divinities. Indeed a mystic account is given of the parents, in which they appear together as incarnations of deities. Vasudeva, the father, is related to have been born exempt from sin.

The idea of birth from a virgin does not appear to have been attributed to Krishna in the Mahâbhârata or Puranas. In the "Great Bhârata," one of the principal chieftains, who fights against Krishna's friends, has been thus miraculously brought into the world. While virginity has also been assigned to the mother of Buddha, whose name is Mâyâ, curiously coinciding with Maria, in the "Ancient Book of the Blessed," Bhagavat is said to manifest everything in the world by his association with Mâyâ. (This signifies illusion personified, or art, from *mâ*, which signifies "measure;" *mâtri*, "mother.") Mâyâ is sometimes identified with the goddess Dourgâ, who is, under one aspect, as has been shown, the divine virgin Kumari,[1] and she is represented, like all the divine beings of the Pantheon,

[1] Hence Cape Comorin.

as being a manifestation of the Supreme Spirit of the universe. Mr. Lillie observes [1] of Queen Mâyâ that it has been debated whether she was a virgin at the time of Buddha's birth, and that, as she is without doubt Virgo of the sky, he thinks the question must be answered in the affirmative.

"Before Buddha's birth," in Mr. Lillie's words, "the queen receives a presentiment that something unusual is about to occur. The king releases many prisoners, and gives bountiful presents around; and banners, scents, flowers, and parasols are provided in profusion in the upper rooms of the palace, whither the Queen betakes herself. She lies on a couch, jealously guarded by innumerable women." Mr. Lillie observes that he has "shown that the solar god-man is known in the Rig Veda as Mârttânda, and the symbol of Mârttânda is the elephant."

In the Chinese and Burmese versions Mâyâ dreams that Buddha comes down in the form of an elephant. So in spring, when appeared the constellation Visakha (April-May), the Bodhisatwa, under the appearance of a young white elephant, entered the right side of his mother, and she, by means of a dream, was conscious of the fact. In the garden of her royal father, beneath a beautiful palâsa tree (*ficus religiosa*) the infant Buddha was born. The branches of the tree, having bent down to salute, overshadow the queen. "No sooner has the infant touched the earth than a large white

[1] "Buddha and Early Buddhism," p. 70.

lotus springs up. He sits upon it, and gazes upon the four cardinal points with the glance of Purusha." "I am in my last birth," he exclaims; "none is my equal. I have come to conquer death, sickness, and old age. I have come to subdue the spirit of evil, and give peace and joy to the souls tormented in the fire of hell." These words roll forth with mighty sound through all the worlds. Then strains of celestial music are heard, flowers and perfumes fall from the skies, brilliant lights illumine all the worlds, &c. &c., while the sick are healed, the blind receive sight, the hungry are fed, the prisoners released, &c. &c., and the torments of those in the hell Avitchi cease.[1]

Mr. Lillie has ably adduced the points of similarity between the religions of Buddha and Woden. He remarks that Professor Max Müller ridicules the idea that there is any connection between Buddha and Woden; but that, on the other hand, the great archæologist, Professor Holmboe, takes up the opposite view. He comments upon the resemblance of the relic mounds, the symbolism, and mythological conceptions of Northern India and Northern Europe. The warlike spirit of Krishnaism,[2] rather than the peaceful precepts of Buddhism, pervade the old Northern Europeans; but the Scandinavian Balder is gentle and benignant, and seems to be homogeneous

---
[1] Lillie's "Buddha and Early Buddhism," p. 75.
[2] See Appendix XI.

with the divine men who appear in the Old and in what has been termed the New World. The Hiawatha of the Red Indians presents the same character; and traces of a similar ideal—of a beneficent superhuman man—have been discovered amongst the Southern Africans.

Mr. Lillie has given many extracts from Buddhist ritual, which demonstrate undeniably that the hopes of conscious bliss in heaven, and the belief in an actual God, have been great features in that religion, although agnosticism has also existed in it. As has been shown in the inscription from Buddha Gaya, Buddha became associated with Krishna as the Supreme Being manifested to mankind in many forms. Mr. Lillie adduces the inscriptions of Asoka or Piyadasi, of the third century B.C., and much other clear evidence of the ancient Buddhistic faith in an actual God and in a future life.

The following quotations are from page 51, &c. of his "Buddha and Early Buddhism:"—

"I pray with every variety of prayer for those who differ with me in creed, that they, following after my example, may with me attain unto eternal salvation."
—*Delhi Pillar*, Edict vi. (Prinsep).

"All the heroism that Piyadasi, the beloved of the gods, has exhibited is in view of another life. Earthly glory brings little profit, but, on the contrary, produces a loss of virtue. To toil for heaven is difficult to peasant and to prince, unless by a supreme effort he gives up all."—*Rock*, Edict No. vii. (Burnouf).

"May they (my loving subjects) obtain happiness in this world and the next." "This stûpa (religious mound) has been erected for consolation, advantage, and happiness in this world and the next, and thus to the end of time this stupâ will allow my people to gain heaven."—*Second Separate Edict* (Burnouf).

King Asoka's ideas about God.

"Much longing after the things (of this life) is a disobedience, I again declare; not less so is the laborious ambition of dominion by a prince who would be a propitiator of Heaven. Confess and believe in God, who is the worthy object of obedience (Isânameva manyata mânam)! For equal to this (belief) I declare unto you ye shall not find such a means of propitiating Heaven. Oh strive ye to obtain this inestimable treasure."—*First Separate Edict, Dhauli* (Prinsep).

"Thus spake King Devanampiya Piyadasi: The present moment and the past have departed under the same ardent hopes. How by the conversion of the royal born may religion be increased? Through the conversion of the lowly born if religion thus increaseth, by how much (more) through the conviction of the high born and their conversion shall religion increase? Among whomsoever the name of God resteth, verily this is religion."

"Thus spake Devânampiya Piyadasi: Wherefore from this very hour I have caused religious discourses to be preached. I have appointed religious observances, that mankind, having listened thereto, shall be brought to follow in the right path, and give glory to God."—*Edict* No. vii. (Prinsep).

"In like manner, turning his mind to law in an establishment of learned men, he called together the Buddhist priests of Eastern Kalinga, who were settled there under the ancient kings . . . act of devotion . . . all equipages . . . he gives to God."—*Prinsep's translation of a defaced inscription on the Khandagiri Rock, erected by the grandson of Asoka.*

"By love alone can we conquer wrath, by God alone can we conquer evil. The whole world dreads violence. All men tremble in the presence of death. Do to others that which ye would have them do to you.

"Kill not; cause no death.

"Say no harsh words to thy neighbour. He will reply to thee in the same tone.

"I am injured and provoked. I have been beaten and plundered! They who speak thus will never cease to hate.

"That which can cause hate to cease in the world is not hate, but the absence of hate.

"The awakened man goes not on revenge, but rewards with kindness the very being who has injured him, as the sandal tree scents the axe of the woodman who fells it."

CHAPTER LVII.

The Portuguese found Christians on the Malabar coast when they arrived in India in the sixteenth century. But they appear to have been more akin to modern Unitarians than to members of our "orthodox" Churches. They were followers of Nestorius, who was degraded from the position of Patriarch, and eventually, under the stigma of heresy, buried in Upper Egypt, in the fifth century A.D. They obeyed the Patriarch of the Nestorian sect in Syria. In the beginning of the sixteenth century they had a hundred churches in the countries subject to the Travancore and Cochin Rajahs. And at the time when the account of them was written in vol. vii. "Asiatic Researches" (A.D. 1790), they numbered about 150,000. They were styled St. Thomé Christians, Nestorians, Syrians or Malabar Christians by the Portuguese. By the Hindus they were named Nazaranee or Surianee Mâpila. They have been supposed to have arrived during the persecution of the Nestorians under Theodosius in the fifth century. They used the Syrian or Chaldean language in their sacred rites. Many of them observed a similar mode of life to the Brahmins; but they seem mainly to have followed trade or husbandry, and they wore swords and targets.

They rejected the Divine nature of Christ; and called the Virgin Mary only the mother of Christ and not of

God. They also maintained that the Holy Ghost proceeded only from the Father, not from the Father and Son. They allowed no images; only the cross. They held three sacraments—baptism, the eucharist, and Orders; and they would not admit the doctrines of transubstantiation or purgatory. They conceived that saints were kept, neither in heaven nor hell, but in a third place, till the day of judgment. Their priests were permitted to marry, at least once. Their Sunday lasted from the Saturday evening vespers till the first matins of Sunday, and after sunrise they might work again.

The Portuguese endeavoured to convert them to Romanism, and many, in appearance, became united with the Roman Church. But thirty-two churches, called Schismatic Syrians, still remained. The old St. Thomé Christians considered themselves as under the Rajahs of the different districts in which they lived.

It seems evident, at all events, that it was not from these Malabar Christians that the doctrine of the Incarnation in Krishnaism was derived, in those points in which it presents analogies to our Christian doctrine.

A curious story exists in the Mahâbhârata, which has no actual resemblance to that of the death on the cross, but it presents a strange suggestiveness of it. It is related in explanation of the reason why Yama, the king of death, had been compelled to become incarnate upon the earth.

"There was an illustrious Brahmin, named Mandavya, who was full of constancy, and acquainted with all religious duties. He was immoveable in his life of penitence and truth. This great ascetic remained at the foot of a tree, with his arms elevated in the air, enchained in the vow of silence. Some robbers came with a great booty, and being pursued closely by the police, they concealed their booty in the ascetic's hermitage. When the troops in pursuit arrived, they proceeded to interrogate the man 'rich in penitence.' They inquired what road the thieves had taken; but he would not answer a single word, good or bad. Then the police, having searched the hermitage, found the brigands hidden there, and their booty. The anchorite, suspected of being concerned in the robbery, was bound with the rest, conveyed before the king, and condemned to death. The soldiers fixed him upon a stake, and after they had raised it up, they collected the booty, and returned to the palace. The just man remained for a long time upon the stake, still preserving the breath of life. His misfortune caused the saints and anchorites to assemble from all parts, who were deeply afflicted at beholding this most worthy man affixed to the stake, tormented by such torture. By night, transformed to birds, they flew together to the impaled Brahmin. They said that they desired to learn what crime had brought him to the frightful punishment of the stake. He replied, 'I will go to the king of the dead to become informed of this crime, for I know it not; it is he, no other, that inflicts this chastisement upon me.'

"After many days the soldiers announced to the king what had occurred, and the monarch proceeded to deliberate with his ministers, and then came to demand pardon of this most virtuous man fixed upon the stake. 'I beseech you to pardon me, O most excellent of saints,' said the king, 'for this offence which I have committed towards thee, in ignorance and folly; have no animosity towards me.'

At these words the anchorite pardoned him, and the king had the saint lowered, and would have pulled out the terrible stake, but as it could not be extricated, he had it cut off. At the same instant as the stake was severed, the hermit uttered his last sigh. He had conquered by this torturing trial all the worlds, *i.e.*, heaven, earth, and hell, which others so earnestly covet. He is celebrated throughout the worlds under the name of Animandavya. This Brahman, who in his inner soul beheld the universal soul, then descended to the palace of Yama. He saw the king of the dead seated on his throne, and he addressed to him these words: " What evil deed have I committed, for the fruit of which I have merited such a recompense? Let me forthwith know the truth, for you are aware of the power of my penitence." Yama replied, " When a young child you made a needle pierce the tail of a grasshopper; your punishment was in consequence of this action!"

"You have inflicted a heavy punishment for a slight fault," replied Animandavya, "and in consequence you shall be born as man, the son of a slave woman. There is this limit in the world for receiving the fruits of works: till the age of fourteen they shall not be accounted as sin, but after that period evil shall be accounted sin whenever worked." In the Brahman's forgiveness of those who had inflicted upon him this cruel death, and in his descent to hell afterwards, there seems to appear not a similitude, perhaps, but a suggestiveness of incidents attending the crucifixion; and in his silence amongst the robbers, Isa. liii. 7, 12 is recalled to mind: "He was oppressed, and He was afflicted, yet He opened not His mouth." "He was numbered with the transgressors." But the story bears strong signs of Indian originality in respect to the ascetic's vow, and the idea of the incarnation of Yama.

It seems to testify to the ancient appreciation of the Christian precepts of patience, long-suffering, and forgiveness, and the King of death is conquered by the saint. The name Animandavya signifies that he had been impaled.

CHAPTER LVIII.

The Bible appears clearly to allow that a more expansive view of the dealings of the Divine with the human should be adopted than is often set forth in the teachings of the Church. In it are only related, at length, the dealings of the Almighty with the patriarchs of the Hebrew race. But it shows, in the account of Melchizedek, king of Salem, that truth was on the earth (Gen. xiv. 18). The Epistle to the Hebrews, vii. 3, demonstrates that those who accept the Bible as inspired revelation must acknowledge the verities of religion to have been within the cognisance of Melchizedek. He is said to have been "made like unto the Son of God, and abideth a priest continually." Here, then, is a centre of what must be admitted by Biblical Christians to have contained true religion in ancient days.

Apart from the apparent birth of the eastern Aryan faiths on the ground of India itself—if it should be held that in Palestine only was true religion revealed, in Palestine in the 20th century B.C., according to Archbishop Usher's chronology, was a "king of righteousness." He is also styled a "king of peace"—without father, without mother, without descent; having neither beginning of days nor end of life (Heb. vii. 3). He was the "priest of the most high God;"

and Jesus is said to have been "made an High Priest for ever after the order of Melchizedek."

According to the orthodox chronology of Archbishop Usher, Abraham is assigned to 1950 B.C. While Abraham and his descendants were wandering about till they became temporarily settled in Egypt, whence they emerged after some two hundred years, there was, according to the Bible, a high priest of righteousness and king of Salem (stated by orthodox commentators to be Jerusalem). When the Jews took possession of that city, we are not informed of the existence there of this high priest, or of any descendant of his, spiritual or other. But in the meantime it may be reasonably asserted, on the authority of the Bible, to those by whom Divine inspiration may be denied to the further East, that the knowledge of the truth may have been disseminated eastwards from him. The expressions concerning him in Hebrews are such as are applied to Christ Himself, and would be held, according to the Eastern-Aryan conceptions, to indicate a previous incarnation. He is described as personally blessing Abraham, and bringing forth bread and wine (Gen. xiv. 18). He has neither beginning nor end according to the Epistle to the Hebrews. A reasonable explanation would be that he was regarded as the Almighty on earth; for there can be but One without beginning or end. He is distinctly described as personally present. In him the Bible itself seems to afford an indication of a source whence revelation of the truth could have been given in Palestine 1900 B.C. for the benefit of the ancient world, to be again revealed there for our own times by Christ, "made an High Priest for ever after His order."

The word Salem appears to be Sanscrit, derived from Śaileya, mountainous or rocky; equivalent to Founded on a rock. That the Bible, though dealing especially with the Israelites and their origin, contains this idea of righteousness in the East, seems sufficiently proved by the texts in Isa. xli. 2-4, commencing with, "Who raised up the righteous man (Hebrew *righteousness*) from the East."

It is held in our Biblical chronology to have been about the year 1706 B.C. that "all the souls of the house of Jacob which came into Egypt were threescore and ten" (Gen. xlvi. 27). It is held to have been in the year 1491 B.C. that "all the hosts of the Lord went out from the land of Egypt" (Ex. xii. 41). These consisted of "about 600,000 on foot that were men, besides children." "And the Lord went before them by day in a pillar of a cloud, to lead them the way; and by night in a pillar of fire, to give them light." During this period which was passed by the Hebrews in Egypt, we are not informed of any special revelation till "the angel of the Lord appeared unto Moses in a flame of fire out of the midst of a bush," and "God said unto Moses, *I am* hath sent me unto you" (Ex. iii.) From the time, therefore, when Melchizedek, "priest of the most high God," blessed Abraham, in about the year 1913 B.C., till this revelation to Moses, some 400 years elapsed. During this period vast civilisations were flourishing in arts, laws, commerce, and appreciation of the moralities of life. On the great Chinese and Indian rivers, as well as on the Euphrates and on the shores of the Mediterranean, millions of people were spending their lives in a manner more approximate to our own modern life apparently than ever that of the Jews has been in Palestine. The remote antiquity of the incarnation doctrine thus seems to be suggested in the case of Melchizedek, as well as in the appearances of the Almighty upon earth, as recorded in the Old Testament. He is mentioned in Gen. iii. 8 as "walking in the garden in the cool (Hebrew *wind*) of the day." He talked with Abraham (Gen. xvii. 3). He then appeared unto him in the form of three men (Gen. xviii. 1, 2). The Almighty also wrestled with Jacob, and "when He saw that He prevailed not against him, He touched the hollow of his thigh, and the hollow of Jacob's thigh was out of joint as he wrestled with Him" (Gen. xxxii. 24–32). But no system seems to have been deduced from these recorded appearances. The favour of the Almighty was thereby held merely to have been assured to the chosen prophet. But in the acknowledged commercial intercourse between Eastern and Western Asia, some knowledge of the Aryan doctrine of the incarnations must have passed. At all events this intercourse was flourishing in the epoch of Solomon, about 1000 B.C., according to orthodox chronology. If our Western world will not admit that the Eastern can have rightly apprehended divine truth, the mysterious Melchizedek may be held to have disseminated, in ancient days, the doctrine realised subsequently in Christianity.

APPENDIX.

I.

Mr. H. S. ASHBEE, in a description of a visit to the Library of Tanjore, published in the French "Livre" in 1881, states that it contains 18,000 manuscripts, of which 8000 are written upon palm leaves. This library, which also possesses a fine collection of European books, was founded at the end of the sixteenth century, when Tanjore was under the government of the Telugu Naiks, who came from Vijayanaga, and deposed the Chola princes. The manuscripts are written in the Telugu character but in the Sanscrit language, and also in the idioms of later days; and works on architecture and kindred topics are mingled with the religious writings which constitute the greater portion. Mr. Ashbee informs us that—"Les livres imprimés sont rangés sur des rayons à la manière Européenne, tandis que les manuscrits, soigneusement enveloppés dans des morceaux de soie ou coton, sont tenus dans des armoires." For the inditing of these Mr. Ashbee tells us that "on n'emploie ni plumes ni encre. Un simple stylet de fer suffit. Prennant la palme, longue de plusieurs pieds, dans la main gauche, on trace rapidement dessus avec le stylet un charactère excessivement petit, mais très net. Pour faire ressortir les lettres on frotte la feuille d'un liquide noir, on lave aussitôt la feuille et les lettres restent noires comme si elles avaient été écrites avec une plume. Pupitres et tables sont inconnus. Pour écrire on se tient à terre, assis ou couché. Bien qu'elles n'aient aucun appui les mains écrivent avec une facilité et une vitesse étonnantes" . . . "Il ne nous manque pas de livres où sont décrites les bibliothéques célèbres, en grande partie détruites, de l'Égypte, de l'Assyrie, de la Judée, de Constantinople, de la Grèce et de Rome ; mais, autant que je sache, aucun bibliographe ne s'est occupé spécialement des collections, encore plus importantes de l'Inde, qui nous restent heureusement aujourd'hui."

Mr. Ashbee further observes that it is now almost universally admitted, by those who have deeply studied the subject, that our religion, arts and sciences, have come, not from Egypt, as was formerly supposed, but from India through Greece, the first inhabitants of which were Indian refugees, Buddhists, and others, exiled on account of their religion. He concludes his article by expressing his regret that the greater part of the literature of the Hindus, Buddhists and Jains, remains, and will probably long remain, a dead letter. He quotes Professor Max Müller's observation, that modern history would be incomplete without that of the *moyen âge*, and that this would be incomplete without the history of Greece and Rome. So the entire history of the world must be studied in the first chapter of the life of Aryan humanity, preserved in the Vedic literature. Many noble translations have certainly been made in French and English by the admirable industry of the Sanscrit scholars of our day, as has been shown in this book. A fair exposition of the so-called heathen religions of our Aryan cousins in the East seems to have been made; but as Mr. Ashbee says, What riches are still concealed in the great libraries of India!

II.

The Mahâbhârata commences, as quoted in chapter ii. of this book, with an adjuration to Nara and Narâyana, and to the goddess Sarasvati (divine wisdom). Sir John Froissart commences his Chronicles in not dissimilar terms: "To thentent that the honorable and noble aventures of featis of arms, done and achyued by ye warres of Frâce and Inglande, shulde notably be inregistered, and put in perpetuall memory, whereby the prewe and hardy may have example to encourage them in theyr well doyng, I, Syr Johñ Froissart, wyll treat and recorde an hystory of great louage and preyse; but or I begyn, I require the Sauyour of all the worlde, who of nothyng created all thynges, that He wyll gyue me suche grace and vnderstandyng that I may cōtinue and perseuer in suche wyse, that whoso this proces redeth or hereth, may take pastance, pleasure, and ensample."

"Fyrst by the grace of God and of the blessed Virgyn, Lady Saynt Mary, from whom all comfort and consolation procedeth, I wyll take my foundation out of y\^e true cronicles, sometime cōpyled by the right reverend, discrete, and sage Maister John la Bele, sometyme chanon in Saint Lambartis," &c. &c.—*Lord Berner's Translation.*

III.

The Buddhist temple in the Japanese village, on view in London in 1885, affords a striking instance of the similarity between the Roman and Buddhist forms of ecclesiastical decoration. The altar, with its super-altar, candles, lamps burning before it, &c., is almost identical with a Roman Catholic altar, making allowances for the general differences between Europe and Japan. Instead of the crucifixion, Buddha, under a canopy, occupies the place above the altar. Instead of the stations of the cross, Buddha, in some of the forms which he has assumed during his transmigrations, is seen in the images ranged along the super-altar. Although not crucified in the flesh for humanity, he is related to have often sacrificed his body for the welfare of human beings. The red garb of the priest is certainly again in accordance with the vesture of the priests of the Romish Church. In the old religion of Japan, called the Sin-Sin (faith in gods), the Supreme Deity was held to be too great to be addressed in prayer, save through the mediation of the Mikado, the Son of Heaven, or of inferior spirits called *Kami*, of which 492 were born spirits, and 2640 were canonised mortals. For these *Kami* temples were especially erected. Japanese dwellings had invariably a kind of oratory, in which prayers were offered morning and evening.

IV.

In the "Annual Register" of 1803, p. 93, is an extract from "Mr. Percival's Account" of the Island of Ceylon. After descriptions of the Buddhistic religion there prevailing, &c. &c., he says: "The mountain called Hannoralleel, or Adam's Peak, is one of the highest in Ceylon. It is from the summit of this mountain, as tradition reports, that Adam took his last view of Paradise before he quitted it, never to return. The spot on which his foot stood at the moment is still supposed to be found in an impression on the summit of the mountain resembling the print of a man's foot, but more than double the ordinary size. After taking this farewell view, the father of mankind is said to have gone over to the continent of India, which was at that time joined to the island; but no sooner had he passed Adam's Bridge than the sea closed behind him and cut off all hopes of return. This tradition, from whatever source it was originally derived, seems to be interwoven with their earliest notions of religion, and it is difficult to conceive that it can have been engrafted on them without forming an original part. I have frequently had the curiosity to inquire of black men of different castes concerning this tradition of Adam. All of them, with every appearance of belief, assured me that it was really true; and in support of it produced a variety of testimonies, old sayings, and prophecies, which have for ages been current among them. This mountain, which is looked upon as the original residence of Adam, is held in great veneration not only by the natives of Ceylon, but also by a variety of persons of different castes and persuasions throughout India. Most of these have particular places of worship on it, to which they make pilgrimages at certain seasons of the year. The Roman Catholic priests have also taken advantage of the current superstitions to forward the propagation of their own tenets."

V.

Mr. R. Mitra, in his work on Buddha Gaya, gives expression to doubts concerning the authenticity of this inscription, with its mingling of Krishnaistic and Buddhistic ideas. One argument urged against its appertaining to the age at which it is dated is that it describes Buddha Gaya as being in a forest. But it does not appear necessarily to say this, but merely that Buddha took up his abode in a forest. There are certainly wild forests in the district of Bahar; but doubtless the temple would have been erected in the open and cultivated country for the convenience and consolation of worshippers. Another argument is that the mingling of Brahminical and Buddhistic conceptions is unnatural. But in the illustratration in this work of Buddhistic ritual in Nepaul, it will be seen that there is a similar association of the Brahminical conceptions of deity with Buddhism.

VI.

SPECIMEN VERSES OF THE HYMNS OF THE RIG-VEDA, TRANSLATED FROM THE ORIGINAL SANSCRIT BY H. H. WILSON, M.A., F.R.S., &c.

First Ashtáka, First Adhyáya, Súkta II.

1. Hasten hither, friends, offering praises; sit down and sing repeatedly the praises of Indra.

2. When the libation is poured forth, respectively praise Indra, the discomfiter of many enemies, the lord of many blessings.

3. May he be to us for the attainment of our objects; may he be to us for the acquirement of riches; may he be to us for the acquisition of knowledge; may he come to us with food.

4. Sing to that Indra, whose enemies in combats await not his coursers harnessed in his car.

5. These pure *soma* juices, mixed with curds, are poured out for the satisfaction of the drinker of the libations.

. . . .

Anuváka III, Sukta I.

1. Indra, bring for our protection riches, most abundant, enjoyable, the source of victory, the humbler of our foes.

2. By which we may repel our enemies, whether (en-

countering them) hand to hand, or on horseback, ever protected by thee.

3. Defended by thee, Indra, we posses a ponderous weapon, wherewith we may entirely conquer our opponents. . . .

7. The belly of Indra, which quaffs the *soma* juice abundantly, swells like the ocean.

8. Verily the words of Indra to his worshipper are true, manifold, cow-conferring, and to be held in honour; (they are) like a branch (loaded with) ripe (fruit).

First Ashtáka, Second Adhyáya, Súkta III.
To Agni.

1. Lord of sustenance, assume thy vestments (of light), and offer this our sacrifice.

2. (Propitiated) by brilliant strains, do thou, ever youthful Agni, selected by us, become our ministrant priest (invested) with a radiance.

3. Thou, Agni, art verily as a loving father to a son, as a kinsman to a kinsman, as a friend to a friend. . . .

10. Agni, son of strength, (accept) this sacrifice, and this our praise, with all thy fires, and grant us (abundant) food.

Fourth Adhyáya, Súkta V.

1. Ushas, daughter of heaven (the personified dawn or Aurora), dawn upon us with riches; diffuser of light, dawn upon us with abundant food; bountiful goddess, dawn upon us with wealth (of cattle).

2. Abounding with horses, abounding with kine, bestowers of every sort of wealth, (the divinities of morning) are possessed of much that is necessary for the habitations of men.

3. The divine Ushas has dwelt (in heaven of old); may she dawn to-day, the excitress of chariots, which are harnessed at her coming, as those who are desirous of wealth (send ships) to sea.

Fourth Adhyáya, Sukta V.

1. The amplitude of Indra was vaster than the (space of) heaven; earth was not comparable to him in bulk; formidable and most mighty, he has been ever the afflicter (of the enemies of) those men (who worship him); he whets his thunderbolt for sharpness as a bull (his horns).

2. The firmament-abiding Indra grasps the widespread waters with his comprehensive faculties, as the ocean (receives the rivers); he rushes (impetuous) as a bull, to drink of the *soma* juice; he, the warrior, ever covets praise for his prowess.

3. Thou, Indra, hast not (struck) the cloud for (thine own) enjoyment; thou rulest over those who are possessed of great wealth; that divinity is known by us to surpass all others in strength; the haughty (Indra) takes precedence of all gods, on account of his exploits. . . .

6. Ambitious of renown, destroying the well-built dwellings of the *Asuras*, expanding like the earth, and setting the (heavenly) luminaries free from concealment, he, the performer of good deeds, enables the waters to flow for the benefit of his worshippers.

Professor H. H. Wilson observes, in a note, that the sun and the constellations were obscured by the same cloud which detained the aggregated waters.

Sukta VI.

... 2. His (Indra's) adorers, bearing oblations, are thronging around (him), as (merchants) covetous of gain crowd the ocean (in vessels) on a voyage. Ascend quickly with a hymn to the powerful Indra, the protector of the solemn sacrifice, as women (climb) a mountain.

3. He is quick in action and mighty; his faultless and destructive prowess shine in manly (conflict) like the peak of a mountain (afar), with which, clothed in iron (armour), he, the suppressor of the malignant, when exhilarated (by the *soma* juice), cast the wily Sushûa into prison and into bonds.

Sukta II.

To Agni, in the form of Vaiswánara (from viswa, all, and nara, a man).

1. Whatever other fires there may be, they are but ramifications, Agni, of thee; but they all rejoice, being immortal in thee; thou Vaiswanara art the navel of man, and supportest them like a deep-planted column.

2. Agni, the head of heaven, the navel of earth, became the ruler over both earth and heaven; all the gods engendered thee, Vaiswánara, in the form of light, from the venerable sage.

3. Treasures were deposited in the Agni, like the per-

manent rays (of light) in the sun; thou art the sovereign of all the treasures that exist in the mountains, in the herbs, in the waters, or amongst men.

4. Heaven and earth expanded, as it were, for their son. The experienced sacrificer recites, like a bard, many ancient and copious praises addressed to the graceful-moving, truly vigorous, and all-guiding Vaiswánara.

5. Vaiswánara, who knowest all that are born, thy magnitude has exceeded that of the spacious heaven; thou art the monarch of Manu-descended men; thou hast regained for the gods in battle the wealth (carried off by the Asuras).

6. I extol the greatness of that showerer of rain whom men celebrate as the slayer of Vritra: the Agni, Vaiswánara, slew the stealer (of the waters) and sent them down (upon earth) and clove the (obstructing) cloud.

7. Vaiswánara by his magnitude is all men, and is to be worshipped as the diffuser of manifold light in offerings of nutritious viands. Agni, the speaker of truth, praises with many commendations Purunítha, the son of S'atávani.

Seventh Adhyáya, Sukta II.

To Agni.

1. Two periods of different complexions (black and white, or night and day) revolve for their own purposes, and each, in succession, severally nourishes a son; in one Hari is the receiver of oblations, in the other the brilliant Agni is beheld.

2. The vigilant and youthful Ten beget, through the

wind, this embryo Agni, inherent (to all beings), sharp-visaged, universally renowned, shining among men; him they conduct (to every dwelling).

3. They contemplate three places of his birth, one in the ocean, one in the heaven, one in the firmament; and dividing the seasons of the year, for the benefit of earthly creatures he formed, in regular succession, the eastern quarter.

4. Which of you discerns the hidden Agni? a son, he begets many mothers by oblations; the germ of many (waters), he issues from the ocean; mighty and wise, the recipient of oblations. . . .

7. Like the sun, he stretches forth his arms, and the formidable Agni, decorating both heaven and earth (with brightness) labours (in his duties); he draws up from everything the essential (moisture), and clothes (the earth) with new vestments (derived) from his maternal (rains).

Sukta IV.

1. May our sin, Agni, be repented of; manifest riches to us; may our sin be repented of.

2. We worship thee for pleasant fields, for good roads, and for riches; may our sin be repented of. . . .

7. Do thou, whose countenance is turned to all sides, send off our adversaries, as if in a ship (to the opposite shore); may our sin be repented of.

8. Do thou convey us in a ship across the sea, for our welfare; may our sin be repented of.

APPENDIX.

Second Ashtáka, First Adhyáya, Súkta I.

To Vayu (Wind).

1. Let thy swift coursers, Vayu, bring thee quickly hither, that thou mayest be the first to drink—the first (of the gods) to drink of the *soma* libation. May our upraised, discriminating, and sincere (praise) be acceptable to thy mind. Come with thy steed-yoked car for (the libation) to be presented to thee; come, Váyu, (for granting) the objects of our worship.

2. May the exhilarating drops (of the libation) exhilarate thee, Vayu, being fitly prepared, doing their office, administered opportunely, rendered efficacious by (our) praises, and flowing (in due season); for which purpose thy docile and active steeds, the Niyuts, attending (thy presence, bring thee) to the sacrificial hall to accept the offering; to the sacrifice in which the pious (priests) represent their desire.

3. Vayu yokes to his car his two red horses; Váyu (yokes) his purple steeds; Váyu (yokes) his two unwearied (coursers) to his car to bear their burden, for most able are they to bear the burden. Arouse, Váyu, the intelligent (sacrificer), as a gallant (awakens) his sleeping mistress; summon heaven and earth; light up the dawn; light up the dawn (to receive) thy sacrificial food. . . .

6. These *soma* juices, poured out in our rites and borne by the priests, are prepared for you both (Indra and Váyu).

The pure juices were passed through the oblique filter; the *soma* juices, intended for you both, pass through the woolly fleece.

First *Ashtáka*, Fifth *Adhyáya*, *Súkta VII*.

TO THE MARUTS (WINDS COLLECTIVELY).

1. Offer earnest praise to the company of the *Maruts*, the senders of rain and ripeners of fruit, deserving of adoration.

2. They were born handsome and vigorous from the sky, the sons of Rudra, the conquerors of their foes, pure from sin, and purifying (all), radiant as suns, powerful as evil spirits, diffusers of rain drops, and of fearful forms. . . .

4. They decorate their persons with various ornaments; they have placed, for elegance, brilliant (garlands) on their breasts; lances are borne upon their shoulders, and with them and their own strength they have been born leaders from the sky. . . .

6. The munificent *Maruts* scatter the nutritious waters as priests at sacrifices the clarified butter; as grooms lead forth a horse, they bring forth for its rain the fleet-moving cloud, and milk it, thundering and exhausted.

7. Vast, possessed of knowledge, bright shining, like mountains in stability, and quick in motion, you, like elephants, break down the forests when you put vigour into your ruddy (mares).

8. The most wise *Maruts* roar like lions; the all-knowing are graceful as the spotted deer; they come with their

antelopes and their arms (to defend the sacrificer) against interruption. . . .

11. Augmentors of rain, they drive with golden wheels the clouds asunder, as elephants (in a herd break down the trees in their way). . . .

15. Grant us, *Maruts*, durable riches, attended by posterity, and mortifying to our enemies.

Second Ashtáka, Fifth Adhyáya, Súkta XII.

1. Some creature of little venom, some creature of great venom, or some venomous aquatic reptiles, have anointed me with their poison.

2. (The antidote) coming (to the bitten person) destroys the unseen (venomous creatures); departing, (it destroys them) by its odour; being ground, it pulverises them. . . .

4. The cows had lain down in their stalls, the wild beasts had retreated (to their lairs), the senses of men were at rest, when the unseen (venomous creatures) anointed me (with their venom). . . .

6. Heaven (serpents) is your father; Earth, your mother; Soma, your brother; Aditi, your sister; unseen, all-seeing, abide (in your own holes), enjoy (your own) good pleasure.

7. Those (who move with their) shoulders, those (who move with their) bodies, those who sting with sharp fangs, those who are virulently venomous, what do ye here, ye unseen? Depart together far from us.

8. The all-seeing sun rises in the east, the destroyer of the unseen, driving away all the unseen (venomous creatures) and all evil spirits. . . .

10. I deposit the poison in the solar orb, like a leather bottle in the house of a vendor of spirits; verily that adorable (sun) never dies, nor (through his favour) shall we die (of the venom); for though afar off, yet drawn by his coursers, he will overtake (the poison). The science of antidotes converted thee (poison) to ambrosia. . . .

12. May the thrice-seven sparks (of Agni) consume the influence of the venom; they verily do not perish, nor shall we die; for, although afar off, the sun, drawn by his coursers, will overtake the poison. The science of antidotes has converted thee, poison, to ambrosia.

13. I recite the names of ninety and nine (rivers), the destroyers of poison.

14. May the thrice-seven pea-hens, the seven sister rivers, carry off (O body) thy poison, as maidens with pitchers carry away water.

15. May the insignificant mungoose (carry off) thy venom (poison): if not, I will crush the vile (creature) with a stone, so may the poison depart (from my body) and go to distant regions.

16. Hastening forth at the command (of Agastya), thus spake the mungoose: The venom of the scorpion is innocuous; scorpion, thy venom is innocuous.

Sixth Adhyáya, Sukta VI.

1. Address worshippers, after the manner of Angiras, a new (hymn) to that Indra, whose withering (energies) were developed of old; who, in the exhilaration of the *soma*, forced open the obstructed and solid clouds. . . .

APPENDIX.

7. As a virtuous (maiden), growing old in the same dwelling with her parents (claims from them her support), so come I to thee for wealth; make it conspicuous, measure it, bring it (hither), grant (a sufficient) portion for my bodily sustenance, (such as that) wherewith thou honourest (thy worshippers.)

. . . .

Sukta IX.

1. We bring to thee, Indra, (sacrificial) food, as one desiring food brings his waggon; regard us benevolently, when glorifying thee, rendering (thee) illustrious by (our) praise, and soliciting such guides as thou art to felicity. . . .

7. Indra, the slayer of Vritra, the destroyer of cities, has scattered the black-sprung servile (hosts). He engendered the earth and the waters for Manu; may he fulfil the entire prayer of the sacrificer.

8. Vigour has been perpetually imparted to Indra by his worshippers (with oblations), for the sake of obtaining rain; for which purpose they have placed the thunderbolt in his hands, wherewith, having slain the *Dasyus*, he has destroyed their *iron cities*.

9. That opulent donation which proceeds, Indra, from thee, assuredly bestows upon him who praises thee the boon (which he desires); grant (it) to (us) thy adorers; do not thou, who art the object of adoration, disregard our prayers; so that, blessed with worthy descendants, we may glorify thee at this sacrifice.

Seventh Adhyáya, Súkta V.

1. I present continually, with the ladle (of speech), these oblation-dropping hymns to the royal Adityas. May Mitra, Aryaman, Bhaga, the multi-present Bhaga, the multi-present Varuna, the powerful Ansa, hear us. . . .

4. The divine Adityas are the upholders (of all things), moveable or immoveable; the protectors of the universe; the provident in acts; the collectors of rain; the possessors of veracity; the acquitters of our debts.

5. May I be conscious, Adityas, of this your protection, the cause of happiness (and security) in danger; Aryaman, Mitra, and Varuná, may I, through your guidance, escape the sins which are like pitfalls (in my path). . . .

7. May Aditi, the mother of royal sons, place us beyond the malice (of our enemies); may Aryaman lead us by easy paths; and may we, blessed with many descendants and free from harm, attain the great happiness of Mitra and Varuná.

8. They uphold the three worlds, the three heavens; and in their sacrifices three ceremonies (are comprised); by truth (Adityas) has your great might (been produced), such as is most excellent—Aryaman, Mitra, and Varuná.

9. The Adityas, decorated with golden ornaments, brilliant, purified by showers, who never slumber nor close their eyelids, who are unassailable and praised by many, uphold the three bright heavenly regions for the sake of the upright man.

Anuváka IV., Súkta I.

To Rudra.

1. Father of the Maruts, may thy felicity extend to us; exclude us not from the sight of the sun, (grant that) our valiant (descendants) may overcome (foes), and that we may be multiplied, Rudra, by (our) progeny.

2. Nourished by the sanatory vegetables which are bestowed by thee, may I live a hundred winters; extirpate mine enemies, my exceeding sin, and my manifold infirmities.

3. Thou, Rudra, art the chiefest of beings in glory; thou, wielder of the thunderbolt, art the mightiest of the mighty; do thou waft us in safety over (the ocean) of sin; repel all the assaults of iniquity.

4. Let us not provoke thee, Rudra, to wrath by our (imperfect) adorations; nor, showerer (of benefits), by our unworthy praise, nor by our invocation (of other deities); invigorate our sons by thy medicinal plants, for I hear that thou art a chief physician among physicians.

. . . .

Súkta II.

13. They, the Rudras, (equipped) with melodious (lutes) and decorated with purple ornaments, exult in the dwelling of the waters; and scattering the clouds with rapid vigour, they are endowed with delightful and beautiful forms.

Sukta III.

To Apám-napát (son of the trees, or fuel, the progeny of the rains).

... 4. The young and modest (waters) wait upon the youth, assiduous in bathing him, and he, although unfed with fuel, yet cleansed with clarified butter, shines with bright rays amidst the waters, that abundance (may be) to us.

5. Three divine females present food to that uninjurable divinity, as if formed in the waters they spread abroad, and he drinks the ambrosia of the first-created (element).

6. In him is the birth of the horse, of him is (the origin of) the world; do thou, grandson of the (waters), protect the pious worshippers from the malevolence of the oppressors; those who give no offerings, those who practise untruths, attain not the inconceivable deity, whether abiding in the immature or the perfect waters. ...

9. The grandson of the waters has ascended the firmament above (the region) of the tortuously moving (clouds), arrayed in lightning; the broad and golden-coloured (rivers) spread around, bearing (to all quarters) his exceeding glory.

· · · · · ·

Sukta VII.

To the Aświns (the pervaders or sunbeams; in one hymn they make the lame to walk and the blind to see, and restore an aged man to youth; and they save Bhujyu, who went to sea in an hundred-oared vessel).

1. Descend, Aświns, like falling stones, for the purpose (of destroying our foes); hasten to the presence of the wealth-possessing (worshippers), like vultures to a tree; like two Brahmans repeating hymns, (be present) at the sacrifice, and come like (royal) messengers in the land, welcomed by many people. . . .

4. Bear us across (the sea of life), like two vessels, or (over difficult places) like the poles of a car, the axles, the spokes, the fellies (of two wheels). Be like two dogs, warding off injury to our persons, and like two coats of mail, defend us from decay.

. . . .

Sukta X.

. . . 2. May no kite, no eagle, kill thee; may no archer, armed with arrows, reach thee.

3. Bird, who art ominous of good fortune, the proclaimer of good work, cry from the south of our dwellings.

Third Ashtaka, First Adhyaya, Sukta VIII.

. . . 2. Agni, born of sacrifice, three are thy viands, three thine abiding places, three the tongues satisfying (the gods); three verily are thy forms, acceptable to the deities, and with them, never heedless (of our wishes), be propitious to our praises. . . .

4. The divine Agni is the guide of devout men, as the sun is the regulator of the seasons; may he, the observer of truth, the slayer of Vritra, the ancient, the omniscient, convey his adorer (safe) over all difficulties.

Sukta XIII.

1. Agni, who art omniscient, and the discriminator (of acts), thou art the son of heaven or the son of earth; do thou, who art intelligent, worship severally the gods on this occasion.

5. Agni, son of strength, Játadevas[1] the eternal, traversing the inhabited regions with thy protection, thou art kindled in the dwelling of the waters.

Sukta XVII.

1. This, the apparatus of attrition, is ready. . . .

3. Let the intelligent priest place the lower of the sticks with the face upwards, the upper (with the surface downwards), so that, quickly impregnated, it may generate the showerer (of benefits) Agni; then the bright blazing son of Ilá, whose light dissipates the darkness, is born of the wood of attrition. . . .

6. When they rub (the sticks) with their arms, the radiant Agni bursts forth from the wood like a fleet courser.

7. As soon as born, Agni shines, intelligent, swift moving, skilled in rites, whom the gods have held as the bearer of oblations at sacrifices, adorable and all-knowing.

---

[1] He in whom wisdom is inborn.

Adhyaya II., Sukta VII.

To Indra.

... 6. As the rivers pursue their course, the waters rush to the ocean like the drivers of cars (to a goal); so the vast Indra (hastens) from his dwelling (in the firmament) when the humble *soma* libation propitiates him.

Sukta VIII.

... 11. Come to us, Sakra, whether from afar or nigh: whatever, Indra, wielder of the thunderbolt, be thy region, come from thence hither.

Adhyaya III., Sukta VII.

1. Come, Indra, with thy exulting, peacock-haired steeds.
2. The fracturer of the cloud, the sender of the waters, the demolisher of cities, Indra, the destroyer of powerful enemies, has mounted his chariot to urge his horses to our presence.

It should be observed that the hymns of the Vedas invariably suggest the origin of the Aryan race on the river plains of Hindustan or the Panjab, not in the region to the north-west of the Hindu Kush. Allusions are made to spotted deer, antelopes, peacocks, &c. Elephants trample down the woods. Allusions are made to the ocean, rainy season, &c.; not to the necessary camel of the Bactrian district. This point has been put forward in the author's "Cradleland of Arts and Creeds," chap. xii., &c. Earlier forms of language doubtless preceded the Vedic Sanscrit, and travelled westward before the Vedas had assumed their present aspect. There is nothing to show that the *Dasyus* (p. 325) were a conquered indigenous race. The word means enemies of gods or men in the sense of robbers. The "black sprung servile hosts" were probably to the south of the Panjab.

Fourth Ashtaka, Fourth Adhyaya, Sukta VII.

To Mitra and Varuna.

1. Guardians of water, observers of truth, you ascend your car in the highest heaven; to him whom you, Mitra and Varuna, protect, the rain sends down the sweet (shower) from the sky.

2. Imperial rulers of this world, you shine, Mitra and Varuna, at this sacrifice, the beholders of heaven; we ask of you the wealth (that is) rain, and immortality, for your forms traverse earth and heaven.

. . . . . .

Sukta IX.

1. The wise apply their minds; they perform sacred rites for the propitiation of the intelligent, great, adorable Savitri; he alone, knowing their functions, directs the priests; verily great is the praise of the divine Savitri.

2. The wise Savitri comprehends all forms (in himself); he has engendered what is good for biped and quadruped; the adorable Savitri has illumined the heaven, and shines in sequence to the passage of the Dawn. . . .

5. Thou alone rulest over (the actions of) living beings; thou art Pushan, divine (Savitri) by thy movements; thou art sovereign over the whole world; Syavaswa offers praise, Savitri, to thee.

Fourth Ashtaka, Seventh Adhyáya, Sukta IV.

. . . 10. Make me happy, Indra; be pleased to prolong my life; sharpen my intellect like the edge of an iron sword. . . .

18. Indra, the prototype, has assumed various forms, and such is his form as that which (he adopts) for his manifestation: Indra, multiform by his illusions, proceeds (to his many worshippers), for the horses yoked to his car are a thousand. . . .

22. Prastoka has given to thy worshipper, Indra, ten purses of gold, and ten horses, and we have accepted this treasure from Divodása. . . .

23. I have received ten horses, ten purses, clothes, ample food, and ten lumps of gold from Divodása. . . .

29. War-drum, fill with your sound both heaven and earth.

Fifth Ashtaka, Sixth Adhyaya, Sukta VI.

1. This Saraswati, firm as a city made of iron, flows rapidly with (all) sustaining water, sweeping away in its might all other waters, as a charioteer (clears the road)....

6. Auspicious Saraswati, for thee Vasishtha has set open the two doors (the east and west) of sacrifice: white-complexioned (goddess), be magnified; bestow food on him who glorifies thee; and do you (gods) cherish us with blessings.

Sukta XI.

... 5. Resplendent Vishnu, I, the master of the offering, knowing the objects that are to be known, glorify to-day thy name. I, who am feeble, praise thee who art powerful, dwelling in a remote region of this world.

. . . .

Sixth Ashtaka, First Adhyaya, Sukta V.

TO INDRA.

... 7. May this *soma*, invested (with milk), approach thee, observant Indra, like a bride (clad in white apparel).

. . . .

Sukta VIII.

... 14. Praise them, praise the Maruts, for we are (dependent) upon those agitators (of all things), as a menial is upon his lord; therefore are their donations (characterised) by munificence.

Sukta VIII.

... 25. Whatever medicaments there may be in the *Sindha*, in the *Aśikari*, in the oceans, in the mountains, Maruts, who are all gratified by sacrifice . . .

RIG-VEDA, Vol. III., p. 175 of Translation by H. H. WILSON. Appearance of the Doctrine of Transmigration and Allusion to Iron.

1. Being still in the germ, I have known all the births of these divinities in their order, a hundred bodies of iron confined me, but as a hawk I came forth with speed. . . .

3. (I the archer Kriṣánu), when the hawk screamed with exultation, on his descent from heaven, the guardians of the soma perceived that the soma was carried away by it. Then the archer, Kriṣánu, pursuing with the speed of thought, and stringing his bow, let fly an arrow against it.

As to the Unity of the Deities in AGNI (p. 236), *Sukta III.*—

1. Thou, Agni, art born Varuna, thou becomest Mitra when kindled; in thee, son of strength, art all the gods: thou art Indra, son of strength, to the mortal that presents oblations. Thou art Aryaman in relation to maidens. . . .

5. For thy glory the winds sweep the firmament. When thy birth, Rudra, is beautiful and wonderful, the middle step of Vishnu has been placed, so that thou cherishest the mysterious name of the waters. . . .

11. Agni, youngest of the gods, verily thou bearest thine adorer safe beyond all calamities.

VII.

In the "Journal of the Asiatic Society of Bengal" for 1877, an account is given of a discovery of a burial ground, with crosses, by Mr. W. King, Deputy Superintendent of the Geological Survey of India. He describes them as being in the midst of forest and scrub jungle, near Mungasset in the Nizam's dominions, on the right bank of the Godaveri. He states that he found four large cruciform monoliths, one still standing upright and perfect, near a number of stone tombs. One of the crosses was 13 feet in height, with an unbroken arm of 3 feet 8 inches in length. In the diagrams which accompany his article the crosses seem to resemble our Christian crosses. The arms are near the summit; and the crosses altogether look perfectly adapted for erection in our burial grounds or old crossways. The tombs are constructed of worked stones, and contain coffin-like cavities, which suggest the embalming of bodies. They number about 150; and the four crosses do not appear to have any special connection with individual tombs. Mr. King states that he thinks them prehistoric. Of course the hypothesis, as he observes, may be entertained that they are Christian, though it is difficult to conceive that an old Christian burial-place can have been formed so far inland. The general style of the tombs and of the crosses seems not to have suggested Christian work to him altogether, though the latter certainly have the aspect of Gothic crosses in the diagrams. The surrounding natives called the place the Village of Demons, and its history appears to be quite enveloped in mystery.

VIII.

Professor Curtius, in his "History of Greece," observes that "In the entire religious life of the Greeks no great epoch is more clearly marked than the first appearance of Apollo. It resembles a second day of creation in the history of their spiritual development. In all the Greek towns, from which a rich treasure of myths has been handed down to us, there attaches itself to his blessed arrival a lofty revolution of the social order of things, a higher development of life. The roads are levelled, the quarters of the towns are marked out, the castles are encircled with walls, things sacred are separated from things profane. The sound of song and stringed instruments is heard, men approach nearer to the gods. Zeus speaks to them through his prophets; and guilt, even the guilt of blood, no longer rests inexpiable, like a leaden weight, on ill-fated man; no longer drags itself, as a curse, from generation to generation. Rather as the laurel cleanses the sultry air, so the laurel-crowned god purifies Orestes from his stains of blood, and restores to him serenity of soul; the dread power of the Erinnys is broken; and a world of higher harmony, a reign of grace, is founded." This Apollo the Greeks of the hither side only knew as one who had come to them from abroad, and his chief sanctuaries they only regarded as the terminating points of the path along which he had entered among them.

IX.

The antiquity of the idea that the Supreme Spirit may be present on earth as Hari-Krishna, or any other manifestation, seems evident. He may, at the same time, be in himself all the divine beings, and all that which is spiritual in the universe. It is a spiritual pantheism in which the divine is in the non-sensual human. The remnants of the Orphic hymns which have descended to us bear testimony to this. M. De la Barre (in Mem. de l'Acad. des Ins., tom vi. p. 28) makes observations upon these which seem to display the exact affinity of the ancient religions of Greece with that set forth in the Indian "Great Bharata" poem and "Ancient Books." He was apparently quite unacquainted with the spiritual pantheism of our cousins in the East, and only perceives contradictions and absurdities in the Orphic system. He remarks: "Mais l'examen leur est infiniment désavantageux ; puisqu'il y découvre un mélange monstrueux d'idées philosophiques qui se croisent, et qui n'ont pas plus de rapport entre elles qu'avec la religion commune, qui ne laisse pas de s'y trouver partout. C'est la en effet qu'Hercule est tout à la fois le premier des êtres qui a paru, né de lui même et production de la terre, celui qui porte autour de sa tête l'Amour et la nuit, et celui aussi dont le bras délivra la terre des scélerats qui troubloient la tranquilité publique. [Hari, or Krishna, seems evidently repeated in this conception.] C'est la encore que, suivant je ne sais quelles idées, l'an est le monde entier, dont le ciel, la terre, la mer, et le feu éternel sont les membres ; et que suivant les idées Grecques c'est un dieu qui court les forêts, qui se cache dans les antres, qui se plait à faire peur, à s'entretenir avec l'écho, à danser avec les nymphes. Jupiter est représenté ici comme l'auteur de la nature, celui qui a produit la terre, la mer et tout ce que les cieux enserrent ; il est, dit on, le commencement et la fin de toutes choses, et tout de suite on lui donne pour femme Junon considerée comme l'air. Il me paroit d'ailleurs assez plaisant de voir que Atrea soit dans un hymne fille de Protogone et mère de ciel, et que dans un autre hymne le ciel soit son père."

The Orphic hymns seem to be acknowledged to be of uncertain origin and remote antiquity ; and they are only found scattered amongst the writings of philosophers and historians. Certainly the cosmogony expounded in them seems in absolute accord with that developed in the Bharatan or ancient Indian books. We find the universe created by one Supreme, Self-existent Being. We have the primeval egg which opens into two halves, and forms heaven and earth, &c. &c.

X.

According to the "Preliminary Discourse to Sale's Koran," an heretical sect amongst the Mohammedan Shiites seems to have maintained doctrines quite identical with the Indo-Aryan. "They unanimously held a metempsychosis and what they call *al Holûl*, or the descent of God on His creatures; meaning thereby that God is present in every place, and speaks with every tongue, and appears in some individual person, and hence some of them asserted their Imâms to be prophets, and at length gods. The Nosairians and Ishâkians taught that spiritual substances appear in grosser bodies; and that the angels and the devil have appeared in this manner. They also assert that God hath appeared in the form of certain men; and since, after Mohammed, there hath been no man more excellent than Ali, and, after him, his sons have excelled all other men, that God hath appeared in their form, spoken with their tongue, and made use of their hands; for which reason, say they, we attribute divinity to them.

And to support these blasphemies they tell several miraculous things of Ali, as his moving the gates of Khaibar, which they urge as a plain proof that he was endued with a particle of divinity and with sovereign power, and that he was the person in whose form God appeared, with whose hands He created all things, and with whose tongue He published His commands; and therefore they say he was in being before the creation of heaven and earth. In so impious a manner do they seem to wrest those things which are said in Scripture of Christ by applying them to Ali. These extravagant fancies of the Shiites, however, in making their Imâms partake of the Divine nature, and the impiety of some of these Imâms in laying claim thereto, are so far from being peculiar to this sect, that most of the other Mohammedan sects are tainted with the same madness, there being many found among them, and among the Sûfis especially, who pretend to be nearly related to Heaven, and who boast of strange revelations before the credulous people."

Professor Weber observes that the Samkhyayoga system of Indian philosophy had an important influence upon the growth of the Sûfi philosophy. So that it appears that the Indo-Aryan religious conceptions had obtained a footing in Arabia. And the Sabian religion, which was the most prevalent faith of the Arabs before Mohammed, seems to have been connected with the ancient Vedic system of the Indo-Aryans.

"They do not only believe one God," says Sale, "but produce many strong arguments for this unity, though they also pay an adoration to the stars, or the angels and intelligences which they suppose reside in them, and govern the world under the Supreme Deity. They endeavour to perfect themselves in the four intellectual virtues, and believe the souls of wicked men will be punished for nine thousand ages, but will afterwards be received to mercy. They are obliged to pray three times a day: the first, half an hour or less before sunrise, ordering it so that they may, just as the sun rises, finish eight adorations, each containing three prostrations; the second prayer they end at noon, when the sun begins to decline, in saying which they perform five such adorations as the former; and the same they do the third time, ending just as the sun sets. They fast three times a year: the first time thirty days, the next nine days, and the last seven. They offer many sacrifices, but eat no part of them, burning them all. They abstain from beans, garlic, and some other pulse and vegetables. Besides the book of Psalms, the only true Scripture they read, they have other books which they esteem equally sacred, particularly one in the Chaldee tongue which they call the book of Seth, and is full of moral discourses. Travellers commonly call them Christians of St. John the Baptist, whose disciples also they pretend to be, using a kind of baptism, which is the greatest mark they bear of Christianity."

"The idolatry of the Arabs, then, as Sabians, consisted chiefly in worshipping the fixed stars and planets, and the angels and their images, which they honoured as inferior deites, and whose intercession they begged as their mediators with God."

"Manah was the object of worship of the tribes of Hodhail and Khazâah, who dwell between Mecca and Medina. This idol was a large stone, demolished by one Saad in the eighth year of the Hegira (A.D. 630), a year so fatal to the idols of Arabia. The name seems derived from *manu, to flow*, from the flowing of the blood of the victims sacrificed to the deity." Its sound seems suggestive of the Aryan manu.

"Some of the pagan Arabs believed neither a creation past nor a resurrection to come, attributing the origin of things to nature, and their dissolution to age. Some believed a metempsychosis. The Persians had, by their vicinity and frequent intercourse with the Arabians, introduced the Magian religion among some of their tribes. Christianity had likewise made a very great progress among this nation before Mohammed."

"Mohammed taught that God had the goodness to re-inform and re-admonish mankind by several prophets, of whom Moses and Jesus were the most distinguished till the appearance of himself, who is their seal, no other being to be expected after him."

Mohammed, then, like the Christian Church, ignored the possibility of divine knowledge amongst the millions of the Eastern civilisations, and contemned the Aryan conception of the Incarnation, which seems to have invaded Arabia from both East and West. He fell back upon what seems to be the Mosaic doctrine of God in heaven communicating personally His will to His chosen prophet on earth.

XI.

The life and attributes of Krishna, regarded under his warlike aspect, certainly present well-defined aspects of being the originals of those of the Odin of ancient Germany. Odin is related to have effected great changes in government, manners, and religion. Colonel Vans Kennedy observes that divine honours were paid to him, and that in the midst of dangers the invoking of the name of Odin was an unfailing resource. He is said to have instituted Asiatic rites and ceremonies, to have taught magic and performed miracles. He would sometimes appear transformed into a fish, bird, or serpent. After his death his body was said to have been burnt. Sacrifices of captives taken in war were instituted in his honour.

According to the Edda of Northern Europe, one supreme God created heaven and earth. A mystic cow appears in the account of the creation, which suggests ancient Indo-Aryan legends.

www.ingramcontent.com/pod-product-compliance
Lightning Source LLC
Chambersburg PA
CBHW033532304026
4367ZCB00007B/684